THE ACADEMIC ACCELERATION OF GIFTED CHILDREN

Edited by

W. THOMAS SOUTHERN
ERIC D. JONES

Teachers College, Columbia University
New York and London

Published by Teachers College Press, 1234 Amsterdam Avenue
New York, NY 10027

Library of Congress Cataloging-in-Publication Data
The academic acceleration of gifted children / edited by W. Thomas
    Southern, Eric D. Jones.
       p.   cm.—(Education and psychology of the gifted series)
    Includes bibliographical references and index.
    ISBN 0-8077-3068-8
    1.Gifted children—Education—United States.   2. Educational
acceleration.   I. Southern, William T. (William Thomas), 1948–
II. Jones, Eric D., 1950–   .   III. Series.
LC3993.9.A65   1991
371.95—dc20   90-19218
                                                             CIP

Printed on acid-free paper

Manufactured in the United States of America

97 96 95 94 93   8 7 6 5 4 3 2

I would like to dedicate this work to my most valued professional colleagues:

> To Howard Spicker, who worked to make a writer of me.
> To Dale Underwood, who taught me what it is to be a teacher.
> And to Jan, who forgives me for what I am not.

Thank you. W. Thomas Southern

I would like to dedicate this book to the people who have been an inspiration:

> To Natalie, who wanted to go to school—sooner.
> To Nathaniel, a bright boy who may someday ask to be red-shirted for football.
> To Akiko, our *kyōiku*-mama, who keeps us all learning.
> And to my parents, who worried that I would not finish high school.

Thank you. Eric Jones

EDUCATION AND PSYCHOLOGY OF THE GIFTED SERIES
James H. Borland, Editor

Planning and Implementing Programs
for the Gifted
James H. Borland

Patterns of Influence on Gifted Learners:
The Home, the Self, and the School
Joyce L. VanTassel-Baska
Paula Olszewski-Kubilius
EDITORS

Reaching the Gifted Underachiever:
Program Strategy and Design
Patricia L. Supplee

The Academic Acceleration of Gifted Children
W. Thomas Southern
Eric D. Jones
EDITORS

Understanding the Gifted Adolescent:
Educational, Developmental, and Multicultural Issues
Marlene Bireley
Judy Genshaft
EDITORS

Contents

Foreword

Academic acceleration is an educational issue about which everybody, educator and layperson alike, appears to have a strong opinion. Moreover, although I have not conducted systematic research on the question, I would wager that, in more cases than not, this opinion is a negative one. For some, especially those outside the field of the education of the gifted, acceleration as an educational option is simply out of the question. These individuals seem to view the prospect of a child deviating from the one-grade-per-year lockstep not simply as a modification of a somewhat arbitrary administrative convenience, but rather as a contravention of the laws of nature. Others, however, have objections to academic acceleration that are more substantive in nature.

Writers such as David Elkind and Neil Postman have correctly warned us of the dangers inherent in forcing children to grow up too fast. These concerns are in many cases legitimate, and they are often fueled by striking and undeniable cases of abuse. However, when applied to the education of gifted children, they can lead to some simplistic and unfair equations. For there is a world of difference between, on the one hand, Better Baby Institutes and beauty contests for children and, on the other, attempts to bend the curriculum and the administrative arrangements of the schools to the needs of children who significantly deviate from the norm. Pushing children unnaturally is wrong, just as forcing a child to mark time in a lockstep that is educationally frustrating is wrong. In both cases, the mistake is the result of allowing adult needs instead of the processes of natural development to guide the unfolding of children's lives.

Simplistic thinking is not to be found only among the opponents of acceleration, however. Reading some of the more vigorous advocates of this practice, one might easily conclude that these educators see themselves as a beleaguered but enlightened minority, justifiably appalled by the persistence with which the benighted masses hold fast to their superstitions rather than attending to the unequivocal implications of the research literature. The more radical advocates of acceleration (not to be confused with the advocates of radical acceleration) seem to believe that if the research demonstrates the efficacy and beneficence of acceleration for children in general, it is fatuous to question the wisdom of its application in any specific instance.

Within the field of the education of the gifted, the controversy takes on another dimension. When one encounters the word *acceleration* in the literature of this field, it is as often as not in the context of a dichotomy, a stark choice between acceleration or enrichment. Those who aggressively promote enrichment argue that when acceleration is adopted as an educational approach for the gifted, the core curriculum—which is usually inappropriate for gifted students although it dictates most of their educational activities—will remain unchanged. Those who single-mindedly advocate acceleration, on the other hand, express the fear that enrichment too often leads to supplementary activities that are irrelevant at best, vacuous at worst. Fortunately, many others recognize the compatibility of the two approaches and the frequent necessity of their combination in the special education of gifted learners.

All of this underscores the timeliness and value of the present volume, the fourth in the Education and Psychology of the Gifted Series from Teachers College Press. W. Thomas Southern and Eric D. Jones have made a major contribution to the literature on acceleration by bringing together between the same covers papers by some of the most knowledgeable and capable scholars who have turned their thoughts to this controversial topic. The contributors constitute an eclectic and synergistic mix of researchers, theorists, and practitioners, and their insights, opinions, and experiences have a serious claim on our attention.

This book will not resolve conclusively the various controversies that rage around the topic of acceleration. That hardly detracts from its utility or its quality, however. In fact, I would argue that the contrary is the case. For the value of the present volume derives not only from its summary of what we know about acceleration but also, as the editors state in their introduction, from the fact that it underscores what we do not know. And the extent of what we do not yet know about this contentious issue belies the claims to absolute truth of those who make confident pronouncements, pro and con, about acceleration.

Thus, I am pleased to be able to introduce and to commend to you this most impressive anthology. Professors Southern and Jones have given us an up-to-date and comprehensive collection of writings on a crucial topic, the implications of which touch on many of the leading educational issues of the day. For this they deserve our congratulations and our thanks.

James H. Borland, editor
Education and Psychology of the
Gifted Series

Acknowledgments

A great many people were instrumental in developing this book. We would first of all like to thank the individual chapter authors who worked diligently and carefully to produce some extraordinary work. Their attention to detail and to deadlines made this project much easier for us. We would also like to thank our friend and department chairman, Dr. Edward Fiscus. In addition to helping us with our research, he was supportive, patient, and helpful throughout the process. He also leavened our work with a bit of humor and good cheer when we needed it. We wish to acknowledge the special contributions of Brian Ellerbeck, our editor at Teachers College Press. Besides being a very skillful editor, he knew precisely how much pressure to apply to get us cracking—without cracking the whip.

The secretaries in the department and in word processing in the College of Education were superb. Donna Beam, Amy Chapman, Judy Maxey, Sherri Haskins, and Mary Beam deserve our hearty thanks. We would also like to extend a special thank you to Jayne McKanna and Beth Cochran, who spent hours reading the manuscripts to each other and checking various revisions for transcription errors.

We would like to thank the students, parents, and school personnel who responded to our research efforts on surveys and on the phone. Their patience and cooperation were instrumental in providing background for much of our chapters. Additionally, we want to thank Marvin Myers who conducted some of the research and maintained data files in the midst of the chaos of one editor's office.

Introduction

In the late 20th century in the United States, a set of commonly held expectations govern schools. Children enter school at 5-plus years of age, embarking on a kindergarten curriculum that emphasizes school readiness and socialization. As these children progress through grades, they will all require approximately the same amount of time to master common elements of the curriculum tied to each grade level. The interval that measures progress is the school year, and children are tied to age/grade advancement.

Unfortunately, it is readily apparent that many children do not fit these basic expectations. Some children enter school with fewer of the skills and experiences assumed by the curriculum, or they may require more than a year to master a year's content demands. Others may reach school entry age with a larger store of skills and knowledge. They may know their colors, numbers, even simple arithmetic operations. Some have been reading for a number of years before entering kindergarten. Still others proceed rapidly through the academic materials they are presented, covering a year of instruction in a fraction of the time it takes others.

For those children whose development is either slower or more rapid than the norm, schools can be inhospitable places. Schools are not well equipped to deal with anomalous patterns of development. The problems inherent in keeping all children tied into discrete age/grade advancement have sparked a number of controversies. For students who experience difficulty, the issues of developmental primary grades, special education, and promotion and retention have raged now hotter, now cooler over the years. For those who surpass expectations, the controversies have been no less heated and no less complex. Educators and parents have worried over issues of admitting students into school earlier than the mandated age. They also are concerned with potential harm from advancing students ahead of their chronological peers. The term used to characterize these and similar processes designed to deal with the problems of the capable student is academic acceleration, and it remains for educators, parents, and students an issue of concern and debate.

For much of the past century there has been a welter of claim and counterclaim, often accompanied with confident assertions that one set of studies or another has finally resolved the issue once and for all. Despite the confidence of the debaters, parents and educators confronted by the phenomenon of a gifted, achieving child will be the recipient of advice that is at once as confident as it is contradictory. The book you now hold is a recognition that for parents, for students, and for school personnel, the issues surrounding academic acceleration are still lively, vital, and problematic. This book was designed to assist readers to digest and critique what has become a very substantial body of literature regarding academic acceleration. The authors who contribute to the volume provide guidance to the practitioner in assessing, implementing, and evaluating acceleration decisions in schools. They provide a wealth of practical considerations and proffer some potential strategies for reaching decisions about whom to accelerate, when, and how, as well as some practical considerations about building and maintaining acceptance for the decisions that have been made.

Chapter 1 examines the history of academic acceleration and the current controversy over the multitude of options described as accelerative. The authors make a distinction between acceleration as a process and a more general function of acceleration in school as an administrative response to curriculum mismatch. This distinction is useful in putting much of the latter literature reviews in perspective as well as in suggesting pragmatic issues for educators and parents to address in decision making.

Chapters 2 and 3 deal with the debate over early admission. In Chapter 2, Robinson and Weimer review the literature concerning achievement and performance of carefully selected students admitted early. In addition to reviewing studies that examine the potential benefits and drawbacks for such children, the authors also provide some guidelines for decision makers concerning who may be likely candidates for the process.

Jones and Southern in Chapter 3 examine the literature from the related field of general studies of children who are young-in-grade. That body of literature is often cited in response to efforts to admit students prior to suggested school entry age. Although these studies seldom deal with the kind of highly selected populations of gifted children who represent the concerns of this book, their results often discourage educators and parents from placing children in school early. The authors note that this literature cannot provide substantive evidence that should deter decisions to accelerate. Despite this finding, they note that the effect of the literature on educational decision making is pervasive and results in greater reluctance to employ accelerative options.

The greatest concern expressed by all parties to decisions about acceleration is whether or not there will be adverse effects on the accelerant's social and emotional development. In Chapter 4, Cornell, Callahan, Bassin, and

Ramsay adopt a cautious tone in examining the literature on this point. Although they remain convinced of the efficacy of acceleration for some students, they note that the dearth of well-designed empirical studies does not justify the enthusiastic support shown by many proponents of acceleration. They also point out that the evidence is not wholly positive. They speculate that the mixed results may arise from interacting personal variables among the general group of students who are accelerated. They offer several guidelines for research and identify some of the most important issues still unresolved in a concluding research agenda.

Perhaps no name has been connected more strongly with the development of accelerative techniques than Julian Stanley, and perhaps no part of his work is more notable than his research and development of radical accelerative options. Certainly, for the general public, news stories of exceptionally young children attending and graduating from college provide the most striking image of acceleration and the controversies that the practice engenders. In Chapter 5, Brody and Stanley present a series of historical case studies that illustrate both the dangers and benefits of acceleration. Far from uncritically accepting the process, Brody and Stanley review case histories with a view to extracting the elements that result in successful and unsuccessful accelerative experiences. Moreover, they provide this examination in the context of burgeoning opportunities in public schools for gifted children. The chapter is primarily anecdotal, but it provides illustrations of typical and atypical students who have undergone radical acceleration.

In Chapter 6 Feldhusen follows with a view of how accelerative options fit in with other provisions for the gifted and talented. His chapter is far more than a reprise of the enrichment/acceleration debate, however. Feldhusen examines the research base for many of the programmatic responses to the needs of the gifted. He points out that wholesale adoption of one technique or the other ignores the range of differences within the population we term gifted and talented. He provides a summary of available information as well as a sophisticated agenda for further research needed to answer some nagging questions remaining in the field.

In Chapter 7 Van Tassel-Baska's contribution is a look at the administrative implementation of accelerative options. The author strongly advocates the process of acceleration. An examination of the range of options available to decision makers is followed by some general guidelines about assessment and placement. Two valuable contributions are the suggestions for developing accelerative curricula and a consideration of the requirements teachers face in dealing with gifted students who are accelerated. She notes the hesitancy on the part of school personnel and offers some suggestions for a minimum program option for acceleration as well as strategies for addressing reluctance on the part of school officials, parents, and students.

Piper and Creps are coordinators of gifted programs, and Chapter 8 outlines procedures developed in their districts to make acceleration and placement decisions. They adopt a team decision-making approach that serves to build consensus and protects the interests of all parties in the process. The emphasis is on pragmatic rather than theoretical concerns, and this chapter may prove the most useful to school personnel who must make and monitor such decisions.

The two chapters that follow are an acknowledgment that parents and schools deserve accountability after the decisions are made. In Chapters 9 and 10 Callahan and Hunsaker offer evaluations of programs and individual students who have been accelerated. After providing a rationale for evaluation, the authors systematically examine the techniques and guidelines that will provide reliable and valid information. Perhaps most important, they provide the reader with a view of individual student responses to accelerative options. As the earlier reviews dramatically point out, much of the existing literature in the controversy suffers from broad generalizations about group tendencies. Parents and school personnel are interested, primarily, in the effects of acceleration on the individual child. These chapters provide strategies for making such assessments in a timely and meaningful fashion.

No debate in education ends with unequivocal answers, and this one is no exception. Chapter 11 is both a summary and an initiation. On one hand, the authors in this book hope to have been able to clarify the issues surrounding academic acceleration. Some preliminary help has been furnished to the reader in determining who potential, successful candidates for acceleration might be. Instruments and procedures are suggested, and strategies for gauging results have been noted. On the other hand, the effect of many of the chapters will be to point out how little we do know. The book ends, as do most articles and chapters in education, with a look at the need for further study, a situation comforting for researchers who have more worlds to explore but disquieting for those facing the dilemmas of decisions.

CHAPTER 1

Academic Acceleration: Background and Issues

W. Thomas Southern and Eric D. Jones
Bowling Green State University

Academic acceleration is a process that encompasses a large number of practices. In its earliest incarnation, acceleration referred merely to the process
of putting students ahead in school grade placement. In this guise, the process addressed the predicament of providing appropriate academic instruction for students whose performances clearly exceeded the demands established for their chronological peers. The obvious intervention was to place
them in groups of older, more academically accomplished students. However,
the increasing rigidity of curriculum raised the possibility of a mismatch
between the student and the expectations for learning. Some students would
perform in a marginally superior manner, but others potentially could move
faster. These students could assimilate material, consolidate concepts, or acquire knowledge and skills at rates far greater than average.

ACCELERATION: EXAMINING THE CONCEPT

Pressey (1949) defined acceleration as "progress through an educational
program at rates faster or ages younger than conventional" (p. 2). This definition notes that acceleration includes the provision to bypass intervening
instructional demands and also suggests processes that move students
through material at faster rates than average students progress. Three points
are notable about this definition. First, it assumes the existence of an established set of materials, tasks, skills, and acquired knowledge for each level of
instruction. Skipping grades or increasing the pace of instruction presupposes a content that is specified and, to some extent, logically sequenced.
The curriculum is seen implicitly as a discrete set of skills and knowledge
that may be the basis for judging student competence. Second, the definition
presupposes that there is a desirable, specified rate of progress through the
curriculum suitable for most students. Third, it presumes that, compared

1

Table 1.1   Range and Types of Accelerative Options

1. Early entrance to kindergarten or first grade	The student is admitted to school prior to the age specified by the district for normal entry to first grade.
2. Grade skipping	The student is moved ahead of normal grade placement. This may be done during an academic year (placing a third grader directly into fourth grade), or at year end (promoting a third grader to fifth grade).
3. Continuous progress	The student is given material deemed appropriate for current achievement as the student becomes ready.
4. Self-paced instruction	The student is presented with materials that allow him or her to proceed at a self-selected pace. Responsibility for selection of pacing is the student's.
5. Subject-matter acceleration	The student is placed for a part of a day with students at more advanced grade levels for one or more subjects without being assigned to a higher grade (e.g., a fifth grader going to sixth grade for science instruction).
6. Combined classes	The student is placed in classes where two or more grade levels are combined (e.g., third and fourth grade split rooms). The arrangement can be used to allow younger children to interact with older ones academically and socially.
7. Curriculum compacting	The student is given reduced amounts of introductory activities, drill, review, and so on. The time saved may be used to move faster through the curriculum.
8. Telescoping curriculum	The student spends less time than normal in a course of study (e.g., completing a 1-year course in 1 semester, or finishing junior high school in 2 years rather than 3).
9. Mentorships	The student is exposed to a mentor who provides advanced training and experiences in a content area.
10. Extracurricular programs	The student is enrolled in course work or summer programs that confer advanced instruction and/or credit for study (e.g., fast-paced language or math courses offered by universities).
11. Concurrent enrollment	The student is taking a course at one level and receiving credit for successful completion of a parallel course at a higher level (e.g., taking algebra at the junior high level and receiving credit for high school algebra as well as junior high math credits upon successful completion).

Table 1.1 (continued)

12. Advanced placement	The student takes a course in high school that prepares him or her for taking an examination that can confer college credit for satisfactory performances.
13. Credit by examination	The student receives credit (at high school or college level) upon successful completion of an examination.
14. Correspondence courses	The student takes high school or college courses by mail (or, in more recent incarnations, through video and audio course presentation).
15. Early entrance into junior high, high school, or college	The student is admitted with full standing to an advanced level of instruction (at least 1 year early).

with age-level classmates, a superior student will be capable of more rapid progress through a standard instructional program. Thus, there is a dual criterion for advancement: existing achievement and ability to move more rapidly than the norm.

There are several instructional interventions that could fit this definition. Passow, Goldberg, Tannenbaum, & French (1955) note eight options: grade skipping, double promotion (seen as a different process), rapidly moving classes, early admission to first grade, extra course work, single-subject acceleration, concurrent enrollment, and extracurricular course work. Options for acceleration have proliferated in the intervening years. Gallagher (1985) lists seven major methods, Davis and Rimm (1988) nine, and Kitano and Kirby (1986) detail no less than thirteen. Table 1.1 lists a group of options identified by various writers in gifted education as accelerative.

The options presented vary along two dimensions. The first dimension is the degree or extent of differentiation in the intervention. A student who interacts for only a portion of the day with older students, or who takes a fast-paced summer math course with other junior high students, is experiencing a less radical acceleration intervention than one admitted to college at 14, for example. In fact, theorists make a strong distinction between accelerative options in this regard. The age discrepancy between the subject and his or her academic peers, the factor by which instructional time is reduced, and the degree of maturity required of the student in the level into which he or she is placed are dimensions along which this variable is measured. Students who are skipped more than two grades, complete yearlong courses of study in exceptionally brief periods of time (e.g., algebra and advanced algebra in 3 weeks), or enter a higher level of schooling more than 2 or 3 years ahead of average are said to experience radical acceleration (Stanley, 1977).

The second dimension involves which of two major objectives are addressed in the acceleration. The range of program options in Table 1.1 indicates the dichotomy suggested in Pressey's (1949) definition. The first part of the definition assumes that some students are already achieving at a level higher than chronological peers. Indeed, some of the interventions in Table 1.1 appear designed to deal administratively with the already achieved potential of the student. Others indicate a recognition that the student has the ability and inclination to proceed at a faster pace through the curriculum. Certainly, each of the following options—early admission to school, grade skipping, advanced placement through examination, and concurrent enrollment—functions to provide administrative recognition of the student's readily apparent superior achievement. Other program interventions, such as curriculum compacting, telescoping grade levels, and fast-paced course work, are concerned with the needs and abilities of gifted learners to move through curriculum at a faster pace.

The philosophical implications associated with rapid-paced instruction seem much different from those involved in placing a student in a program with older peers. For interventions that offer recognition of the existing states of the learner's achievement, the primary concern is to provide workable administrative provisions. To that end, interventions should provide adequate "credit" without subjecting the student or the school system to negative consequences. Interventions that result in penalties such as reducing the likelihood of admission to selective schools or depriving the student of sports eligibility may do more harm than good for students who target those goals. If the problem is merely to determine whether the needs of a particular student warrant administrative intervention to recognize achievements, then the most serious concern would be only the documentation of superior performance. The questions would be whether it is likely that the performance is truly equal to that of older students, the student is sufficiently advanced in skills and attainments, and current achievement is likely to continue in higher demand settings.

Other options, such as fast-paced course work, telescoping of grades, and curriculum compacting, seem to imply that the student is engaged in programs that radically depart from the expected norm of school in terms of the level of demand, the level of performance, and the nature of the interaction expected with other students. With this sort of program, as with any educational intervention of a radical nature, we are obliged to ascertain certain findings before implementation. If students are engaged in vastly different programs, it means that we must be absolutely sure that we have explored all the potential negative consequences of the intervention. Identification issues are more complex. There must be assurance that those candidates most likely to benefit from such a radical departure have been identified and that adequate documentation of benefits of the process are provided to justify its application.

Recognizing achievement seems less fraught with potential peril than actively changing the pace and expectations for students in school. Although the distinction seems apparent, it has not been generally made in the literature. Few authors distinguish between active interventions and administrative recognition, yet this distinction can be important. Critics of acceleration may concentrate on the implications inherent in more active interventions. Increasing the speed of student learning, apparently through an external agency, sounds potentially harmful. On the other hand, recognizing student-demonstrated achievement is more easily represented as fair and equitable. To the extent that acceleration is merely administrative recognition, there should be less peril from the process of acceleration itself (though concerns of placement with older children remain at issue with many forms of acceleration). Indeed, some research findings become clearer when the two possible purposes of acceleration are kept in mind. It would be well to consider both dimensions of accelerative options when reviewing the history of the controversy.

There are some factors contributing to the confusion of the two purposes for academic acceleration. The first is the result of generalizing the literature about one form of acceleration to all forms of acceleration. Southern, Jones, and Fiscus (1989a, 1989b) found that parents and school personnel tended to make no distinction among (1) either of the dimensions indicated above, (2) the age of the accelerant, (3) the salience of the intervention, or (4) whether the program was directed to an administrative recognition or a modification of the pace and delivery of instruction.

Practitioners, parents, and researchers also tend to collapse findings for or against acceleration across all the types of program interventions. Thus, findings about the dangers or effectiveness of acceleration may be generalized from studies of school readiness to early college admission without distinction or clarification. Distinctions between extracurricular programmatic interventions and school-level interventions may be blurred. Evidence or assertions about school interventions are applied equally to extracurricular options. This aggregation of claims makes the debate more chaotic and decreases the clarity of the issues being argued. It is important to untangle the sources of various claims in order to focus the debate. Examining the historical forces involved and the nature of the specific claims provides an initial framework for understanding how concerns originally developed and how they have informed and misinformed various research efforts.

History of the Acceleration Debate

The controversy over acceleration is relatively recent. Kett (1974) asserts that before the mid 19th century the notion that children should remain with chronological peers was not widely held. In both rural and urban districts, the expectation was that student performance would mandate the disposition of placement and graduation. Students frequently remained in grade or level only long enough to achieve some locally determined assessment of the limits of curriculum for that level. Indeed, "the structure of grades only gradually approached uniformity in the early part of the twentieth century" (Pressey, 1949). As late as 1925, school districts such as Salt Lake City were experimenting with lowering the number of grades from 12 to 11. The goal was to save student time and local tax money by educating students more efficiently (Arneson, 1929). Concerns were rarely expressed about whether students of younger ages might adjust to or fit with older students.

Four factors emerged in the 20th century to modify this belief: (1) mandatory attendance for all children, (2) increased educational expectations, (3) the rise of developmental theories in child psychology, and (4) huge increases in the number of students being educated. In movements commencing in the early 20th century and culminating in extensive legislation in the 1920s and 1930s, students were required to stay in school until they reached a certain age. The movement was probably grounded in the efforts to address issues of child welfare and conditions of employment for minors. It also addressed the need of the country to assimilate large numbers of immigrants. During the early 20th century, the problems of child labor and exploitation emerged as important targets for social reform movements. The limitation and regulation of child labor received widespread support. The tide of immigration that swelled in the latter part of the 19th century and early years of the 20th century added impetus for reformers. School was an ideal institution to train and acculturate the children of these immigrants. The final impetus, however, for establishing far-ranging and inclusive legislation was the Great Depression of 1929. Shrinking job markets and resultant concern about young persons' competing for limited opportunities presented an unspoken but convincing argument for enacting laws requiring students to stay in school and, hence, out of job markets (Pressey, 1949).

With regard to the second factor, the availability of school training contributed to rising expectations among employers and the general public for students in school. During the 20th century the average level of educational achievement rose markedly. In 1910, only 8.6% of all 17- and 18-year-olds held high school diplomas. By 1950, that figure had risen to 57.4% (Bureau of the Census, 1975). Veterans returning from World War II made extensive use of educational benefits in the Serviceman's Readjustment Act of 1944. In the early 1920s only 4.5% of the population between 18 and 24 were pursuing an undergraduate or graduate degree. By 1950, this percentage had risen to 16.5% (Bureau of the Census, 1975). The population was becoming more highly educated, and employers were able to expect increasingly higher levels of school attainment from people in entry-level positions.

The third factor that contributed to an increasingly rigid grade structure was the rise in developmental concerns expressed in educational circles. Developmental psychologists, such as Piaget, theorized that children showed stable and invariant progression in cognitive as well as physical development. Interpretations of developmental theories strongly implied that it was futile and potentially hazardous to attempt to instruct students in areas for which they were developmentally unprepared. The clear implication was that children vary in readiness for certain types of instruction and, more importantly, that children of similar ages were more alike in their development and readiness than they were different.

The fourth factor was the curricular implications of schooling large numbers of students across the country. States and localities began to move toward institutionalizing the skills and knowledge that were being taught at particular grade levels. Textbook writers and teacher trainers became increasingly aware that there was some basic set of knowledge and skills that should be imparted at each grade level. As the curriculum evolved, it contained a more rigid scope and sequence of knowledge and skills than it had in earlier years. Textbook companies formalized curricula in print and disseminated the results to mass markets of schools and teachers. The curriculum became a scope and sequence for 12 years of study that was widely accepted. The demands and expectations resulting from this process have become traditional and desirable.

The first two factors were social and economic. They predisposed schools to accept large numbers of students, then tied them to age-related attendance demands. Schools did not resist the use of chronological age as a guide for student placement. After all, the age of a student is readily obtainable, and it provides a convenient benchmark for entry, progress, and exit. The popularity of theories of cognitive development served to legitimize these predispositions and allowed districts to provide curriculum and make placements on the basis of concrete indicators of age and grade. Necessity is often the mother of theory, and, in this instance, the developing school bureaucracy constructed a logic for placement that confirmed the most convenient placement structures.

Daurio (1979) noted that the debate about acceleration was initiated in the late 1920s with assertions that placing students ahead of chronological peers threatened social and emotional development. The onset of the Depression and the widespread passage of laws requiring mandatory attendance quieted the controversy. The advocates of academic acceleration were effectively silenced by historical forces. Students needed to remain in school. The requirements of the economy made less likely research into the implications of addressing students' needs for more rapid pacing, reduced time to meet minimum career standards, or the socioemotional results of placing younger students with older ones.

World War II changed both the social and the economic zeitgeist. It suddenly became desirable to increase the availability of young populations of prime draft age for induction into the armed forces and to refill the ranks of professionals that had been reduced by the draft. The climate had changed, and the new emphasis on acceleration spurred interest about issues surrounding it. Pressey published extensive studies through the 1940s that clearly indicated there was no harm—and, indeed, positive benefits—from academic acceleration at the college level from both early admission and telescoped college programs. Terman and Oden (1947) in their follow-up of the *Genetic Studies of Genius* commented extensively and quite positively on the effects of acceleration among the group they had been following. The end of the war and the influx of veterans attending universities at older ages cooled the climate for this kind of study. There was once again little social or economic impetus for early entry to or more rapid completion of college (Pressey, 1949; Daurio, 1979).

Skepticism about acceleration held sway for the next several years. But, simultaneously, anxiety escalated about the threat of a technological race with the Soviet Union. There had already been a series of reports and commissions asserting that American schools were declining in their ability to train students in mathematics and engineering. A crisis of public concern was triggered by the launch in 1957 of a Soviet satellite months ahead of a successful U.S. launch. *Sputnik* seemed to spur Americans to find and develop scientific talent quickly and efficiently. Talent searches and accelerative programs in science proliferated. Several universities developed extensive plans for accelerating students in advanced studies (Fund for the Advancement of Education of the Ford Foundation 1953, 1957). Interestingly, at the same time, the issue of early entrance gained increasing prominence. A number of studies (e.g., Baer, 1956; Forester, 1955; King, 1955) were published that seemed to condemn the practice as one that would lead to reduced achievement and higher failure rates for young-in-grade children. It is important to note that at the time elementary schools were subject to pressures different from those on the secondary schools. Like colleges in the 1940s, school districts in the 1950s were inundated with students. The baby boom increased demands on facilities at an extraordinary rate. Interventions that increased the already heavy demand were viewed skeptically. Some districts, undoubtedly, learned about potential harm from early admission with a sigh of relief.

New priorities in the nation's history once again changed the emphasis from exploiting talent to redressing social injustices. The move to compensatory education reduced the concern with the discovery and exploitation of talent that had been the focus of the late 1950s. Instead, the potential range of individual differences was minimized as the educational establishment concentrated on interventions that posited equivalent potential ability among students. In consequence, there was increased concern with students who were characterized as educationally disadvantaged. Any intervention that targeted students who were already achieving received reduced emphasis. During the 1960s and early 1970s, official concern with acceleration steadily diminished.

The programs instituted at Johns Hopkins University in the early 1970s departed from the prevailing educational mood and began to illustrate the potentials of students who received accelerative learning experiences, especially in mathematics. Stanley (1977) described initial events that led to the establishment of the Study of Mathematically Precocious Youth. During the latter part of the 1970s and the 1980s, the programmatic efforts of "talent searches" focused attention on the ability of students to exceed the normal level of demand in schools and exceed dramatically the normal expectations of school curricula. Most recently, the nation has been bombarded by a new wave of national studies (e.g., Boyer, 1983; Goodlad, 1984; National Commission on Excellence in Education, 1988; National Commission on Excellence in Teacher Education, 1985) warning that schools are failing in their responsibility to educate students. These studies hand down the explicit indictment that schools are expecting less and less of students and that certain students are receiving increasingly inadequate education.

It is more than coincidence that the renewed interest in gifted education occurred at the time this new wave began. During the 1970s and 1980s, many districts instituted new programs for gifted students, and more and more districts realized that many of the students identified for service represented a mismatch between performance and expectation.

Rationale for Acceleration

In the acceleration controversy, the obvious question is, What are the benefits that argue for its employment? Advocates note potential benefits for gifted students in the following areas:

1. *Increased efficiency.* Students who are ready for instructional material, who have already mastered curricula at earlier levels, will learn better and more efficiently (e.g., Feldhusen, Proctor, & Black, 1986).
2. *Increased effectiveness.* Students engaged in learning at the level they are

prepared for, and for which they have mastered the prerequisite skills, are the most effective learners. Instruction at a level below the students current achievement will be ineffective and repetitious (e.g., Davis & Rimm, 1988).

3. *Recognition*. Students who have achieved at certain levels deserve to be recognized for this accomplishment. If a student masters algebra, the student needs to receive official recognition (i.e., high school credit) for the accomplishment. This is a recognition of fairness and appropriate credit for accomplishments.

4. *Increased time for careers*. Currently, many professional careers require a major commitment of years of study to qualify for entry into the profession, for example, medicine. For students who are accelerated, the reduced time commitment increases earning power, scholarly productivity, and the time available for personal-life enhancement (Pressey, 1955).

5. *Increased productivity*. Studies of notable achievements and contributions in various fields reveal that many of the most important were made by very young professionals, especially in math and physical sciences (Lehman, 1953). Apparently, then, it is beneficial to expose students to advanced study if they show early talent in a discipline.

6. *Increased options for academic exploration*. Brody and Stanley (Chapter 5) describe several students who were able to engage in advanced education in areas outside their major interest or who were provided opportunities to study abroad, travel, or intern in other environments.

7. *Exposure of the student to a new peer group*. The accelerated student may be exposed to a new group of peers more likely to contain members who share intellectual and academic interests. Proponents of acceleration point out that these students often prefer interaction with older companions (Clark, 1988). This will potentially increase their number of contacts and friends.

8. *Administrative economy*. Schools that employ accelerative options reduce their need for specially trained teachers of the gifted (Stanley, 1979b). They may also save taxpayers a year or more of support in the education of a student who is accelerated (Passow, 1958).

Theorists have also advanced a set of negative consequences that might accrue to students who are advanced in achievement and potential, but who are not accelerated. Some of these include:

1. Instruction for the student will be at too slow a pace, and the knowledge and skills presented will be those already in the student's repertoire. Hence, the student will be subject to a seemingly endless, repetitive cur-

riculum. The result may be maladjustment in school characterized by frustration and boredom (Stanley, 1979b; Morgan, Tennant, & Gold, 1980).

2. Students who are infrequently challenged will be unlikely to maintain excitement about the learning process. They may develop antipathy toward formal schooling. This will result in lowered achievement motivation and productivity (Passow, 1958).
3. Lowered achievement motivation can have even more dire effects. Unchallenged students may reject career options that require a long-term commitment to schooling, and in extreme cases they may drop out before graduation. Marland (1972), for example, provided evidence that gifted and talented students were dropping out of school at both the secondary and postsecondary level in great numbers. If students are dropping out, one contributing cause may be the inappropriateness of the curriculum.
4. Lowered expectations in school will allow students to get by with less and less effort. This will occasion the development of slovenly study habits, inaccurate perceptions about the kind of effort required for study at advanced levels, and stunted patterns of attention and persistence.
5. Reduced motivation, poor study habits, and lowered attention in school may result in initially high-achieving students missing out when appropriate skills are presented. Thus the bright student may begin a pattern of poor learning and performance that will mask high potential ability. When clear evidence of potential ability exists, the student may be characterized as an underachiever or even a learning-disabled gifted child.
6. The student who is far advanced in academic skills and attainments may have difficulty adjusting to peers who do not share his or her interests and concerns. There is a risk that the student will not be accepted by peers in the normal placement. Such a student may become isolated or rejected by classmates (Hollingworth, 1942; Terman & Oden, 1947; Newland, 1976).

It is the position of advocates of acceleration that it is one essential tool that can provide bright students with the appropriate educational opportunities in settings with other students of comparable interests and attainments (e.g., Stanley, 1979a, 1979b; Kitano & Kirby, 1986; Davis & Rimm, 1988). The process will allow students to maintain their enthusiasm and excitement for learning. It will present them with continuing challenges that will better prepare them for the rigors of advanced education and adult productivity. It will grant them additional years for exploration at advanced levels, travel, and study in a variety of settings. It will allow students to enter a profession at an earlier age (if the student wishes), providing increased opportunities for productive work.

The Case Against Acceleration

As indicated above, opposition to acceleration developed steadily in the 1920s through the confluence of a variety of social, economic, and educational forces. Opponents, over the years, have posited a large number of potential harmful effects that could result from the process. In general terms, they may be characterized under some broad headings: (1) harmful academic outcomes, (2) emotional maladjustment, (3) disruption of socialization experiences, and (4) reduction in extracurricular opportunities. Since each of these represents a broad constellation of concerns, it is helpful to detail concerns in these areas, each in turn.

Academic outcomes. Ironically, critics claim that the decision to accelerate someone because of academic precocity can result in reduced productivity and achievement. Several potential negative outcomes for the academic progress of an accelerated student have been suggested.

1. The advanced level of content in the accelerated placement may be far too advanced for the student. Accelerants will be unable to adjust to new demands, will fall behind their new peers, and will become mediocre, even failing, students (Uphoff & Gilmore, 1986).
2. The appearance of advanced abilities in early grades may be a temporary phenomenon. As other chronological peers develop, they will match and surpass the rate and achievement of those who were precocious in their development. Thus, the need for accelerative options is ephemeral, and a student would be better served to remain with chronological peers until they catch up (McCluskey & Walker, 1986).
3. Students who are accelerated will have gaps in the development of basic academic skills. Because accelerants "leapfrog" over the curriculum, they will not have had systematic instruction and assessment of skills. Hence, early performance advantages for these students will disappear because they are lacking certain vital, prerequisite skills (Passow, 1958; Khatena, 1982).
4. Students who are accelerated, though qualified academically, may be too immature socially, physically, and emotionally to achieve at the higher level of placement (McCluskey & Walker, 1986). Attention, discipline, and school-related fine motor skills of early entrants may be inadequately developed for coping with school regimes (Uphoff & Gilmore, 1986). Early entrants may be unable to perform in the kind of group learning activities required in higher grades. As students advance through the curriculum, young-in-grade students may perform in ways qualitatively dif-

ferent from those of older classmates. Students unable to meet expectations held for older students may fail in school (Passow, 1958).

5. The process of acceleration may require a student to commit to career decisions much earlier than is the norm. Students simply may not be equipped to make such choices at early ages. At best, this would eventually require expensive and inefficient retraining in new careers. At worst, it might mean commitment to a career unsuitable for the student.

6. An accelerant may develop a "specious precocity," knowledge without appropriate experience (DeHaan & Havighurst, 1957, p. 122). Such a child might have sophisticated knowledge of decoding and comprehension skills, for example, but be unable to understand complex character motivations in a classic novel. Hence, advanced grade placement may make too great a demand on the child's level of experience and sophistication.

7. The most appropriate experiences for a gifted child may not be a part of the curriculum. Some students need access and exposure to knowledge and experiences that are not normally taught in school. Acceleration is bound to the traditional curriculum in ways that enrichment, for example, is not (Renzulli, 1977).

8. The level of demand for students will be so great that they will have to concentrate on convergent academic production. Hence, they will lack opportunities to develop creativity and divergent thinking abilities. This will result in rather sterile and segregated kinds of performance that will not lead to productivity in advanced studies or as an adult (Renzulli, 1977).

Social adjustment. According to many who adopt conservative attitudes toward acceleration, removal of a student from his or her peer group can occasion difficulties in social adjustment. Four objections are listed below:

1. The student who is accelerated will be pushed to perform academically, reducing the time available for age-appropriate activities. Students who are pushed to learn faster sacrifice their childhood on the altar of academic precocity. For these students, the world of play and wonder is lost to the world of adult expectations of performance (Elkind, 1986).

2. Accelerated students will miss out on important age-appropriate social activities. Those cited range from adequate time to explore peer relations in grade school to driving or attending the prom in high school. One consequence is that students will later regret these lost opportunities. Another, more serious, is that missing important formative opportunities as a child will lead to social maladjustment as an adult. Accelerants may be

handicapped in their relations with others because they lacked important exposure in childhood (DeHaan & Havighurst, 1957).

3. Older classmates might reject the young accelerant. Placement with these older peers will also reduce the amount of time available for the accelerant to interact with same-age peers. Thus, there is the possibility that acceleration reduces the number and frequency of contacts with friends (Sumption & Leuking, 1960).

4. It is unlikely that students who are older will accord as much attention or respect to classmates who are substantially younger. Hence, the accelerant has less opportunity to develop leadership skills. In later life, this can adversely affect career and social development (Mawhinney, 1964).

Reduced extracurricular opportunities. School is more than the sum of its academic parts, say the critics of acceleration. It offers the student opportunities to develop personal interests, to participate in group and team activities, and to find other outlets for self-expression. From interscholastic athletics to art and science clubs, modern American schools offer a wide range of activities of potential value to any student. There is some cause for concern if academic acceleration reduces the potential participation of students in these activities. A number of theorists have hypothesized just such a set of outcomes for the accelerant:

1. Many extracurricular activities are age related. In such cases participants may militate against the inclusion of young classmates. Accelerated students thus will have reduced opportunities to participate in potentially important and rewarding activities outside the normal school curriculum. This may result in decreased exposure to important career and avocational experiences that are normally available to students in the course of their school careers.

2. Participation in varsity athletics can be extremely important for many students. For the student who is young-in-grade, such participation is greatly reduced in likelihood. Although accelerants may be academically advanced, it is unlikely that they will also be equally well developed physically. It is not reasonable to expect that a student who is young-in-grade can compete a full four years in high school against older, stronger, and more skilled opponents. In fact, the recognition that a year or two of development may be crucial for athletes is widespread. In some states, the practice of "redshirting" students in junior high or high school has become prevalent. This entails retaining students in a grade, not for academic reasons, but to allow time for physical development in order to increase their opportunity to play varsity sports (Stover, 1988). The accel-

erant could easily become discouraged from participating against older competitors, perhaps withdrawing from athletics altogether.

Emotional adjustment. It has also been claimed that the student who is accelerated may run a risk of emotional maladjustment. Many of the claims are direct consequences of adverse effects in academic and social areas. Lack of friends, increased pressure, and reduced outlets for expression outside of schoolwork may result in emotional maladjustment.

1. Students who are accelerated will become frustrated with the level of pressure and demand. A constant push to perform will induce unacceptable levels of stress. Accelerants will eventually burn out under the pressure, reducing their level of career attainment and even becoming underachievers or dropouts.
2. Accelerants with fewer opportunities to form childhood and adolescent friendships will become isolated or aggressive toward others. They may become antisocial to the extent that they will not be able to obtain normal adult relationships in dating, marriage, and family life. Unhappy, maladjusted children will become unhappy, maladjusted adults.
3. They will be less well adjusted in later careers, because either they are misplaced in those careers, they have not had the opportunity to adjust to pressures and stress generated throughout their life, or they are unable to work effectively with others.
4. The early pressure to perform, the lack of opportunities to develop appropriate outlets in the form of personal creativity or hobbies (Passow, 1958), and the potential isolation from others may result in marital difficulties or even suicide (Uphoff & Gilmore, 1986).

For critics of academic acceleration, it seems clear that it is a process fraught with risk and potential harm. Young children who are accelerated will be hurried through a curriculum and miss essential childhood experiences, lose appropriate peer contacts, and face adult pressures prematurely. The accelerant potentially will miss much of the subsidiary benefits of the school career and be deprived of experiences than can contribute to the development of a well-adjusted adult career, home, and family. These risks are run in order to address an academic mismatch that may be temporary or illusory. For these critics, the danger of violating developmental appropriateness of curriculum and expectation far outweighs the potential benefits of the little time gained through acceleration or early admission.

The Course of the Debate

Contradictory claims of both sides should have resulted in easily clarified research hypotheses, where final answers could be obtained. In fact, the lit-

erature concerning academic acceleration is quite large, characterized by spo-
radic fits of activity and long periods of relative silence. A recent trend of the
last decade has been to examine the existing research base through a series
of reviews and meta-analyses. Cornell, Callahan, Basin, and Ramsay (Chapter 4) note that it is becoming quite difficult to review even the reviews ex-
haustively. Although several later chapters in this book deal with the specific
findings of these studies, it should be noted that certain objections to academic acceleration of older students have been fairly effectively dismissed.
Kulik and Kulik (1984) found that students who were grade-skipped did not
suffer any negative academic consequences. These students continued to
achieve at a high rate, often performing as the best students in the new placement. These findings have been confirmed by reviewers such as Daurio
(1979), Pollins (1983), and Feldhusen et al. (1986). Although there are critics
who might contradict these findings, very few recent writings cite potential
academic difficulties. The conclusions of researchers even appear to have
been shared by practitioners. Southern et al. (1989b) found in a survey of
principals, teachers, school psychologists, and coordinators of gifted programs that relatively few respondents expected academic performance to be
harmed by acceleration.

On the other hand, the evidence concerning social and emotional harm
and the effects of early admission to school is not nearly so convincing. Contradictory results from a host of early-admission studies and the difficulty of
defining appropriate measures have made it difficult to conclude whether or
not acceleration clearly contributes to social-emotional harm. Practitioners
in the Southern et al. (1989b) study were much less sanguine about the effects
of acceleration on the social and emotional development of the young child.
Many expressed reservations about whether they would recommend such a
practice for any child. In contrast to the relative absence of claims of academic harm in grade skipping, the literature is replete with warnings about
the danger of early admission and the threat to the social and emotional adjustment of all accelerants.

Social and emotional issues are different from academic ones in several
ways. Academic outcomes are much more easily defined, and there are a
battery of acceptable, reliable, and valid measures that can be employed to
determine whether or not a child is performing at a certain level. Teachers
are accustomed to make assessments frequently of a student's academic progress and feel competent to do so. Social adjustment and emotional maturity,
on the other hand, are not so easily measured or observed. Even the definitions of these constructs vary wildly from setting to setting and from individual to individual. Instruments do not have the same reliability as academic
achievement measures, and definitional problems make assessment of validity problematic. Teachers, too, are generally less confident in the assessment

of these qualities. Whereas we know to some extent the importance of certain broad academic skills for later development, we have no way of knowing the relative importance of certain experiences nor can we gauge the impact of small or large events on later development. Not knowing the signs to look for or the potential impact of what we might observe raises the discomfort we feel in recommending interventions with reputed negative effects.

It is plain that the literature has had a strong effect on the general practice of early admission. Jones and Southern (Chapter 3) discuss school-readiness literature at length, because findings from this field seem to influence attitudes toward acceleration among a wide range of the population. It is also important to point out that the results from studies of unselected children, admitted to school at relatively early ages, have been widely generalized to other accelerative practices. Thus, though much of that literature is not about academic acceleration of gifted students, or about practices applied chiefly to older students, or about programs that do not remove students completely or permanently from their age-mates, it has a decided influence on practitioner and parent attitudes.

There are a series of assumptions that critics and proponents of acceleration share that contribute to the difficulty of finding definitive research answers. One is the treatment of all accelerative options as the same. Referring to Table 1.1, it is clear that such options vary widely in salience and in the degree to which students are separated from age-mates and the normal school program. Summer classes and extracurricular programs seem intuitively different from grade skipping. This is true both for the level of need the intervention might address and for its potential to cause harm. In many studies, little is done to discriminate between the type and level of program service. These programs provide differing degrees of integration of participants with their age-level peers and hence should probably vary in the impact they might have on any of the effects cited.

In addition, the age level at which the option is provided is often ignored as a potential variable. It is possible that benefits and harmful effects are not the same for the same intervention provided to children at different age levels. Is separating first graders from age-mates the same as separating high school students from theirs? Although some writers have addressed the question of when one should accelerate (e.g., Proctor, Black, & Feldhusen, 1986; Davis & Rimm, 1988), very few researchers have provided empirical evidence about differential age effects of academic acceleration. Where it has been done (e.g., Feldhusen et al., 1986; Brody & Benbow, 1987), it is often confounded by the problem of treating various levels of acceleration as equivalent.

One confusion that has been noted by Cornell, Callahan, and Loyd (in press) is the practice of generalizing favorable results to all potential accelerants. Research to date has concerned itself with the documentation of benefit or harm for large, general populations of accelerants. In many instances, potentially rich sources of data about individual difficulties have been ignored in the aggregation of group data (see Chapter 4). Cornell et al. (in press), Maddux (1983), and Maddux, Stacey, and Scott (1981) have pointed out that the question of whom to accelerate is a much more important question than whether acceleration is good. It is essential to find out if there are students for whom acceleration is not a viable programming option.

Accelerative Options and the Concept of Mental Acceleration

Whereas many confusions muddy the questions one might ask about the effectiveness or potential harm arising from academic acceleration, there is an even more basic problem that afflicts writers, researchers, and practitioners. In part it is a semantic confusion. Saying that a student has been accelerated, we seem to imply that some process has been employed to speed that student along. The term *accelerate* in everyday usage means, after all, to speed up. In the real world of schools, however, this is rarely the case. Quite often, acceleration is the administrative recognition of a student's current academic performance. When a student skips a grade, it is because the school realizes that the student has mastered all the knowledge and skills to be taught at the current placement. Students admitted to college early are recognized to have substantially completed all the material available in the public school setting. In practice, the student is rarely "sped along."

Although in theory a student can be accelerated because a prediction is made that he or she will learn at a rate faster than other students and will subsequently be frustrated by a normal instructional pace and sequence, this is rarely the case. In fact, when examined in the light of actual school practices, most of the options listed in Table 1.1 are probably only matters of administrative recognition and convenience. Early admission, for example, usually results from an entering student's having clearly and demonstrably mastered material at a level far beyond the expected demands of kindergarten or first grade. No systematic search is undertaken to find likely candidates for the practice of early admission. Parents, and receiving teachers at the kindergarten or first-grade level, note that the child seems to be achieving at advanced levels, and they institute some sort of referral process.

The same is true of the practice of grade skipping. The student becomes a salient candidate for grade skipping because of clear demonstrations of precocious achievement to teachers and parents. The decision to skip a grade comes from a realization that the student will not be exposed to new material for a considerable amount of time, and something must be done to bring the student closer to new instructional material. Such a student has already sped through the curriculum, generally in informal ways through outside reading and experiences. Given teachers' reluctance to employ acceleration, it is probable that the performance level that confers candidacy is more than just marginally superior. Such students are likely to be performing at the upper levels of even most new placements that may be considered. Small wonder, then, that research has found accelerants to be performing with the upper ability groups even in accelerated placements.

Options like continuous progress and self-paced instruction are rare and do not involve external modification of the pace or demands of instruction. The student is responsible for setting the pace, and the material presented theoretically conforms to the student's internal needs. Differentiation of the student from peers is limited because these options are implemented in the student's broad age band. In the case of self-paced instructional materials, the actual presentation may take place entirely within the student's normal grade-level assignment; only the materials are different. Subject-matter acceleration, on the other hand, does imply that the student will spend at least a portion of each day with peers. This method, however, is largely a matter of recognition that the student is performing in some content area at a level far beyond grade-level demands. As with grade skipping and early admission, the performance must be clearly recognizable as advanced, and the discrepancy with age-level peers will probably be enormous.

Some options are clearly evident as administrative recognition. Concurrent enrollment, advanced placement, credit by examination, and correspondence courses all have built-in criteria for documenting achievement, an examination or product of some sort. These options also are applied at the student's normal grade level or in extracurricular settings. Concurrent enrollment and advanced placement are most often employed for groups of achieving students. Credit by examination and correspondence courses are individual, but they are also self-paced and take place outside the school. They do not preclude interaction with chronological peers, nor do they provide external pacing for learning.

Some options do appear to impose external pacing changes. Curriculum compacting, telescoping curriculum, and some mentorships and extracurricular options such as fast-paced classes strongly imply that the pace of instruction may be intensified outside the student's control. Moreover, there are elements of an active search for likely candidates involving assessment of potential as well as actual achievement. The fast-paced math program associated with the Search for Mathematically Precocious Youth (SMPY) at Johns Hopkins University is a notable example. In this program, a national search is undertaken to identify potential mathematical talent through the agency of the Scholastic Aptitude Test (Stanley, 1979b). In telescoping, mentorships, and compacting, some groups of target students are identified as likely participants, and the level and pace of instruction are modified. Such practices may seem extreme and invoke all the questions about the dangers of acceleration attendant to misidentification and inappropriate pacing. In reality, these interventions are still based primarily on the attained achievement of the student, and the amount of overt differentiation of students may be quite small.

Fast-paced classes, for example are basically extracurricular in nature. Most fast-paced instruction takes place outside of the school and during the summer. The students choose to participate, and the classes are filled with age-level peers. It is only when a large enough group of these classes has accumulated to allow early admission to high school or college that these programs result in age differentiation in school. One might argue that the identification methods used also concentrate on achievement. Although the SAT was selected as the test of mathematical aptitude, it may also test the effects of informal experiences in mathematics garnered from parents, reading, or educational experiences outside of school. Like the students who enter school reading, a number of children have had informal math experiences that have provided the equivalent of high school math courses.

Even telescoping may be less drastic than it appears. It most often arises as a program option at the secondary level, perhaps most frequently at junior high/middle school. Taking 3 years of instruction and collapsing it into 2 years is certainly a salient intervention. The practice, however, is almost always connected with acceleration of groups of students, maintaining for the accelerant a substantial group of age-level peers. The nature of the intervention in junior high school also identifies students who might be likely to benefit, and these are precisely those students who are the most highly achieving. Given the nature and history of the rationale for the establishment of junior high schools, it is not surprising that there are students who are achieving at levels far above average. Historically, the junior high school was instituted to allow students to consolidate learning, develop social skills, and gain some respite from the turbulence of development in early adolescence (Brimm, 1963; Eichhorn, 1966; Tye, 1984). The average curriculum expectation in junior high is pitched at a much less demanding rate than in either elementary or high school. Large numbers of students have already achieved much or even all of the material targeted in the junior high school, and these are the perfect candidates for telescoping instruction. Similar efforts at the high school level are not radical in effect either. For example, it is quite common that unselected students, on their own and with no assistance or demands from external agents, take sufficient course work to graduate a semester early. Attempts to accomplish this on a programmatic basis are probably no more taxing or difficult.

Programs that advance students into new levels of school, such as early admission to high school or college, do result in a serious discrepancy between the accelerant and the new peer group. Many, if not most, of them, however, are based primarily on the achievement of the student. Educators do not seek out likely talent and then speed instruction or raise placements to new levels. Students who are accelerated already have accomplished superior levels of achievement to justify admission to the new level. Indeed, given the conservatism with which such a practice would be viewed, it is likely that the student exceeds those minimums by a considerable margin.

If acceleration is not a process of speeding students along (hurrying them, in other words), some reevaluation is called for in the way we view acceleration research. In the first place, we should realize that much of the literature that exists noting the favorable consequences for acceleration actually chronicles the situation for students who are functioning at levels markedly higher than chronological peers in the classroom (Kulik & Kulik, 1984). Their continued high levels of achievement should come as no surprise. Moreover, concentration on the effects of some interventions that apparently make the student appear quite different from peers is to some extent unjustified. The normal candidate for acceleration is a student who is currently functioning in a manner that marks him or her as very positively deviant in performance. Much of the retrospective research on adjustment that shows some maladjustment, or research that purports to show superior adjustment, may be an artifact of the student's initial differences.

It is difficult to show that any effect we witness with accelerated students is a function of the treatment as opposed to a consequence of the condition that nominated them as candidates for acceleration. We can never be sure that effects come from the intervention or from the condition that targeted the intervention. For example, it is a strong possibility that students, parents, and teachers may attribute any positive or negative events after acceleration to the fact of acceleration itself. Experimental controls are hard to establish. No subject can function as his or her own control in this sort of experiment, and meeting the requirements of adequate between-groups design is quite impossible.

Two very human errors in causational attribution function to make it likely that observed problems will be attributed to acceleration. The first is *post hoc, ergo propter hoc.* Because one event precedes another in time, the first can be perceived as the cause of the second. Acceleration is a particularly salient event. Hence, it is likely to receive the attribution of cause for many subsequent events. In addition, we may exercise selective memory over events connected with a major decision. Those occurrences that are suspected to be connected with major events are remembered; those that do not associate themselves strongly are more easily forgotten. Prejudice makes it likely that confirmatory events are noted more strongly than disconfirmatory ones. Practitioners, parents, students, and researchers are subject to the phenomenon, and resultant associations and attributions may not be accurate.

That critics of acceleration are confused is evident from the manner in which they describe acceleration solely in terms of a process intervention. For example, Elkind (1988) talks about the danger that acceleration will rob students of time and experience. Authors in gifted education often describe acceleration as finding an appropriate pace for students (Kitano & Kirby, 1986). Acceleration is described as an identification/needs-assessment process rather than a process of recognition of achievement. Because school districts rarely seek out candidates for acceleration, this is also probably an inappropriate characterization. As an ironic aside, the major proponent of enrichment options, Joseph Renzulli (1977), is also a proponent of performance-based identification of the gifted. In nearly all districts, and for nearly any programmatic option, the performance base of the students is the delineator of candidacy for acceleration.

The Acceleration Versus Enrichment Fallacy

Many authors write about acceleration and enrichment as if they were completely discrete processes (e.g., DeHaan & Havighurst, 1957; Passow, 1958; Sumption & Leuking, 1960; Daurio, 1979; Renzulli, 1977). Although few totally negate the value of one process or the other, they often treat acceleration and enrichment as if they are segregated options. In fact, a number of authors have pointed out that the processes of enrichment and acceleration have definitions that overlap considerably (Stanley, 1979a; Kitano & Kirby, 1986; Davis & Rimm, 1988). The concept of enrichment as broadening the curriculum to include elements that are not normally present also implies that these elements are not part of the normal curriculum at that level. It is unrealistic and futile to seek subjects and courses of study that are not part of the curriculum at any level. If a second grader is interested in chemistry, eventually the instruction of that student will entail an element of acceleration. Moreover, acceleration is often indicted for a failure to modify instruction in any way other than speed. In truth, advanced study in any discipline may entail the kind of activities normally associated with enrichment. Some of these include original investigations, productive and critical thinking in the content area, moral and ethical implications of procedures, and advanced levels of analysis, synthesis, and evaluation.

Treating the two processes as though they were distinct from each other often obscures the real issues of the debate. For example, suggesting that acceleration will reduce the amount of time for exploration and development of creative abilities ignores the inherent potential of acceleration to deal with those elements in advanced study. Asserting that gifted students need advanced content instruction ignores the fact that enrichment will always contain an element of advanced material if it is to address student ability and achievement. Many claimants in the debate have generally asserted that acceleration is effective but harmful or acceleration is harmless but ineffective. Proponents of acceleration seem to attempt continually to prove that the process is not harmful. Proponents of enrichment seem most concerned with documenting that the process is effective. The opposite propositions, or the examination of questions concerning for whom these processes are effective or harmful, have virtually been ignored.

Pragmatics Versus Theory

There are two levels to problems that gifted students and their parents want to discuss. The first involves the issues most discussed in the literature. Will the student be able to handle the new placement? Will he or she have friends? Will the student adjust to the academic demands, and will valuable academic and social experiences be missed in consequence of being advanced? At the second level, the parents and students want to know if the decision will have an adverse effect on grades, athletic eligibility, or the prospect of admission to a selective college (Southern et al., 1989b). Although an administrator or teacher can comment on research conducted to answer the traditional issues, the practical ones are little researched and little discussed.

When addressing accelerative options for individual students, a school professional needs to be prepared to answer questions about practical consequences inherent in the process of acceleration. The discussion should indicate that the district has examined options for students and predicted whether difficulties are likely. Six areas are important for districts to examine, if they are to guarantee the success of accelerants in a wide range of probable outcomes.

First, students who are accelerated are subject to new placements, with new demands and increased competition. The student and parents may be anxious to know if there will be some grace period for meeting those new demands, or if the student will be expected to perform without differential assessment. Piper and Creps (Chapter 8) describe the acceleration process as one with a built-in trial period, and the implication is that this is also a grace period.

A second problem arises in the assignment of credit for work done. Schools generally have minimal requirements for course taking, content specialization, and so on. Accelerants may innocently be caught with credits in the wrong areas when they attempt to graduate. In addition, university requirements may operate to the prejudice of accelerants. In one case, a student with 5 years of high school math was admitted on probation to a state university because the high school transcript did not reflect algebra and advanced algebra he had taken as a junior high student.

Third, students who enroll in advanced placement courses, concurrent high school and college courses, or credit by examination options with high school credit are currently in a position of caveat emptor. Options portrayed as desirable and economical may have hidden traps that result in wasted effort and money. Not all colleges accept the credit offered through such programs. Often, the student and parents don't know which options are more likely to be accepted. For very able students, the kind of course credit offered is very important. For example, in one offering, a student received simultaneous credit for high school senior English and college introductory composition for the cost of college credit only. It may turn out, however, that a student with high SAT scores and a strong academic record could enroll in an honors course that yielded credit for several hours of composition. The student enrolled in the high school option would lose money, time, and contact with students capable of qualifying for the honors course. Nor is this unusual. Often advanced placement and concurrent enrollment courses screen participants from honors courses at the college level, because the student receives credit for or is enrolled in the first of a sequence of ordinary college offerings.

Fourth, parents and students are often concerned about grades received in these new placements. Such concerns are often dismissed as unimportant, even petty, by school officials. Frequently, students who apply for admission to prestigious schools, or who seek competitive scholarships, are assured that college admission officers consider differential course taking and honors options. But is this true? Little empirical information exists to support this contention. Admissions officers do consider these elements, but comparative importance assigned to this kind of information and the amount of time given to its consideration almost assuredly vary. Nairn et al. (1980) point out that despite demurrals by colleges and by the Educational Testing Service (ETS), scholarships and admissions are still being decided on the basis of small differences in scores on the Scholastic Aptitude Test. It is likely that minor differences in grade-point average may also spell the difference between admission to and rejection from selective colleges. Schools that receive many more applications than they can accept may simply not have time to weigh the differences in course taking and academic demand adequately.

Fifth, the problems of the student who is accelerated do not end at the level of high school transcript. This student requires earlier and more extensive career counseling. An accelerant may be faced with course taking and career decisions at an earlier age than other students. Yet a divided status in terms of school level (e.g., junior high or high school) or class standing in high school may allow an oversight in the normal counseling mechanisms. Falling through the cracks may have dire consequences for the students who need the most timely advice about registration for admission testing, scholarship applications, and selecting an appropriate curriculum to maximize academic attainment.

Finally, students who are accelerated for a significant part of their school day may find that they are giving up a major part of their athletic eligibility. For example, in Indiana, students who attend high school classes for 50% of the day are considered high school students in terms of athletic eligibility. Consequently, students, no matter what their age, who take two or three courses at the high school level may find that they cannot participate for four years at the high school level in interscholastic athletics.

The problems above are of real concern to students and parents. Some problems, such as questions of athletic ability, have immediate consequences for the student and his or her adjustment to a new setting. Other concerns, such as grades or appropriate credit, may have an impact several years later. Assessing the way these concerns interact with particular students is the responsibility of the school district, not solely of the parent. Professional counselors assessing the advisability of various accelerative options need to realize that many of these issues are more real than the ones that have been at the center of the last seven decades of controversy.

CONCLUSION

The issues involved in accelerating students have had a major impact on educational decisions in 20th-century America. It would be easy to say that the efforts of researchers have been wasted. Opinion remains divided. Research that validates the academic attainment of accelerants seems to have found rather wide-scale acceptance. Most practitioners, parents, and students discount the danger that students who are accelerated will fail academically in the new placements (Southern et al., 1989a, 1989b). Moreover, there is an increasing realization that all students may not be affected equally by various interventions. Several of the authors in this volume have called for concentration on the question of which, if any, of the students we recommend for acceleration will be harmed by the process. This is in stark contrast to the tenor of the literature of the distant past, which posited either universal benefits or general harm from any accelerative option.

On the other hand, some basic misapprehension remains about many of the processes we described as accelerative. As this chapter has pointed out, there is a wide gulf between what is theoretically possible in acceleration and the way acceleration is generally practiced in the field. The normal candidates for acceleration are students who are already very different from their peers in achievement. The existing divergence between the accelerant and peers in performance works to mitigate many of the apparently radical effects of moving students away from age-level peers into settings of higher academic demand.

It is also apparent that in the concern for exploration of potential harm, some very practical and immediate problems for the accelerant may have been overlooked. For the school professional in gifted education, these issues may be much thornier and more difficult to predict and address.

REFERENCES

Arneson, A. (1929). Shortening the preparation for college in Salt Lake City. *School Review, 41*, 531–538.

Baer, C. J. (1956). The school progress and adjustment of underage and overage students. *Elementary School Journal, 55*, 331–336.

Brimm, R. P. (1963). *The junior high school.* New York: Center for Applied Research in Education.

Brody, L. E., & Benbow, C. P. (1987). Accelerative strategies: How effective are they for the gifted? *Gifted Child Quarterly, 3*, 105–110.

Bureau of the Census. (1975). Bicentennial edition of historical statistics of the United States: Colonial times to 1970. Washington DC: United States Government Printing Office.

Clark, B. (1988). *Growing up gifted* (3rd ed.). Columbus, OH: Merrill.

Cornell, D. G., Callahan, C. M., & Loyd, B. (in press). Socioemotional adjustment of adolescent girls enrolled in a residential acceleration program. *Gifted Child Quarterly.*

Daurio, S. P. (1979). Educational enrichment versus acceleration: A review of the literature. In W. C. George, S. J. Cohn, & J. C. Stanley (Eds.), *Educating the gifted: Acceleration and enrichment* (pp. 13–63). Baltimore: Johns Hopkins University Press.

Davis, G. A., & Rimm, S. B. (1988). *Education of the gifted and talented* (3rd ed.). Englewood Cliffs, NJ: Prentice-Hall.

DeHaan, R. F., & Havighurst, R. J. (1957). *Educating gifted children.* Chicago: University of Chicago Press.

Eichhorn, D. H. (1966). *The middle school.* New York: Center for Applied Research in Education.

Elkind, D. (1988). Mental acceleration. *Journal for the Education of the Gifted, 11*(4), 19–31.

Feldhusen, J. F., Proctor, T. B., & Black, K. N. (1986). Guidelines for grade advancement of precocious children. *Roeper Review, 9*(1), 25–27.

Forester, J. J. (1955). At what age should a child start school? *School Executive, 74*, 80–81.

Fund for the Advancement of Education of the Ford Foundation. (1953). *Bridging the gap between school and college*. New York: Research Division of the Fund.

Fund for the Advancement of Education of the Ford Foundation. (1957). *They went to college early*. New York: Research Division of the Fund.

Gallagher, J. J. (1985). *Teaching the gifted child* (3rd ed.). Boston: Allyn and Bacon.

Hollingworth, L. (1942). *Children above 180 IQ*. New York: Macmillan.

Kett, J. (1974). History of age grouping in America. In J. S. Coleman (Ed.), *Youth: Transition to adulthood, a report to the panel of youth of the President's Science Advisory Committee* (pp. 6–29). (Publications No. 4106–00037) Washington DC: U.S. Government Printing Office.

Khatena, J. (1982). *Education and psychology of the gifted*. New York: John Wiley & Sons.

King, I. B. (1955). Effect of age of entrance into grade 1 upon achievement in elementary school. *Elementary School Journal, 55*, 331–336.

Kitano, M. K., & Kirby, D. F. (1986). *Gifted education: A comprehensive view*. Boston: Allyn and Bacon.

Kulik, J. A., & Kulik, C. C. (1984). Effects of accelerated instruction on students. *Review of Educational Research, 54*(3), 409–425.

Lehman, H. C. (1953). *Age and achievement*. Princeton, NJ: Princeton University Press.

Maddux, C. D. (1983). Early school entry for the gifted: New evidence and concerns. *Roeper Review, 5*(4), 15–17.

Maddux, C. D., Stacy, D., & Scott, M. (1981). School entry age in a group of gifted children. *Gifted Child Quarterly, 4*, 180–183.

Marland, D., Jr. (1972). *Education of the gifted and talented*. Report to the Congress of the United States by the U. S. Commissioner of Education. Washington, DC: U. S. Government Printing Office.

Mawhinney, P. E. (1964). We gave up on early entrance. *Education Digest, 30*, 8–9.

McCluskey, K. W., & Walker, K. D. (1986). *The doubtful gift*. Kingston, Ontario, Canada: Ronald Frye.

Morgan, H. J., Tennant, C. G., & Gold, M. J. (1980). *Elementary and secondary programs for the gifted and talented*. New York: Teachers College Press.

Nairn, A., et al. (1980). *The reign of ETS: The corporation that makes up minds*. The Ralph Nader Report on the Educational Testing Service. Washington, DC: Ralph Nader.

National Commission on Excellence in Education. (1983). *A nation at risk: The imperative for educational reform*. Washington DC: Author.

National Commission on Excellence in Teacher Education. (1985). *A call for change in teacher education*. Washington DC: American Association of Colleges for Teacher Education.

Newland, T. E. (1976). *The gifted in socioeducational perspective*. Englewood Cliffs, NJ: Prentice-Hall.

Passow, A. H. (1958). Enrichment of education for the gifted. In N. B. Henry (Ed.), *Education for the gifted, 57th yearbook. National Society for the Study of Education* (pp. 193–221). Chicago: University of Chicago Press.

Passow, A. H., Goldberg, M., Tannenbaum, A., & French, W. (1955). *Planning for talented youth: Considerations for public schools.* New York: Bureau of Publications, Teachers College, Columbia University.

Pollins, L. D. (1983). The effects of acceleration on the social and emotional development of gifted students. In C. P. Benbow & J. C. Stanley (Eds.), *Academic precocity* (pp. 160–178). Baltimore: Johns Hopkins University Press.

Pressey, S. L. (1949). *Educational acceleration: Appraisal of basic problems.* (Bureau of Educational Research Monographs, No. 31). Columbus: Ohio State University Press.

Pressey, S. L. (1955). Acceleration: Basic principles and recent research. *Proceedings of the 1954 Conference on Testing Problems, Educational Testing Service.* Princeton, NJ: Educational Testing Service.

Proctor, T. B., Black, K. N., & Feldhusen, J. F. (1986). Early admission of selected children to elementary school: A review of the research literature. *Journal of Educational Research, 80,* 70–76.

Renzulli, J. S. (1977). *The enrichment triad model: A guide for developing defensible programs for the gifted.* Mansfield, CT: Creative Learning Press.

Southern, W. T., Jones, E. D., & Fiscus, E. D. (1989a). *Academic acceleration: Concerns of gifted students and their parents.* Paper presented at the annual meeting of the National Association for Gifted Children, Cincinnati, OH.

Southern, W. T., Jones, E. D., & Fiscus, E. D. (1989b). Practitioner objections to the academic acceleration of young gifted children. *Gifted Child Quarterly, 33,* 29–35.

Stanley, J. C. (1977). Rationale for the study of mathematically precocious youth (SMPY) during its first five years of promoting educational acceleration. In J. C. Stanley, W. C. George, & C. H. Solano (Eds.), *The gifted and creative: A fifty year perspective* (pp. 75–112). Baltimore: Johns Hopkins University Press.

Stanley, J. C. (1979a). Identifying and nurturing the intellectually gifted. In W. C. George, S. J. Cohn, & J. C. Stanley (Eds.), *Educating the gifted: Acceleration and enrichment* (pp. 172–180). Baltimore: Johns Hopkins University Press.

Stanley, J. C. (1979b). The study and facilitation of talent in mathematics. In A. H. Passow, (Ed.), *The gifted and talented: Their education and development, 78th yearbook of the National Society for the Study of Education* (pp. 169–185). Chicago: University of Chicago Press.

Stover, D. (1988). What to do when grown-ups spoil the fun of school sports. *American School Boards Journal, 175*(7), 19–22.

Sumption, M. R., & Leuking, E. M. (1960). *Education of the gifted.* New York: The Ronald Press.

Terman, L. M., & Oden, M. H. (1947). *Genetic studies of genius: Vol. 4. The gifted child grows up: Twenty-five years' follow-up of a superior group.* Stanford, CA: Stanford University Press.

Tye, K. A. (1984). *The junior high school: School in search of a mission.* Lanham, MD: University Press of America.

Uphoff, J. K., & Gilmore, J. (1986). Pupil age and school entrance—How many are ready for success? *Young Children, 41*(2), 11–16.

CHAPTER 2

Selection of Candidates for Early Admission to Kindergarten and First Grade

Nancy M. Robinson and Linda J. Weimer
University of Washington

All children—bright or otherwise—tend to learn best when they are appropriately challenged at a level for which they are ready. Achieving an optimal match between child and challenge is a test of its own for parents and teachers. Among the options that can offer appropriate learning environments to young children is early entrance to kindergarten or first grade, provided that the children are intellectually advanced and within 6 months of the usual entry age.

Early school entrance is attractive from many viewpoints. Economically, for example, it relieves parents of the costs of a year of preschool and enables bright students to enter college, and subsequently their careers, at an earlier age. As one of several ways for providing for bright children, it is the least disruptive option from an administrative point of view. Unlike other forms of acceleration, such as grade skipping, early school entry enables children to develop stable friendships and avoids discontinuities in the curriculum. Among the most important aspects of acceleration are that it promises greater intellectual stimulation for children who would be bored with a program that satisfies other children of their age and it offers a potentially better match with their readiness for challenge and growth. There is plenty of evidence, as we shall see, that bright children carefully selected for early entrance tend to do very well indeed, both academically and socially.

Why, then, is this option utilized so infrequently, why do educators oppose it so strongly, and why are so many parents reluctant to take this step? This chapter will address these questions by, first, mentioning some of the issues that give concern to parents and educators; second, reviewing the literature that deals with outcomes of early entrance for carefully selected, capable children; and finally, considering guidelines and measures that schools and parents can use to arrive at and live with decisions.

ACHIEVING AN OPTIMAL MATCH: SCHOOLS FOR CHILDREN OR CHILDREN FOR SCHOOLS?

Increasingly, since about 1925, education in the United States has become locked into age grading (Angus, Mirel, & Vinovskis, 1988). Birthdate has become the mandate for admission or exclusion, with little regard to children's readiness for school or, in fact, the readiness and flexibility of the school to support them once they arrive. Indeed, children born prematurely and at some increased risk for school problems may, by an accident of birth, be admitted a year earlier than if they had been born at term, whereas children who are clearly advanced must wait. To be sure, some parents (typically, middle-class parents of boys) elect to keep back children who would be young-for-grade, making them, the following year, old-for-grade. Aside from the problem presented by these children, the tyranny of the calendar prevails. Unfortunately, the experiences awaiting new kindergartners or first graders are not necessarily matched to their needs and abilities. This is especially the case for brighter children. Those who are at risk for or are actually exhibiting problems in school achievement are much more likely to make special claims on the attention of the teacher and to be provided targeted programs. Very few districts pay systematic heed to kindergartners who have already mastered the goals of the curriculum, leaving it up to their already burdened teachers to make provisions. Because many districts favor only enrichment programs, special planning for advanced students does not begin until late into the elementary school years, after basic skills have been mastered. Leaving these students locked into standard grade-level curriculum, which does not match their learning pace or interest level, means that children with advanced conceptual and academic skills, so eager at first to enter school, are in clear danger of becoming casualties of the system. Although it is no panacea, early entrance can ameliorate some of these problems by matching child to system, since most systems lack sufficient flexibility to adjust to the child.

RESEARCH BACKGROUND

There are four distinct bodies of research about early school entry that the unwary reader may fail to distinguish. One small set of studies deals simply with teachers' and administrators' attitudes about early entry. A second set examines *unselected* children who happen to be younger than the average child in their class. The third, and much more relevant set of studies, deals with children who have been *selected* for early school entry by reason of their intellectual, academic, and social readiness. Finally, there are studies about the stability of advanced development: Do bright children remain bright over time, so that it is all right to make long-term decisions when the children are quite young? We will discuss questions raised by each of the four sets of studies considering some methodological issues that need to be taken into account.

Issues of Research Design

The research question. Both the questioner and the question should be considered when designing a study. From a school district's point of view, for example, it may be sufficient to discover whether, in comparison with classmates, children accepted early will as often survive without blatant school failure. The district has a stake in minimizing the demands made on teachers by children who are not doing well and wants to avoid the expense of retaining some fraction of them for an extra year. What the parent really wants to know, however, at the fork in the road, is how the child will fare academically, socially, and emotionally as an earlier or a later entrant. To respond to this question, the most relevant comparison groups are children comparable in birthdate, ability, academic skills, maturity, and personality, who do or do not enter early.

Selective factors. Such comparable groups are very difficult to identify not only because children who are significantly advanced are few in number but also because there are subtle selective factors, unrelated to intellectual development, that underlie even the initial consideration of early entry. For example, some of the applicants may already be exhibiting signs of boredom and discontent with incipient behavior problems in preschool or kindergarten; or they may be outstandingly mature, physically large, and socially skilled; or the parents may have agendas of their own (such as reducing day-care costs). Application will not be made for all eligible children.

Documentation. Some aspects of a child's development can be measured more objectively and reliably than others. For example, by age 5, intelligence test scores tend to be more stable than behavior ratings made by parents or teachers. It is often difficult to document adults' impressions of the child's abilities, temperament, and maturity. Yet, when one attempts to ferret out how decisions might have been made more effectively, it is essential to have records that are complete and comparable across children. This ideal has seldom been reached.

Longitudinal designs. It is important to follow children's school careers from the point of school entry and not simply to compare, at some later grade, those who were "let in" early and those who were not. Despite the cost of longitudinal studies, without them one would miss the children who were retained in grade as well as children who left the system altogether.

Despite all these caveats, the questions remain and therefore answers must be sought. Fortunately, most of the studies make up in concurrence what they lack in methodological rigor. We report here a few individual studies, as well as reviews available for detailed reading.

Reluctance of Teachers and Administrators

A few investigators have surveyed teachers and administrators, invariably reporting negative attitudes toward early entrance. Braga (1971), for example, found negative attitudes toward early entrance expressed by primary-grade teachers, some of whom maintained these views even after positive experiences with such children. One the whole, however, primary-grade teachers with early entrants in their classes were more likely to respond favorably. Kindergarten teachers asked by Jackson, Famiglietti, and Robinson (1981) to rank the probable achievement of hypothetical cases—highly advanced children, moderately advanced children, and average children—consistently gave low ranks to early entrants. First-grade teachers were less consistent, suggesting that the first-grade teachers recognized the value of early entrance but preferred that kindergarten teachers manage the period of adaptation. Southern, Jones, and Fiscus (1989) similarly found conservative attitudes expressed by school personnel, though they also found that personal experience (self or family member) with accelerative options was associated with more positive views; gifted coordinators and school psychologists were also somewhat more accepting of the practice than were teachers and administrators. Proctor, Black, and Feldhusen (1988) surmise that administrators are predisposed against early entrance mainly because it is administratively messy, requires expensive assessment, and risks the ire of parents whose children are excluded.

Educators, when queried, consistently indicate worries about the social and emotional maturity of accelerated children, not about their academic success. Perhaps they are not aware of research that points to the social maturity that characterizes brighter children as a group; perhaps they give greater weight to social goals; perhaps they overgeneralize from a few younger children who do exhibit problems (as do some older children as well). Since the monumental research of Lewis Terman and his colleagues (e.g., Terman & Oden, 1947), confirmed with consistent redundancy by educators ever since (Daurio, 1979; Janos & Robinson, 1985), we have known that, as a group, gifted children prefer older friends, show mature patterns of communication, and exhibit high levels of social skills and social/moral reasoning, although there are, of course, broad individual differences. The fact that the personality and maturity of the child will weigh heavily in the decision to admit or exclude is often forgotten by educators.

Unselected Populations: Younger Versus Older

Studies comparing the achievement and school problems of young-for-grade children with those of their classmates make use of easily accessible indices such as school grades, achievement test scores, referrals to psychologists, and grade retention. Probably because they are easy to do, such studies abound. Earlier reports (e.g., Bigelow, 1934; Carter, 1956; Green & Simmons, 1967; Hall, 1963; King, 1955) agree remarkably with later ones (e.g., Breznitz & Teltsch, 1989; DiPasquale, Moule, & Flewelling, 1980; Drabman, Tarnowski, & Kelly, 1987): At least through elementary school, those children whose birthdays are later in the school year tend to fall short on all indices, a phenomenon that holds true across countries (Husen, 1967), even though standard ages of school entry differ significantly by state and country (Shepard & Smith, 1986). The effect is usually found to diminish over time (Shepard & Smith, 1986).

It is disheartening that so many school settings expect all the children in a grade—differing by as much as 12 months in age and usually more than that in developmental level—to be alike. By doing so, we create failures and exaggerate the significance of transient or mild learning problems. These are unfortunate outcomes, but they are not particularly relevant to capable children who have been carefully selected and are expected not merely to hold their own in the class but to be among the top students.

Selected Populations: Early School Entry

A very different picture emerges when we examine the literature dealing with early school entry for children who have been carefully evaluated. The several comprehensive reviews available (Braga, 1971; Daurio, 1979; Proctor, Black, & Feldhusen, 1986; Reynolds, Birch, & Tuseth, 1962; Worcester, 1956) tend to produce optimistic expectations. Even by 1962, reviewers could state:

> It may be concluded . . . early admission to school of mentally advanced children who are within a year of the ordinary school-entrance age and who are generally mature is to their advantage. . . . There are few issues in education on which the research evidence . . . is so clear and so universally favorable to a particular solution. (Reynolds et al., 1962, p. 16)

A review by Proctor et al. (1986) includes 21 studies, some comparing early entrants with their unselected classmates and others comparing them with matched samples. Of the first group, 16 of 17 studies found early entrants the equal of or surpassing their classmates in achievement, with several studies showing progressive improvement in academic standing. There were hints of some social adjustment problems for a small percentage of children in the early grades, although these disappeared over time. Only one study (Obrzut, Nelson, & Obrzut, 1984) found increased incidence of retention, primarily for social reasons. A careful reading of the data, however, suggests that teacher judgment, "the determining element that discriminated the success or failure of the students (p. 76)," may have been biased against acceleration. The accelerated children may often have been placed in settings where they were not well tolerated, and their behavior may have been rated by adults with biased perceptions.

Especially significant were the several studies of early entrants who were in junior and senior high schools; the students were excelling academically, participating in numerous extracurricular activities, and exhibiting strong, positive self-concepts. Perhaps best known of these studies is one by Hobson (1963), who followed a group longitudinally and found that by high school, the early entrants exceeded their classmates by 2 to 1 in honors, awards, and other graduation distinctions despite greater involvement in extracurricular activities (including athletics and social honors as well as more intellectual pursuits).

In a definitive experimental study, children who are eligible for early admission would be randomly assigned to early versus standard year of entrance. No one, however, has undertaken such a study, which would certainly be unpopular with parents (who have definite ideas about what they want for their children) and well might raise questions of ethical responsibility. There is, however, a very small group of studies that has made an attempt at control by comparing early entrants with nonaccelerated children matched in ability. Such methods do not escape the selective factors that determine which children were, or were not, accelerated, but they are a step in the right direction. Mueller (1955) and Pennau (1981) compared early entrants with matched samples one year behind them in school.

In Mueller's study, children who had met the criteria and had entered kindergarten early were rated by their teachers in grades 1–5, on traits of achievement, health, coordination, popularity, school attitude, and emotional adjustment. Early entrants were rated as superior on all traits to all other groups, including regular classmates, children who had not met the criteria, and even eligible children who had been kept back a year.

Pennau (1981), also using a matched sample, found few differences; in fact, any differences in adjustment tended to favor the early entrants, although, as Proctor et al. (1986) point out, there may have been subtle differences in adjustment between the groups prior to school entry.

One can conclude that early admission is almost certainly not a bad idea and may even be helpful when selection is careful and admissions criteria relatively stringent. For example, in the eight matched-control studies cited by Proctor et al. (1986), those finding mildly negative effects tended to be the minority with relatively low requirements, such as an IQ of 115 or an MA of 5–0, so that the early entrants did not have a "running start."

Although not limited to early school entrants, the major analysis by Kulik and Kulik (1984) of school accelerants clearly demonstrates that academic achievement advantage lies with the student who is accelerated. In that meta-analysis of a large number of studies, students who were a year advanced in placement were equally advanced in academic achievement.

Children who enter early may not be admitted as frequently to their district's special program for gifted children (Maddux, 1983). This consideration will vary in importance according to the nature of the program itself and the strength of the child's abilities. By implication, at least in the early grades, the needs of some of these children may be effectively met in the regular classroom. Since most "gifted" programs occupy only a fraction of a child's school week, this trade-off may be positive in some instances, negative in others.

To which variables should most weight be given? Very few investigators have asked this question. With early entrance clearly a viable option, it is time that investigators turn to specific issues such as this so that decisions can be better informed.

Stability of Developmental Advancement

By the time a child is of school age, scores on tests of general intelligence tend to remain fairly stable over time. A very long-term follow-up of the California segment of the original preschool standardization sample for the 1937 Stanford-Binet is probably the best study available of an unselected young population. By heroic efforts, Bradway was able to track 111 subjects into early adulthood (Bradway & Robinson, 1961), 62 of them into their middle adult years (Kangas & Bradway, 1971). The correlation between first test in 1931 and the Wechsler Adult Intelligence Scale administered 25 years later was an impressive 0.64 (0.80 over the 15-year period from junior high to adulthood).

Using data from a large study of twins in Louisville, Humphreys and Davey (1988) report that IQs at age 4 were correlated 0.79 with those at age 6 and 0.60 with IQs earned at age 15; age 5 IQs yielded higher correlations, 0.87 to age 6 and 0.67 to age 15.

Despite the tendency for scores to remain relatively constant over a period of years, the IQs of some individuals do change dramatically sometimes steadily upward or downward, sometimes in an irregular pattern (Honzik, Macfarlane, & Allen, 1948; McCall, 1970; McCall, Appelbaum, & Hogarty, 1973), the larger changes tending to occur in brighter children. Even the high follow-up correspondences reported by Bradway et al. concealed some large shifts; in the first 10 years after the preschool tests, 22% changed by more than 15 points, and between the second and third, 7% changed by the same amount. Using deviation IQs rather than ratio IQs has, however, reduced the magnitude of some of these shifts (Pinneau, 1961).

With respect to specific skills identified in young children, early reading is a standout easily identified by adults and exhibiting some stability during the early years. Mills and Jackson (in press), following children to second grade who had been identified as precocious readers in kindergarten, found them later to be advanced readers but not as remarkably so as when first assessed. In a longitudinal study following children whose parents had identified them as gifted during the preschool years, Robinson, Robinson, and Stillman (cited in Robinson, in press) found preschool reading skills to be modestly stable to age 6, more stable than within-domain skills in spatial, numerical, or verbal reasoning.

Longitudinal studies of this nature can yield some hints about the direction of changes to be expected for an individual child. Some part of the instability is simply error of measurement; an initially high score is likely to be followed by a slightly lower one. Bradway and Robinson (1961) found that changes could be predicted by an index of familial attainment stretching over two generations; often the changes tracked by Honzik et al. (1948) were accompanied by changes in family situation, social adjustment, and mental health. Sontag, Baker, and Nelson (1958), interestingly, found that the most significant gains in IQ between ages 3 and 10 were earned by children high in achievement motivation; more passive, lackadaisical children decreased in relative standing. There are, then, no easy answers, but for a child who is active and curious, who exhibits personal maturity, and whose family is supportive, the picture is a relatively positive one not only for stability but possible growth.

CONTEXTUAL ISSUES OF ASSESSMENT AND DECISION MAKING

In this section, we consider some contextual issues bearing upon application for early entry. Subsequently, we discuss specific areas of ability and suggest methods of assessing a child's status to inform such a decision.

Assessment and decision making do not occur in a vacuum or in a uniform educational setting. The legal standards and common practices of the school system in question are important, as are the characteristics of the particular school, its curriculum, and its population.

Legal entry dates vary such that a child deemed old enough in one state may be several months too young in another, although there is a trend to make the cutoff as early as September 1. Additionally, local communities evolve their own patterns, a frequent variant being the custom of waiting a year to enroll boys with spring or summer birthdays in kindergarten. Many of these are bright children whose parents hope to give them a "competitive edge." The result is an older average age and increasing within-classroom ranges of chronological and developmental ages, both of which need to be considered in determining the readiness of a young child.

Differences among state and school systems also influence the results of standardizing testing. Tests standardized nationally or in states with late cutoff dates are likely to underestimate the proficiency of children in areas with earlier cutoffs (older average ages). It is easy to be misled by an impressive score on a nationally normed test. Young children's reading and calculating skills make significant leaps in a short period of time, so that one must be very careful about the normative group with which they are being compared.

The openness and flexibility of the school system are also important considerations. No matter how ready a child may be, early entry in a setting where teacher and administrators are opposed to this strategy may be setting up the child for failure. A cooperative spirit of partnership among teachers, counselors, and parents will greatly increase the likelihood of success. The ease of grade-placement adjustments up or down during the kindergarten to second-grade period, and the support given to students who experience such adjustments, can also greatly facilitate the match between student ability and class setting and reduce the risks of a decision (for or against early entry). The likelihood that being young-in-grade may lessen chances of later placement in special "gifted" programs (Maddux, 1983) may be an argument, in some settings, for delaying entrance in spite of a child's readiness, depending upon the child's intellectual advancement. Weighing in such a decision, too, are the alternative interim options (including private options) to maintain the child's interest and developmental progress.

Individual and family factors must also be taken into account. Regardless of advancement, a child undergoing significant personal stress such as adjustment to divorce, serious illness in the family, frequent moves, or family financial crisis may not have the emotional energy available for a transition that requires more than the usual adjustment of beginning school. Gathering background information, preferably in a face-to-face parent interview, should be included in any careful assessment. Additionally, a trained examiner can sometimes provide clues to the child's anxiety, stress, and resilience.

Although this chapter focuses on assessment to determine the advisability of early entry for intellectually advanced young children, it is important that the clinician not narrow the focus of an individual evaluation to questions of grade placement alone. A thorough assessment is also an opportunity to screen for real problems that may impact a child's learning or social-emotional adjustment. Intervention that is likely to help the child's development or adjustment should be planned whether the child is admitted as an accelerant or not.

AREAS OF ASSESSMENT

When development is evenly advanced across the board in all domains, the process of determining the child's "fit" with chronologically older children is greatly simplified. The difficult decisions occur where there is unevenness of development, probably a more common circumstance.

As we have mentioned, there are few studies identifying the best predictors of the success of an accelerative strategy, and therefore decisions at this time rely heavily on clinical and teacher experience. In this circumstance, we suggest that, in light of the goal of improving the match between the child and the educational environment, priority be given to those factors most central to the school experience, namely, intellectual and academic ability. Assessment of perceptual abilities and memory in young children who have not yet become readers and calculators can screen for problems predictive of early learning difficulties, but advancement in these areas is not necessarily predictive of later high attainment. Assessment of social and emotional maturity and physical development also provides essential information about the ease with which the child is likely to function within the peer group. In very bright children, however, social skills may appear "retarded" when in fact they have had no intellectual peers with whom to share play interests or conversation.

Cognitive Abilities

Cognitive, or reasoning, abilities are critical to achieving a match with a child's school placement. Several measures exist that provide not only an estimate of overall cognitive advancement but a sampling of special abilities as well. Included are, for example, measures of vocabulary, verbal reasoning of both an abstract and an everyday nature, quantitative reasoning, construction of figures requiring analytic and integrative abilities, and so on. Scores derived from these tests are the strongest predictors available for later intellectual development and school achievement. Used as an estimate of the child's rate of development (e.g., an IQ of 125 suggests cognitive development roughly 25% more rapid than that of the average child), one can approximate the difference expected over time between the individual child's abilities and the typical age norms that guide curriculum development. A word of caution about use of IQs is in order. Although frequently useful as predictors of how early entrants will fare, IQs should be used only as approximate predictors of successful adjustment to early entrance.

A professionally administered individual intelligence test, such as the Wechsler Preschool and Primary Scale of Intelligence, Revised (WPPSI-R) (Wechsler, 1989), or the Stanford-Binet Intelligence Scale, Fourth Edition (Thorndike, Hagen, & Sattler, 1986), is recommended as the measure of cognitive abilities. These measures are well designed, nationally normed, and comprehensively validated. Both yield IQs (a form of standard score) and age norms for each of the subscales. Other measures such as the McCarthy Scales of Children's Abilities (McCarthy, 1972), or the Kaufman Assessment Battery for Children (K-ABC) (Kaufman & Kaufman, 1983) are popular in some regions, and there is an advantage to using a measure that is familiar to the local schools. These instruments also feature individual achievement tests normed on the same populations.

As mentioned above, individual administration allows the tester to observe the child's reaction to challenge and difficulty, enthusiasm for problem solving, or anxiety in a new situation. Such information is useful in predicting a child's response to early entrance and is also essential (especially for the young child) in estimating the degree to which test performance approximates the child's best effort.

Except, perhaps, where a child misses a cutoff by only a matter of days, or in a school with decidedly low achievement levels, children who show moderate advancement (e.g., an IQ of 115) usually are not strong candidates for early entrance. In mental age, they are unlikely to fall within the top half of the classes in the immediate or distant future. In contrast, for a child who is unusually advanced (e.g., IQ > 145), early entrance may at best represent only a temporary solution to the problem of achieving an ability match with classmates. The question then becomes whether early entrance provides short-term benefit, and what plans can be made when this adjustment is outgrown.

When evaluating a profile from the WPPSI-R or the Stanford-Binet, Fourth Edition, it is helpful, again, to consider the relative significance of the factors assessed. For example, it is reasonable to give special weight to the portions of the tests that assess verbal and quantitative reasoning, because these abilities are most central to school success. Follow-up studies have not supported the expectation that above-average (as opposed to below-average) abilities in visual-motor skills assessed during the preschool era are particularly effective predictors of later academic achievement (Badian, 1988), although short-term memory skills may be of somewhat more importance (Sattler, 1988).

Academic Abilities

In view of the emphasis during the first few school grades on the acquisition of reading and calculation skills, children's interest and readiness for learning these skills is a prime consideration in the early-entrance decision. A child who is entering kindergarten need not already be a reader or calculator but should exhibit an interest in and readiness for such activities. For early advancement to first grade, Proctor, Feldhusen, and Black (1988) recommend what seem to us reasonable minimums: reading comprehension and arithmetic reasoning at the second-semester level of first grade in the local school district. Such achievement assures that the child will not be among those who need a little extra time with these skills, as do many children with age-appropriate or even advanced cognitive development.

Several considerations mandate careful selection of an appropriate academic achievement measure for this decision process. First, current norms are essential, particularly for the earliest grades. With so many children attending preschool, with the advent of educational television for young children and an abundance of academically oriented games and books, and with increased parental interest in early childhood education, children are not entering kindergarten with skills that were formerly acquired during the kindergarten year. Outdated norms yield significantly inflated grade equivalents and raise unreasonably high expectations for the child's performance and relative standing in the classroom. When available, the use of local norms for such tests may also help decision making. Such statistics provide direct comparisons with the group where children are to be placed.

Second, the ceiling effect of some scales will affect the ablest students who take tests designed for their age-mates. Very few items of sufficient difficulty are available to discriminate individual differences among the top group; on some tests, even a perfect score results in a percentile rank of less than 90 (Cohn, 1988). Missing even one item may result in the child's failing to qualify for a program appropriate to his or her educational needs. The ceiling effect is most critical on tests designed for a narrow age or grade range. Bright children need to be tested on a measure that leaves room for advanced performance.

The most appropriate achievement measures for this purpose are those that are designed for individual administration and assess performance across a broad range of academic skills. Individual administration allows observation of the child's interest level, reaction to failure, attentiveness, and working pace. Using a wide-ranging test, the examiner can adapt the level of difficulty to the child's ability level without lengthy administration of easier material. Reading tests should include reading comprehension as well as word recognition; arithmetic tests should include reasoning tasks as well as standard operations. Three achievement test batteries that meet these criteria are the Woodcock-Johnson Psycho-Educational Battery, Revised (Woodcock & Johnson, 1989), the Kaufman Test of Educational Achievement (K-TEA) (Kaufman & Kaufman, 1985), and the Peabody Individual Achievement Test—Revised (PIAT-R) (Dunn & Markwardt, 1989).

Classroom Learning Skills

Although not strictly academic, there also exist a set of learning skills that most children acquire in the course of preschool. These include, for example, the ability to remain engaged in an interesting task for perhaps 15 minutes without adult redirection, the ability to be a member of a group (as, e.g., listening to a story), the ability to listen and remember oral instructions, the ability to translate from one visual stimulus (e.g., a blackboard) to another (e.g., a piece of paper), and a vocabulary that encompasses concepts of relationship and quantity basic to classroom communication. There is no easy measure for any of these behaviors. Perhaps the best source of information here is the preschool teacher, who generally has a good sense of how a child compares with age-mates in these learning skills. A child who has not attended preschool, and therefore has not had the previous experience of developing group social skills, adapting to structured routines, and sharing adult attention, is seldom a good candidate for early school entry.

Screening for Learning Problems

Because some children with advanced intellectual ability still experience significant learning difficulties, and because neuropsychological deficits are associated with reading underachievement among both intellectually average and superior children (Bow, 1988; Mantzicopoulos, Morrison, Hinshaw, & Carte, 1989), it is essential that for children who are not reading fluently, a screening of reading readiness be included in the assessment. It is not necessary that the child demonstrate significant advancement in these areas, only age-appropriate processing abilities for reading acquisition. Significant predictors of successful versus delayed reading achievement include perception of orientation of letters and numbers, phonological awareness and auditory discrimination, and auditory short-term memory.

Some children with quite adequate visual discrimination and orientation may have trouble identifying easily confused letters such as *b*, *d*, *p*, and *q*, or *m* and *w*, simply because of minimal exposure. For them, a measure using other visual stimuli such as the Motor-Free Visual Discrimination Test (Colarusso & Hammill, 1972) or the Visual Discrimination subtest of the Woodcock-Johnson Psycho-Educational Assessment Battery would be appropriate.

Auditory discrimination in kindergarten applicants may be assessed with the Wepman Auditory Discrimination Test (Reynolds, 1987), although norms are inexact and the length of the test taxes the attention of young children. A preferable option is the Word Discrimination subtest of the Test of Language Development—2 Primary Level (Newcomer & Hammill, 1988). The ability is generally developed fully by age 6 and tests of pure auditory discrimination show strong 6-year ceiling effects.

Auditory processing may also be assessed by the Memory for Sentences subtests of the WPPSI-R or the Stanford-Binet, Fourth Edition, which require both word discrimination and short-term auditory memory. Short-term auditory memory has consistently been found to predict reading achievement (Bow, 1988; Sattler, 1988; Stanovich, 1985). We suggest that a child who does well on Memory for Sentences need not be given a further auditory discrimination test. Such tests are unnecessary for children already reading at the late first- or second-grade level, but solid age-level ability in short-term auditory memory is important to ensure the ability to follow classroom instructions.

Information from parent interview will also be helpful in assessing risk for learning problems. Children with reading problems are more likely to have histories of problems such as birth complications, speech delays, or family histories of learning disability. Such background factors are significant for decision making if the child's own development appears questionable. Where some evidence of learning problems is discovered during this step of the assessment process, further evaluation may be needed to determine the appropriate course of action. For some children, the issue is one of maturity; however, parents and educators should be cautious about delaying schooling as a sole treatment. For children with problems in perceptual discrimination, fine motor skills, language, or the like, specific intervention during the intervening year may maximize chances of later success.

Motor Development

The child's competence in motor skills, as well as health and physical stamina, is important in determining a comfortable fit within the peer group and the ability to participate in classroom and playground activities. Fine motor coordination and visual-motor integration are essential to the paper and pencil activities typically introduced in kindergarten, and delays in visual-motor integration are often associated with delays in acquiring reading skills. Well-standardized measures of visual-motor integration are exemplified by the tasks of copying designs that are included in subscales of the WPPSI-R and the Stanford-Binet, Fourth Edition. If the intellectual measure does not include such a subscale, the Test of Visual-Motor Integration (Beery, 1982) may be administered.

Because a quality kindergarten program should include a variety of physical activities, information about physical strength and coordination will help estimate whether the child will stand out as significantly less mature than classmates, thereby increasing the risk of advanced placement. The McCarthy Scales of Children's Abilities (McCarthy, 1972) includes a variety of upper and lower body coordination tasks that are appropriate for 5- and 6-year old activities. In questionable cases, where motor skills may be pivotal to a decision, the lengthier Peabody Developmental Motor Scales (Folio & Fewell, 1982) would provide a more thorough assessment of both fine and gross motor skills. If suspicion arises of a significant problem, then referral to a pediatric occupational therapist would be appropriate.

Social-Emotional Maturity Issues

As described earlier in this chapter, most reviewers have concluded that opposition to acceleration of gifted students is based primarily on concern for the child's social and emotional development. Teachers cite social maturity as the most desired information in assessing adjustment of early entrants, despite the consistent failure of reviewers to document a social-emotional disadvantage for accelerants, and despite the consistent finding that, as a group, gifted children prefer older friends and show mature patterns of communication and social skills. Rather than following an age-based policy based on generalization, assessors need to consider each child's social and emotional maturity. Unfortunately, valid and reliable information regarding social maturity is very difficulty to provide. Favorable information would be reports of adaptation to preschool or group activities and evidence of existing friendships with children within the age range of the proposed class. Yet, the decision process often occurs during the summer, when teachers may be unavailable as informants and when the luxury of observing the child in an appropriate group setting is impossible; in such cases, parent interview and the behavioral observations of the psychologist must be more heavily weighted. The Socialization subscale of the Revised Vineland Adaptive Behavior Scale (Sparrow, Balla, & Cicchetti, 1984), a parent interview measure, will provide an estimate of social maturity but should be supplemented by additional inquiry regarding the child's emotional adjustment and the parents' reasons for considering acceleration. Children who are unready for school tend to exhibit short attention spans, inattentiveness, trouble postponing gratification, impulsiveness, low frustration tolerance, poor task orientation, and behavioral rather than verbal expression of aggression (de Hirsh, 1975).

What appears to be evidence of social immaturity should, however, be considered in light of the child's background and advanced intellect. From our experience in consultation with families and schools, we have seen that lack of success in making friends may be due to lack of common interest and communication style with age peers; what may at first appear to be distractibility may be due to the combination of a quick and curious mind with unchallenging material. In such cases, behavior problems may signal the advisability of advancement rather than its reverse. Well-adjusted, gifted young children, although often considered popular by age-mates, may prefer older children (who share interests) or younger children (whom they can organize in games of imagination) and may believe that they have few "friends" because their notion of friendship is more mature than that of their age-mates (Roedell, Jackson, & Robinson, 1980). Extremely bright children may, moreover, have fewer friends than do other children of their age, and some may experience marked loneliness (Janos, Marwood, & Robinson, 1985).

When adjustment problems are suspected, it is important to distinguish between "immaturity" and a stable personality trait. It seems reasonable to consider that serious adjustment problems such as angry or depressed mood or habitual noncompliance signal additional risk for early entrants. On the other hand, children who are slow to enter a group may not be anxious or maladjusted but may be showing the same family temperament and interactional style as their shy, cautious parents. Such a style is not likely to change significantly with an intervening year. Indeed, intellectually advanced children who lack desirable social skills, such as entering a group or negotiating a shared activity, may have a better setting for developing those skills with peers of similar mental age and interests than in a strictly chronological age group. It is also important to remember that social skills are teachable and that timely instruction and support by teachers and parents can greatly aid a child's adaptation to peers and avoid problems in emotional development

A Suggested Battery

Table 2.1 summarizes the measures we have recommended for an assessment battery suitable to address the issues we have raised. Note that the measures are, in the main, individually administered, recently normed, and broad scale enough to assess advanced levels of functioning.

Table 2.1   Kindergarten and First-Grade Screening Battery

Preferred tests are capitalized; alternatives are also listed in some cases.

MENTAL ABILITY

WECHLER PRESCHOOL AND PRIMARY SCALE OF INTELLIGENCE, REVISED (WPPSI-R) (or)

STANFORD-BINET, FOURTH EDITION

McCarthy Scales of Children's Abilities

Kaufman Assessment Battery for Children

VISUAL DISCRIMINATION

KAUFMAN TEST OF EDUCATIONAL ACHIEVEMENT

PEABODY INDIVIDUAL ACHIEVEMENT TEST, REVISED READING RECOGNITION (for children not reading well, additional visual discrimination measure is needed)

WOODCOCK-JOHNSON PSYCHO-EDUCATIONAL BATTERY, REVISED, VISUAL DISCRIMINATION subscale (if needed)

Motor-Free Visual Discrimination Test

GROSS MOTOR SKILLS

MCCARTHY SCALES OF CHILDREN'S ABILITIES, MOTOR SCALE

Peabody Developmental Motor Scale

Revised Vineland Adaptive Behavior Scale, Motor subscale (kindergartners only)

FINE MOTOR SKILLS

WPPSI-R GEOMETRIC DESIGNS

Peabody Developmental Motor Scale (if detailed assessment needed)

Test of Visual Motor Integration (VMI)

(May be supplemented, as above, by Vineland Motor Scale)

AUDITORY DISCRIMINATION

(ordinarily will not be needed for children reading well)

WPPSI-R MEMORY FOR SENTENCES (this does involve memory load)

TEST OF LANGUAGE DEVELOPMENT—2 PRIMARY, WORD

DISCRIMINATION

Wepman Auditory Discrimination Test

Goldman-Fristoe Auditory Discrimination Test

SOCIAL-EMOTIONAL MATURITY

REVISED VINELAND ADAPTIVE BEHAVIOR SCALE (Socialization, Daily Living Skills)

AVAILABILITY OF OPTIONS

As we have indicated previously, there are a number of issues quite apart from the child's developmental level that impinge on the early-entrance decision. Among these are current and future educational options.

Despite all the findings we have quoted that demonstrate clearly that early entrance is a viable option for carefully selected children, there will always be individual cases that defy the odds. Later circumstances, such as a change in the child's developmental pace, increased family stress, or a child's preference, may call for a change of plans. The availability of options may encourage a bit of risk taking in the early decision; if no options are available, more conservatism may be in order.

Local resources may or may not present a wide variety of choices. We list here but a few to look for:

1. The suitability and availability of gifted programs
2. Ungraded or combined-grade elementary classes through which a child can later move rapidly or more slowly
3. Cross-grade skill-level grouping for academic subjects
4. A suitable private school in which a grade could be repeated
5. Skipping a grade later on (a much more positive option than grade retention)

LIVING WITH JUDGMENT CALLS AND COMPROMISES

Educational options for children who do not fit the "average" mold almost always are compromises. For the very bright child, it is nearly impossible within the common educational system to achieve simultaneously placement with classmates who are (1) age-mates with heterogeneous abilities, (2) at the child's own level of social and emotional maturity, and (3) at the child's level of intellectual maturity and academic achievement. Some families are secretly hoping for heaven on earth. They want their bright children not only to grow with challenge but to be supremely happy in every aspect of their lives, academically successful, outstanding at sports, musically talented, and socially acclaimed. Any sign of stress or minor failure can serve as evidence that the entry choice was a bad one, that all would have been well if the child had (or had not) entered kindergarten early.

Given the careful consideration of intellectual, social, and physical development, available options, and supportiveness of the environment for an individual child, parents and school personnel simply must do the best they can. It is important to recognize, however, that there are drawbacks to any decision, and it is usually unwise to shift back and forth unless conditions prove compelling.

Indeed, some decisions do prove later to have been unwise and need undoing. The majority are, however, worthy and sensible compromises that can and should be lived with. Most children cope well with most circumstances. Children who have the solid backing of parents who appreciate them as people, who attend to their efforts rather than just their successes, and who lend them optimism through life's ups and downs are themselves likely to experience school in a very satisfactory way. Gifted children and their families are destined to live with compromise.

REFERENCES

Angus, D. L., Mirel, J. E., & Vinovskis, M. A. (1988). *Historical development of age-stratification in schooling.* Ann Arbor: University of Michigan School of Education, Bureau of Accreditation and School Improvement Studies.

Badian, N. A. (1988). The prediction of good and poor reading before kindergarten entry: A nine-year follow-up. *Journal of Learning Disabilities, 21,* 98–103.

Beery, K. E., (1982). *Revised administration, scoring, and testing manual for the developmental test of visual-motor integration.* Cleveland, OH: Modern Curriculum Press.

Bigelow, E. B. (1934). School progress of underage children. *Elementary School Journal, 35,* 186–192.

Bow, N. J. (1988). A comparison of intellectually superior male reading achievers and underachievers from a neuropsychological perspective. *Journal of Learning Disabilities, 21,* 118–123.

Bradway, K. P., & Robinson, N. M. (1961). Significant IQ changes in twenty-five years: A follow-up. *Journal of Educational Psychology, 52,* 74–79.

Braga, J. L. (1971). Early admission: Opinion versus evidence. *Elementary School Journal, 72,* 35–46.

Breznitz, Z., & Teltsch, T. (1989, April). The effect of school entrance age on academic achievement and the social-educational adjustment of children: A longitudinal study. Paper presented at the meetings of the Society for Research in Child Development, Kansas City, MO.

Carter, L. B. (1956). The effect of early school entrance on the scholastic achievement of elementary school children in the Austin public schools. *Journal of Educational Research, 50,* 91–103.

Cohn, S. J. (1988). Assessing the gifted child and adolescent. In C. J. Kestenbaum & D. T. Williams (Eds.), *Handbook of clinical assessment of children and adolescents* (pp. 355–376). New York: New York University Press.

Colarusso, R., & Hammill, D. (1972). *Motor-Free Visual Perception Test.* San Antonio, TX: The Psychological Corporation.

Daurio, S. P. (1979). Educational enrichment versus acceleration: A review of the literature. In W. C. George, S. J. Cohn, and J. Stanley (Eds.), *Educating the gifted: Acceleration and enrichment* (pp. 13–63). Baltimore: Johns Hopkins University Press.

de Hirsch, K. (1975). Language deficits in children with developmental lags. In R. Eissler, M. Kris, & A. J. Solnit, (Eds.), *Psychoanalytic Study of the Child, 30*, 96–126.

DiPasquale, G. W., Moule, A. D., & Flewelling, R. W. (1980). The birthdate effect. *Journal of Learning Disabilities, 13*, 234–238.

Drabman, R. S., Tarnowski, K. J., & Kelly, P. A. (1987). Are younger classroom children disproportionately referred for childhood academic and behavior problems? *Journal of Consulting and Clinical Psychology, 55*, 907–909.

Dunn, L., & Markwardt, F. (1989). *Peabody individual achievement test, revised.* Circle Pines, MN: American Guidance Service.

Folio, R. M., & Fewell, R. R. (1982). *Peabody developmental motor scales.* Allen, TX: DLM Teaching Resources.

Green, D. R., & Simmons, S. V. (1967). Chronological age and school entrance. *Elementary School Journal, 63*, 41–47.

Hall, R. V. (1963). Does entrance age affect achievement? *Elementary School Journal, 63*, 391–396.

Hobson, J. R. (1963). High school performance of underage pupils initially admitted to kindergarten on the basis of physical and psychological examinations. *Educational and Psychological Measurement, 23*, 159–169.

Honzik, M. P., Macfarlane, J. W., & Allen, L. (1948). The stability of mental test performance between two and eighteen years. *Journal of Experimental Education, 17*, 309–324.

Humphreys, L. G., & Davey, T. C. (1988). Continuity in intellectual growth from 12 months to 9 years. *Intelligence, 12*, 183–197.

Husen, T. (Ed.). (1967). *International study of achievement in mathematics, Vol. I.* Stockholm: Almquist & Wiksell.

Jackson, N. E., Famiglietti, J., & Robinson, H. B. (1981). Kindergarten and first grade teachers' attitudes toward early entrants, intellectually advanced students, and average students. *Journal for the Eudcation of the Gifted, 4*, 132–142.

Janos, P. M., Marwood, K. A., & Robinson, N. M. (1985). Friendship patterns in highly intelligent children. *Roeper Review, 8*, 46–49.

Janos, P. M., & Robinson, N. M. (1985). Psychosocial development in intellectually gifted children. In F. D. Horowitz & M. O'Brien (Eds.), *The gifted and talented: Developmental perspectives* (pp. 149–195). Washington, DC: American Psychological Association.

Kangas, J., & Bradway, K. (1971). Intelligence at middle age: A 38-year follow-up. *Developmental Psychology, 5*, 333–337.

Kaufman, A. S., & Kaufman, N. L. (1983). *K-ABC: Kaufman assessment battery for children.* Circle Pines, MN: American Guidance Service.

Kaufman, A. S., & Kaufman, N. L. (1985). *K-TEA: Kaufman test of educational achievement.* Circle Pines, MN: American Guidance Service.

King, I. B. (1955). Effect of age of entrance into grade 1 upon achievement in elementary school. *Elementary School Journal, 55,* 331–336.

Kulik, J., & Kulik, C. (1984). Effects of accelerated instruction on students. *Review of Educational Research, 54,* 409–425.

Maddux, C. D. (1983). Early school entry for the gifted: New evidence and concerns. *Roeper Review, 5*(4), 15–17.

Mantzicopoulos, P., Morrison, D. C., Hinshaw, S. P., & Carte, E. T. (1989). Nonpromotion in kindergarten: The role of cognitive, perceptual, visual-motor, behavioral, achievement, socioeconomic, and demographic characteristics. *American Educational Research Journal, 26,* 107–121.

McCall, R. B. (1970). Intelligence quotient pattern over age: Comparisons among siblings and parent-child pairs. *Science, 170,* 644–648.

McCall, R. B., Appelbaum, M. I., & Hogarty, P. S. (1973). Developmental changes in mental performance. *Monographs of the Society for Research in Child Development, 38* (Serial No. 150).

McCarthy, D. (1972). *Manual for the McCarthy scales of children's abilities.* San Antonio, TX: The Psychological Corporation.

Mills, J. R., & Jackson, N. E. (in press). Predictive significance of precocious reading achievement. *Journal of Educational Psychology.*

Mueller, K. J. (1955). Success of elementary students admitted to public schools under the requirements of the Nebraska program of early entrance. *Dissertation Abstracts, 15,* 2103.

Newcomer, P. L., & Hammill, D. D. (1988). *Test of language development—2 primary level.* Austin, TX: Pro-Ed.

Obrzut, A., Nelson, R. B., & Obrzut, J. E. (1984). Early school entrance for intellectually superior children: An analysis. *Psychology in the Schools, 21,* 71–77.

Pennau, J. E. (1981). The relationship between early entrance and subsequent educational progress in the elementray school. *Dissertation Abstracts, 42,* 1478 (4A).

Pinneau, S. R. (1961). *Changes in intelligence quotient, infancy to maturity.* Boston: Houghton Mifflin.

Proctor, T. B., Black, K. N., & Feldhusen, J. F. (1986). Early admission of selected children to elementary school. A review of the research literature. *Journal of Educational Research, 80,* 70–76.

Proctor, T. B., Black, K. N., & Feldhusen, J. F. (1988). Early admission to elementary school: Barriers versus benefits. *Roeper Review, 11,* 85–88.

Proctor, T. B., Feldhusen, J. F., & Black, K. N. (1988). Guidelines for early admission to elementary school. *Psychology in the Schools, 25,* 41–43.

Reynolds, W. (1987). *Auditory discrimination test* (2nd ed.). Los Angeles: Western Psychological Services.

Reynolds, M. C., Birch, J. W., & Tuseth, A. A. (1962). Research on early admissions. In M. C. Reynolds (Ed.), *Early school admission for mentally advanced children* (pp. 7–17) Reston, VA: Council for Exceptional Children.

Robinson, N. M. (in press). The use of standardized tests with gifted children. In A. Tannenbaum & P. Klein (Eds.), *To be young and gifted.* Northwood, NJ: Ablex.

Roedell, W. C., Jackson, N. E., & Robinson, H. B. (1980). *Gifted young children.* New York: Teachers College Press.

Sattler, J. M. (1988). *Assessment of children* (3rd ed.) San Diego: Author.

Shepard, L. A., & Smith, M. L. (1986). Synthesis of research on school readiness and kindergarten retention. *Educational Leadership, 44,* 78–86.

Sontag, L. W., Baker, C. T., & Nelson, V. (1958). Mental growth and personality development: A longitudinal study. *Monographs for the Society for Research in Child Development, 23,* (2, Serial No. 68).

Southern, W. T., Jones, E. D., & Fiscus, E. D. (1989). Practitioner objections to the academic acceleration of gifted children. *Gifted Child Quarterly, 33,* 29–35.

Sparrow, S. S., Balla, D. A., & Cicchetti, D. V. (1984). *Revised Vineland adaptive behavior scale.* Circle Pines, MN: American Guidance Service.

Stanovich, K. E. (1985). Cognitive determinants of reading in mentally retarded individuals. *International Review of Research in Mental Retardation, 13,* 181–214.

Terman, L. M., & Oden, M. H. (1947). *Genetic studies of genius: Vol. 4. The gifted child grows up: Twenty-five years' follow-up of a superior group.* Stanford, CA: Stanford University Press.

Thorndike, R., Hagen, E., & Sattler, J. (1986). *Stanford-Binet Intelligence Scale, Fourth Edition.* Chicago: Riverside.

Wechsler, D. (1989). *Wechsler preschool and primary scale of intelligence, revised.* San Antonio, TX: The Psychological Corporation.

Woodcock, R. W., & Johnson, M. B. (1989). *Woodcock-Johnson psycho-educational battery, revised.* Allen, TX: DLM Teaching Resources.

Worcester, D. A. (1956). *The education of children of above-average mentality.* Lincoln: University of Nebraska Press.

CHAPTER 3

Objections to Early Entrance and Grade Skipping

Eric D. Jones and W. Thomas Southern
Bowling Green State University

If one looks only at the research from gifted education on the effects of acceleration, it appears to have been fairly conclusively resolved that gifted students benefit from acceleration and acceleration poses no direct risks to their achievement or development. If, however, one uses current practices as an indicator of consensus, it becomes readily apparent that the issue is not settled. Teachers and administrators often express serious reservations about the practice, particularly when considering early admission and grade skipping in the primary grades (Jackson, Famiglietti, & Robinson, 1981; Southern, Jones, & Fiscus, 1989b). Indeed, it seems that parents are more likely to initiate referrals than are professional educators. Educators may recognize the precocity of the young candidates, but they rarely recommend either early entrance or grade skipping—even in school systems where other options for gifted children have not been developed.

When considering acceleration in the primary grades, the issues of most concern to public school teachers are frequently different from those that concern parents and specialists in gifted education. Parents typically feel that it is unlikely that instruction offered to age-level peers will be challenging to their academically precocious child. They consider acceleration a viable option because it appears to afford their child an appropriate level of instruction that is not likely to be provided in classrooms of same-age peers. Educators, on the other hand, are more concerned that children who are younger than the rest of their classmates will not be mature enough to meet the various demands of being schooled with older and presumably more mature peers. They consider that the relative difference in chronological age between a child and his or her classmates is a more powerful predictor of future adjustment and success in school than the child's demonstrated achievement. Children who are relatively young compared with their peers are presumed to be less ready for schooling and more apt to confront serious problems in academic achievement and social-emotional adjustment. Educators worry that acceleration places young gifted children at risk for serious problems in adjustment. Educators' apprehensions about the risks presented by early entrance or grade skipping can be substantially accounted for by several factors, including

1. Assumptions about the intellectual, academic, and social-emotional development of children—particularly gifted children
2. Knowledge about and experience with acceleration
3. The extent to which individual differences among students are perceived as impeding the operation of the school programs
4. The extent to which they consider that schools can or should be expected to accommodate individual differences and varied instructional needs

Practitioners' objections to acceleration are based primarily upon their notions of common sense (Southern et al., 1989b). Placing gifted students with older students, in the contexts of increasing demand, would seem to (1) increase academic pressures to perform, (2) decrease opportunities for forming friendships and social interactions, and (3) limit the models and occasions for developing age-appropriate behavior and experiences. The validity of educators' intuitions appears to be bolstered by their recollections of personal experiences and, to a lesser degree, the school-readiness literature. They will not easily set aside their widely shared opinions. Practitioners who hold these commonsense opinions, however, appear to be unaware of the empirical studies from gifted education on the effects of acceleration (Southern et al., 1989b). The results of studies that are inconsistent with their current and highly personal perceptions will not be accepted easily. In order to understand the difficulties that educators have with the acceptability of early admission and grade skipping, it will be necessary to identify and to examine the nature and logic of objections to early entrance and grade skipping and to weigh the nature and persuasiveness of contrary evidence.

In this chapter, three topics related both to understanding practitioners' objections and to providing a more rational basis for making decisions about the appropriateness for acceleration will be examined:

1. Practitioners' perceptions of the effects of acceleration
2. The logic and implications of expressed objections and their perceived implications
3. The importance of information available from teachers, parents, and the students themselves for making informed decisions about the advisability of early entrance and grade skipping

BASES OF PRACTITIONERS' OBJECTIONS TO ACCELERATION

Early entrance and grade skipping were once commonly used options for meeting the instructional needs of gifted students in public education (Daurio, 1979). Currently, however, many practitioners in the public school consider both forms of acceleration to be unacceptable—regardless of a child's demonstrated level of achievement. It appears that their objections are based upon combinations of personal experiences, intuitions, and the literature on school readiness. To some extent it appears that the tensions of the current educational reform movement may have also toughened educators' resistance to early entrance or grade skipping for any children.

Experience and Attitudes Toward Acceleration

Southern et al. (1989b) examined the sentiments of educational practitioners (elementary school principals, teachers in grades K to 3 and 5, school psychologists, and coordinators of programs for gifted children) toward early entrance and acceleration. They found that the practitioners generally regarded these forms of acceleration as unacceptable options for meeting the educational needs of gifted children. The attitudes expressed by teachers and principals were more negative than those expressed by school psychologists and coordinators of programs for gifted children.

The observation that practitioners hold negative attitudes toward acceleration is consistent with an earlier study by Braga (1971). Both studies revealed that practitioners considered that placing young children with older classmates would jeopardize their social-emotional adaptation. Avoiding problems with social-emotional development was clearly their overriding concern. Educators did not consider that the academic achievement of the young accelerants would be directly jeopardized, but the teachers in Braga's (1971) study considered that young accelerants might be indirectly and adversely affected by increased demands for working independently, coping with class routines, remaining attentive and quiet, and tolerating the frustrations of competition in classrooms with relatively older children. Paradoxically, in the Southern et al. (1989b) study, although educators clearly regarded both forms of acceleration as very risky, most also considered that requiring precocious children to be instructed with their age-mates was also potentially harmful.

When asked for reasons for their feelings about acceleration, the teachers interviewed by Braga (1971) referred to their specific experiences with early entrants. In the study by Southern et al. (1989b), very few of the respondents had direct experience with either a referral for acceleration or the instruction of a child who had been accelerated. Nevertheless, respondents cited personal experience as being important to shaping their opinions far more frequently than they did professional literature, teacher training, or the experiences of their peers. It is interesting to note that respondents who either had been accelerated themselves or had family members who had been accelerated were more likely to report favorable attitudes toward early entrance and grade skipping.

Clearly, practitioners consider that personal experiences provide an important basis for their beliefs about the effects of early entrance and grade skipping. It is also evident that because so few practitioners have direct encounters with accelerated gifted students, experiences with students other than gifted accelerants are brought to bear in their judgments of the value of acceleration. Most educators at the primary level have a substantial amount of experience with the academic and adjustment problems of children who are not prepared for school by the time they reach legal age for entrance. Their expressed beliefs about early entrance and grade skipping plainly reveal that they consider that young children—regardless of their demonstrated levels of achievement—will be immature and, thus, at a substantial disadvantage in classes with older students. Recent professional and popular press articles that have issued caveats about trends in highly structured infant instruction and "hurrying of children" developmentally also seem to have sparked their concerns (e.g., Elkind, 1981, 1986). Educators' notions about school readiness and their fears of adjustment problems underpin their beliefs about the benefits and risks of acceleration at the primary level. In order to confront the problems in the validity of their assumptions, it is necessary to examine the concept of school readiness and to review the school-readiness literature.

School Readiness

Interpretations of the construct of school readiness can reasonably be described according to a continuum that ranges from nativist interpretations at one end and environmental interpretations at the other (Smith & Shepard, 1988). The nativist interpretation assumes that intellectual development and social-emotional growth, like physiological development, proceed according to a fixed pattern. The general assumption is that developmental stages cannot be skipped nor can progress be accelerated through the stages. Thus, according to the nativist perspective, there is little chance that children who are developmentally behind their age-mates will be able to catch up. Similarly, children who are developmentally ahead of the age-mates will, barring misfortune, remain ahead of them.

In contrast to the nativist view, the environmental perspective describes both intellectual and social-emotional development in terms of an individual's prior learning. Within the broad limits of normal development, three elements of an individual's environment can account for differences in readiness to meet the demands of instruction and schooling—opportunities to learn, quality of learning experiences, and encouragement to persevere in learning (cf. J. B. Carroll, 1963). The environmental perspective is fundamentally different from the nativist position. First, it conceptualizes readiness in terms of the prior mastery of skills, not in terms of a series of qualitatively different developmental stages. A student is "ready" for a particular instructional task if the requisite preskill behaviors have already been learned. Progress toward readiness can be predicted from previously learned behavior rather than from chronological age. Second, the rate of growth does not necessarily progress evenly. Rate is determined by opportunities for learning, quality of instruction, and perseverance in the learning activity. Third, individual differences are not considered immutable. Differences between students can be minimized or accentuated, depending on the differences in instructional experiences.

Teachers who view child development from a nativist perspective appear to believe that chronological age is a more important predictor of readiness than demonstrated achievement. A study of kindergarten teachers (Smith & Shepard, 1988) suggests that their beliefs about school readiness may mediate their hesitance to consider early entrance or grade skipping as vehicles for meeting the needs of precocious children. Smith and Shepard (1988) observed that kindergarten teachers who had nativist perspectives on school readiness exhibited consistent approaches for dealing with students whom they considered to be immature and, thus, not ready for the demands of school. Nativist educators frequently recommended that children who appeared immature should stay at home an additional year or, perhaps, attend a prekindergarten program. Compared with teachers who adhered to a more environmental perspective, teachers who held nativist beliefs retained high proportions of their students. Students who failed to master academic skills or appeared to be socially immature were likely to be recommended for retention. In schools where the nativist beliefs prevailed, early admission was virtually nonexistent. On the other hand, teachers with more environmental views were more apt to attempt to accommodate individual differences of both gifted students and students needing remedial support.

Smith and Shepard (1988) did not report on the incidence of either early entrance or grade skipping in schools where environmental perspectives tended to prevail, but they did report that teachers in those schools used a variety of strategies to accommodate individual differences, including allowing capable students to accelerate by attending classes in different grades rather than being permanently assigned. Thus, it is reasonable to speculate that teachers' assumptions about intellectual, academic, emotional, and social development in general may influence their sentiments about the acceleration of gifted students.

Teachers who view school readiness more as a product of instruction than of native development may be less resistant to early entrance and acceleration. Although the nativist perspective appears to enjoy greater popularity than the environmental, there is evidence that it is not the more defensible perspective for addressing individual differences. The environmental view has, however, been gaining greater acceptance in special education where there is increasing support for direct instruction. The essence of the environmental perspective is also apparent in both the teaching of performance music and the coaching of competitive age-level sports such as swimming. Proficient young musicians and athletes routinely train and compete with older children. Very few of their mentors would seriously consider delaying advanced and more rigorous training for their most talented and willing proteges.

SCHOOL-READINESS RESEARCH

Although educators considered that personal experiences were the most important bases for their perceptions about acceleration, they sometimes bolstered the validity of their assumptions with reference to the school-readiness literature (Southern et al., 1989b). Some educators referred to specific publications or authors by name. In most cases, however, their references to the conclusions of the literature were general. Educators who were resistant to acceleration tended to believe that there was a body of literature that would support their sentiments. It is interesting to note that, when questioned, none of the respondents could cite an author or a study that supported acceleration, though some indicated a general awareness of the existence of such literature.

School-readiness studies of the academic and social adjustment of children who are relatively young compared with their classmates have often reported that younger children are more likely to have lower levels of academic achievement (Baer, 1958; Bigelow, 1934; M. L. Carroll, 1963; Carter, 1956; DiPasquale, Moule, & Flewelling, 1980; Forester, 1955; Hall, 1963; King, 1955; Langer, Kalk, & Searls, 1984) and more difficulties in social and emotional adjustment (Baer, 1958; DiPasquale et al., 1980; King, 1955). They are also more likely to be at greater risk for retention (DiPasquale et al., 1980; Langer et al., 1984) and for referral to programs for learning-disabled students (Diamond, 1983; DiPasquale et al., 1980). Several writers (e.g., Donofrio, 1977; Frick, 1986; Uphoff & Gilmore, 1985, 1986, 1987) have argued against any early school admission—regardless of an individual child's aptitude. They have also advocated both raising the minimum age for school entrance for all children and advising the parents of young children who appear to be relatively immature at preschool screenings that they be held out of school an additional year.

School-readiness literature has also been used to legitimize recommendations for "best practices" on early admission and retention (e.g., Ohio School Psychologists Association, 1989). It is also apparent that the school-readiness literature has been given more credence than the studies from gifted education. Yet when it comes to the issues of early admission for selected high-achieving students, the school-readiness studies are, at worst, fraught with severe methodological deficiencies and, at best, misapplied. Moreover, policy implications that have been drawn from these studies are inconsistent with most reasonable and currently accepted positions on early intervention and individualization of instruction.

GENERAL METHODOLOGICAL PROBLEMS

Although examinations of research methodologies may seem tedious, school-readiness studies must be scrutinized closely in this regard. The validity of the conclusions of these studies and the generalizations drawn from them depend heavily on the adequacy of the research methodologies that were used. Although school-readiness research, with few exceptions, has received uncritical acceptance among educators, the studies characteristically show grave methodological errors. Many of the threats to the validity of the studies can be related to four important issues: sampling, local contexts in which the studies were conducted, statistical conclusion validity, and selection of criteria for judging the effects of acceleration.

Sampling

Threats to the validity of conclusions drawn from school readiness studies are related to basic problems in the selection of samples—inadequate description and inappropriate restriction. Inadequate sampling procedures severely compromise the validity of any generalizations that can be drawn from the school readiness studies.

Sample descriptions. The validity of generalizations beyond the specific results of the study depends on the extent to which the persons studied are not substantially different from the ones to whom the generalizations are applied. In most school-readiness studies, the only characteristics that have been described are grade level, intelligence, age, and sex. Two variables that should have been explored are the reasons early admission was granted to those children who obtained it and socioeconomic status. Early admission has frequently been sought by single parents or couples who both work outside the home (Carter, 1956; Green & Simmons, 1962; Hall, 1963). In the 1950s and early 1960s when many of the school-readiness studies at issue were done, these situations were related to a family's lower socioeconomic status. The results of studies detailing the performance of young working-class children, whose early school entries were related to their families' economic circumstances and not to academic precocity, may not be useful in making predictions about the performance of academically precocious children. The two groups of students are not similar with respect to either the reasons that early entrance was sought or a host of values and behaviors that educational research has repeatedly associated with successful adjustment to schooling.

Only two studies have attempted to address the effect of socioeconomic status. Green and Simmons (1962) matched their student samples on socioeconomic status. They found no benefit to barring capable young children from early school entrance. Langer et al. (1984) examined correlations between grade retention and several variables for a very large sample of black and white pupils. They observed statistically significant, but trivially small, negative correlation between age-in-grade and achievement. In fact, the data cited in their study revealed that the relationships between achievement and (1) quality of home environment, (2) level of parental education, and (3) quality of the community were much more important than chronological age for predicting success in school.

Sample restriction. None of the school-readiness studies systematically investigated the effects of acceleration in the primary school on children who were selected because of their high achievement. Two of those frequently cited (King, 1955; DiPasquale et al., 1980) intentionally eliminated children who had high intelligence. Some studies did attempt to account for the effect of cognitive ability (e.g., Baer, 1958; Green & Simmons, 1962; Maddux, Stacy, & Scott, 1981; Partington, 1937; Uphoff, 1985, cited in Uphoff & Gilmore, 1986) by using unselected groups of students with fairly high measures of ability such as IQ. Research by Maddux and his colleagues (Maddux et al., 1983; Maddux et al., 1981) deserves attention. That study is presented as a consideration of the effects of early entrance on the performances of gifted students and will likely be used by critics of acceleration to support their contentions that even gifted students are at serious risk from early admission. That study, however, has very little to do with the early admission of precocious children. The young-in-grade students were not early entrants. They were students who were born within 6 months of the final date for school entrance. Although Maddux et al. observed that a significantly larger proportion of the students in gifted programs came from the oldest-in-grade group of students compared with the young-in-grade group, these results merely indicate that there is an advantage in being relatively old-in-grade. Because the students in the Maddux et al. study were not selected for early entrance prior to being labeled, and because none of the students were early entrants, the results of the study have little relevance in discussions of the acceleration of students who were identified as precocious before they were accelerated. Pennau (1981) suggested that it is not legitimate to assume that the performances of unselected students with relatively high IQs can be generalized to those of candidates for acceleration who would be selected on the basis of their demonstrated academic precocity. Students with high IQs who were not provided early admission indicated poorer attitudes toward school and exhibited more behavior problems compared with early entrants with comparably high IQs. Intelligence tests were administered after-the-fact and did not indicate affective variables that would have been likely to contribute to a referral for early entrance.

The descriptions of the unselected samples do not indicate the reasons children were relatively young-in-grade. It is not clear that they were academically precocious. Other factors such as family economics (cf. Carter, 1956) can contribute to a referral for early admission. Some bright children may not demonstrate exceptionally remarkable levels of academic achievement, but they are admitted early because of apparently high levels of social maturity. Finally, some young-in-grade children may appear relatively young simply because they reached the legal age for school entrance during the last months of the legal enrollment period. They may not have entered school early or skipped grades. In practice, students who are considered for academic acceleration because of their demonstrated academic or intellectual precocity exceed the average levels of performance by a substantial margin. The differences between selected and unselected populations of early entrants are apt to be quite marked.

The conflicting results on the effects of being relatively young-in-grade, from studies in the areas of school readiness and the education of gifted and talented children, indicate the critical importance of selecting samples. In the school-readiness literature, primary school students who are relatively young-in-grade consistently achieve at slightly lower levels compared with their older classmates (Shepard & Smith, 1986). The school-readiness literature consistently indicates that those small differences between groups of relatively younger and older classmates substantially disappear around the third grade (DiPasquale et al., 1980; Hall, 1963; Halliwell & Stein, 1964; Langer et al., 1984; Miller & Norris, 1967; Shepard & Smith, 1986).

The results of studies of the performances of students who have been accelerated on the basis of their demonstrated academic precocity differ markedly from the results of the school-readiness studies. Proctor, Black, and Feldhusen (1986) reviewed 21 empirical studies of the effects of early entrance and found that academically precocious students fared as well as or better than their peers in early primary grades. Perhaps more important, the studies that examined the performances of early entrants during their junior and senior high school years indicated that throughout their school careers, they continued to be well adjusted and to excel academically. A meta-analysis by Kulik and Kulik (1984) corroborates Proctor et al.'s (1986) conclusions. Thus, in the school-readiness studies, the superior performances of older students on various outcome measures may be an artifact that is related to the population being studied. To the extent that those differences persist in the literature they seem to be the result of differences in the experimental context, bias in measurement, or inappropriate methodologies.

Local Context

The events that occur during a study or in the general context of a study can threaten the validity of any conclusions that are promoted. It is clear from the reports that most of these studies took place during local controversies over how old children should be when they enter school. Of the studies that reported negative effects due to early entrance, all but two (DiPasquale et al., 1980, Langer et al., 1984) appear to have been conducted by persons employed by the school district in which the study took place (Baer, 1958; Bigelow, 1934; M. L. Carroll, 1963; Carter, 1956; Forester, 1955; Hall, 1963; King, 1955; Mawhinney, 1964; Obrzut, Nelson, & Obrzut, 1984). On the other hand, of the six studies that observed no disadvantage associated with early entrance, four (Deitz & Wilson, 1985; Green & Simmons, 1967; May & Welch, 1984; Miller & Norris, 1967) were conducted by persons outside the employ of the districts in which the studies took place. There is no indication in these reports that the personal or professional integrities of the researchers were compromised, but there is a possibility, too obvious to ignore, that objectivity may have been diminished by the political contexts in which the studies occurred. For example, Obrzut et al. (1984) observed that early entrants were retained at a higher rate compared with that for children who did not enter school early. Teacher judgment, not objectively measured indicators of achievement or adjustment, emerged as the element that determined the successful adaptation of bright young students to early entrance. Vaguely defined nonacademic traits such as short attention span, lack of initiative, or need for supervision were generally given for retaining young accelerants. Neither reading achievement nor serious social-emotional adjustment problems accounted for difficulties experienced by some early entrants.

Obrzut et al. did observe a significant relationship between school success and achievement in mathematics. It is quite possible that the early entrants were at risk as a result of having to confront teachers whose biases against acceleration limited their tolerance for young accelerants—not as a result of the increased academic demands and social stresses. Mathematics is, to a great degree, a curriculum-dependent subject. That is, the skills that a student acquires are apt to be dependent on those that have been taught. Failure to master skills at the lower levels of the hierarchy will have increasingly more serious effects on achievement. Mastery of reading skills is less dependent on instruction: Obrzut et al.'s observation that mathematics, not other academic skills, predicted the school success of early entrants suggests that early entrants may not have been carefully instructed or monitored. Their teachers may have expected that the early entrants would acquire basic academic skills on their own.

Because of potential problems with interpreting studies based on combined samples, the results of Obrzut et al.'s study must be interpreted cautiously. These researchers studied the combined groups of students who had been given early entrance over a 3-year period. If the proportions of accelerants who were retained were the same each year, it is not justifiable to collapse those data from the 3-year period into one group (Cook & Campbell, 1979). Different levels of retentions for each cohort group would indicate differences in the selection or accommodation of early entrants, not the effects of acceleration. If, for example, most of the retentions of early entrants occurred during the first year, the reasonable interpretation would be that whatever problems with the selection or accommodation of early entrants may have existed in the first year of the study were not present in subsequent years.

Validity of Statistical Conclusions

Tests of statistical significance are frequently used to determine whether relationships between variables are sufficiently strong that one could conclude that chance alone would not account for the relationships observed in the study. Obtaining statistical significance does not, however, prove that relationships actually exist. It merely indicates the degree to which the observed relationships would be expected to have occurred at random. Of several possible conditions that can affect the validity of statistically based conclusions, the problems of "fishing rate" (Cook & Campbell, 1979) is pertinent to the school-readiness studies.

The more an investigator "fishes" for relationships, the greater the probability that random associations of variables will be mistaken for systematic relationships. For example, in the study by Baer (1958) at least 70 analyses were conducted. With so many analyses, it is a virtual certainty that some instances of statistical significance will be observed—even if all of the associations between variables actually occurred randomly. Several other studies that reported negative effects of early entrance made only slightly less prodigious pursuits of statistical significance (Bigelow, 1934; M. L. Carroll, 1963; Carter, 1956; Diamond, 1983; DiPasquale et al., 1980; King, 1955; Miller & Norris, 1967). By their casual acceptance of the results of statistical analyses, school-readiness researchers have blurred the differences between random and nonrandom occurrences of relationships.

It is true that the revelation of consistent relationships in a large number of studies might be credible. Certainly many of the studies reveal consistent benefits in academic attainments for older students. Yet the magnitudes of these benefits are quite small (Shepard & Smith, 1986), and the validities of the observations of benefit are not convincing. The consistency of the findings is often muddled by the range and dubious relevance of the variables that have been examined. The next section reviews issues arising from the variables selected as indicators of acceptable adaptation and adjustment.

Selection of Evaluation Criteria

Most of the school-readiness studies used measures of achievement from standardized tests as the basic criteria for evaluating the effects of early entrance. Other measures of academic achievement included teacher-assigned grades (Forester, 1955), discrepancies between expected and observed achievement (Green & Simmons, 1962; Huff, 1984, cited in Uphoff & Gilmore, 1985), rates of retention (Hall, 1963; Langer et al., 1984; Miller & Norris, 1967), and rates of referral to special education programs (DiPasquale et al., 1980; Diamond, 1983). The effects of early entrance on social-emotional adjustment have been evaluated with measures of social maturity (Forester, 1955; Baer, 1958) and leadership (Mawhinney, 1964). Each of the variables listed above has serious limitations on its value as an indicator of achievement and adjustment of children who enter school early.

Standardized norm-referenced achievement tests are, perhaps, the best indicators of achievement that have been used in school-readiness studies. Unless, however, the tests have been carefully selected so that the local curriculum content is reflected in the test, the validity of the evaluation will be seriously compromised (Gredler, 1978). It is unlikely that the tests used in the studies were carefully matched to the curricula. Most local school districts do not conduct such content validations. When districts do attempt the process, they generally require considerable technical assistance (Northwest Regional Education Laboratory, 1979). Problems with the validities of norm-referenced evaluations are minor compared with difficulties encountered with the other measures of academic achievement. Teacher-assigned grades are extremely susceptible to bias—as are other measures that depend on assigned grades, such as discrepancies between expected and observed achievement, retention rates, and rates of referral or placement in special education programs.

Review of the assessments of early entrants' social-emotional adjustment revealed that the school-readiness researchers have demonstrated little regard for (1) the technical quality of the instruments used, (2) the natures of the traits being studied, or (3) the theoretical significance of the traits that they have chosen for evaluation. With the exception of the study by Miller and Norris (1967), which used peer ratings, each of the studies that evaluated emotional or social adjustment used teacher ratings. The theoretical or instructional significance of those differences is not readily apparent, but it is interesting that peer ratings revealed disadvantage for late entrants. Early entrants were not at a disadvantage for social adaptation.

Because teacher ratings depend upon clinical expertise and objectivity, there is reason to question their validity. Research in clinical psychology demonstrates that clinical judgment is often no better than stereotypic diagnoses based upon general information such as age and grade (Mischel, 1968). Furthermore, the observations of untrained observers appear to be as accurate as those of trained clinicians (Kazdin, 1978). Teacher ratings of social and emotional adjustment are highly susceptible to bias. In contexts where early entrance is a political issue, their susceptibility to bias may be even greater.

Part of the problem in assessing social-emotional adjustment is that it is a nebulous concept. It is difficult to describe and measure adequately. The narrow measures that are typically used hardly capture the complex nature of the traits to be measured. This difficulty has been noted in the studies of acceleration of gifted children (Daurio, 1979; Kulik & Kulik, 1984; Pollins, 1983) as well as in school-readiness studies. Some traits such as peer interaction and leadership have been studied as indicators of adjustment, but they are at best only tangentially related to adjustment. With leadership, for example, researchers have concluded that students who were admitted early were later found to be lacking in leadership (Forester, 1955; Mawhinney, 1964, cited in Uphoff & Gilmore, 1985). Leadership is, however, irrelevant to the decision on whether or not a precocious child should be offered academic acceleration. In public school curricula, systematic attempts are generally not made to promote leadership skills at primary levels. Some critics who lament the effects of acceleration on leadership misinterpret their own data. For example, Mawhinney's (1964) study reported that only 20% of the early entrants were outstanding leaders. This report is hardly as discouraging as Mawhinney believes. It indicates that early entrants probably contribute more than their share of outstanding leaders. Even if the reported figure is not spuriously high, it seems to represent quite an accomplishment for a group of students who were accelerated for reasons unrelated to the nature of their peer relationships.

In summary, educators' attitudes toward acceleration have been braced by the school-readiness literature, but virtually none of the conclusions from that research can be justified. The school-readiness studies are, at worst, fraught with severe methodological deficiencies and, at best, misapplied. Policy implications that have been drawn from these studies will do a disservice to precocious children and children who have not been adequately prepared for schooling.

ERRORS OF INTERPRETATION: IMPLICATIONS FOR POLICIES AND PRACTICES

Despite serious methodological problems, the results of school-readiness studies have been uncritically accepted. Unfortunately, these results have been erroneously interpreted to policy makers. Two such interpretations of the school-readiness research are that (1) early admission and grade skipping are causally related to later difficulties in academic achievement and social-emotional adjustment and (2) nonintervention is the preferred intervention for avoiding possible future academic and adjustment problems of young children.

Interpretations of Causation From Correlation

In their rush to explain the relationship between school failure and chronological age, some reviewers (e.g., Diamond, 1983; Uphoff & Gilmore, 1985; Ilg & Ames, 1965) hypothesize a causal link between age-in-grade and negative academic and social effects for school children revealed by correlational data. Some of these assumptions lack even a superficially plausible argument for causality. For example, Uphoff and Gilmore (1985) assert that the immaturity may be related to the higher levels of off-task behavior that they noted among students in their study. Uphoff and Gilmore (1985) imply that this causes interference with learning. Their data reveal that the amount of off-task behavior exhibited by young girls differed more from that of their older classmates than did the rates exhibited by boys. This explanation seems directly at odds with earlier observations that boys are more active and distractible than girls, thereby making adjustment to early admission a more difficult proposition for boys than girls.

In a more sensational claim, Uphoff and Gilmore (1986) also reported that children born later in the year accounted for 45% of the male and 83% of the female youth suicides in Montgomery County, Ohio, in 1983 and the first half of 1984, despite comprising only 35% of the population. The authors considered that the pressures resulting from early admission to school contributed directly to these tragedies. The actual data from the county records office do not support their claims. Uphoff and Gilmore (1986) did not provide information on the sample sizes in their article, so telephone calls were made to Montgomery County. County records that were delivered revealed that only 15 youth suicides occurred in 1983 and 1984. No data were available as to whether or not the youths who committed suicide had been admitted to school early. Nor was there any indication that they were schooled in Ohio or in another state where the minimum age for school entrance might have been different. Intemperate conclusions based on minuscule samples of questionable generalizability are fairly typical of some of the sharpest attacks on early admission.

Diamond (1983) observed a positive correlation between late birth months and future diagnoses of learning disabilities. She suggested that the higher incidence of learning disabilities among children born in the summer months was due to the higher average temperatures in the months when the greatest number of learning-disabled children were carried to term. Diamond's (1983) study was conducted in Hawaii where, she notes, the average monthly temperature ranges from about 72°F in January to 84°F in August. If high temperatures are responsible for educational difficulties, then her study has grave implications for populations in the equatorial zones. It is unclear whether she considers high temperature or mean-temperature variability as the cause, but no attempt is made to construct a mechanism responsible for impact on the developing fetus. Yet, Diamond (1983) is one of the few researchers who even attempted to elucidate a direct link between age and various outcomes. Most other researchers and their reviewers have simply assumed that a relationship established through correlation is powerful enough to stand as the reason.

Prevention of School Failure: A Preference for No Treatment

School-readiness researchers and practitioners have recommended that future academic and adjustment problems may be averted by

1. Raising the minimum school entry age requirements
2. Holding students out of school if they are adjudged immature compared with their peers
3. Strongly discouraging early entrance of precocious children
4. Instituting differential entrance dates for males and other groups of

children who are frequently observed to be at risk for their failure to adjust to schooling (e.g., disadvantaged and minority—see Langer et al., 1984)

These recommendations imply that doing nothing is preferable to addressing individual differences in learning. The school-readiness literature offers the only example in the special education literature where no early intervention is presumed to be preferable to identification and active treatment. There are two basic problems with this no-treatment solution.

First, there is evidence that the no-treatment solution is detrimental to the academic and social-emotional adjustment of some young children. May and Welch (1984) compared the academic performances of three groups of children: (1) children who entered school along with their age-mates, (2) children who, on the basis of a preschool evaluation, were recommended to be held out of school an additional year, but whose parents entered them with their age-mates in spite of the schools' recommendations, and (3) children who were judged to be immature, and whose parents agreed to delay their school entrance one year. May and Welch (1984) observed that children who entered school at the traditional age obtained higher levels of achievement compared with children who were held out of school an additional year. There was no apparent disadvantage to entering school along with age-mates for children who were judged to be relatively immature compared with their peers. Partington (1937) found that the group of students who entered school late actually had the fewest high-achievers and the most low-achievers, compared with groups of students who entered school at the traditional school entry age and students who were provided early entrance. Miller and Norris (1967) reported that children who were old-in-grade tended to have lower levels of achievement and more psychological referrals compared with both early entrants and children who entered school at the normal age. Late entrants were also given the lower sociometric ratings by their peers on two indicators of personal adjustment. It is possible that, rather than preparing immature students better for schooling, delayed school entry actually contributed to their adjustment and achievement problems.

Smith and Shepard (1988) reported that teachers were firmly convinced that delayed entry and kindergarten retentions were beneficial. Parents, however, frequently had different perspectives. Whereas teachers indicated that they were not aware of problems, parents could frequently describe their children's feelings of humiliation, loss of esteem, and discouragement. Whether holding immature students out of school directly contributes to their problems or not, it seems clear that late entry does not increase their relative performance when they finally do enter school. There is no evidence that supports stalling the academic careers of demonstrably precocious children.

The second problem with the no-treatment solution is that it suggests policies that are inconsistent with societal values. The logical conclusion of such a position is that we should legitimize predictions of readiness and establish age cutoffs on the bases of sex, race, and socioeconomic differences as well as chronological age. Clearly, such cutoffs would be discriminatory and inconsistent with our society's values. Instead of public education's being a medium for reducing differences in achievement associated with sex, race, class, and age, it would become an agar for intensifying inequities.

It is dismaying that a body of literature riddled with inadequate methodologies and gross errors in logic could exert influence on educational policies and practices. It is also distressing that some authors in the field of gifted education have recently begun uncritically to accept and incorporate the conclusions of school-readiness literature into their recommendations (e.g., Colangelo & Fleuridas, 1986; Maddux et al., 1981), thus providing ammunition for attacks by critics of academic acceleration for gifted students.

With the current school reform initiatives, many school districts are in the process of reviewing their entrance-age policies. If changes are made, they will probably be to (1) raise the minimum age for school entrance, (2) permit the "academic redshirting" (Frick, 1986) for students deemed too immature to begin school, and (3) make it very difficult for any children— including the academically gifted—to gain early entrance.

The erroneous interpretations of the school-readiness research do not suggest policies that will support efforts to improve the education of children with individual differences. Both gifted and handicapped children face serious risks of being mishandled. Solely for making that point apparent, the earlier objections to the validity and relevance of the data present in the school-readiness literature will be temporarily suspended. Even when that is done, it is apparent that conclusions reflecting the nativist perspective of school readiness will lead to policies that are unwarranted, fundamentally absurd, and potentially detrimental both to children who are academically precocious and to children who are immature or have learning problems.

ADDRESSING THE CONCERNS ABOUT ACCELERATION IN PRIMARY SCHOOL

The process of deciding whether or not to use early entrance or grade-skipping options for particular children should address the concerns of all stakeholders: parents, students, and educators. All parties to the decision will, of course, be concerned about the possible effects that the acceleration will have on the child's academic achievement and social-emotional development. On the surface, data reported in two related studies (Southern et al., 1989a, 1989b) suggested that the different groups were in general agreement in their hesitation about early entrance and grade skipping. They agreed that the acceleration options did not present direct risks to academic achievement but did jeopardize normal social and emotional development. They also shared ambivalence about the wisdom of requiring that gifted children be instructed with age-level peers. Most educators, parents, and students agreed that remaining with age-level peers was potentially hazardous.

Further inspection of the data revealed, however, that the agreements were only on the surface. Sentiments expressed by students and their parents appeared to be neither as consistent nor as negative as sentiments expressed by educators. The differences suggest that the different stakeholders have somewhat different concerns. There appeared to be disagreement about

1. Specifically what sorts of difficulties would be encountered
2. The importance of those difficulties
3. When those difficulties were to be expected

Types of Anticipated Difficulties

Most referrals for early entrance or grade skipping originate with the parents (Southern et al., 1989a), although a considerable number of recommendations for grade skipping in primary grades may come from teachers. The obvious concern is that the child will be performing at a level much higher than the curriculum demands. Teachers making recommendations to advance a child focus on the large observed differences between student performance and instructional demands. To ensure continued high levels of academic achievement is perceived as a primary concern. The underlying assumption is that the student will learn little or nothing in an undemanding setting, and that he or she will become complacent, bored, unmotivated, or even actively hostile to the school experience. Whoever initiates a referral for acceleration will base their decision on data that is different from the information that other education staff bring to the decision. Educators generally base their assumptions about how academically precocious children will fare with acceleration on (1) personal experiences with children whose preschool experiences offered little or no preparation in academics or compliance and (2) assumptions drawn from the badly flawed school-readiness literature. In the Southern et al. (1989b) study, however, the few practitioners who had direct personal experience with early entrance or grade skipping were positively influenced by it (Southern et al., 1989b). Parents, and probably teachers, initiating referrals, however, base their judgments about the advisability of acceleration on their general knowledge of their child and available academic programs. There are several possible sources for their observations, which include performances of age-level peers, earlier performances of older siblings, and acquisition of academic skills that children are expected to learn in school. Personal experience with acceleration (either their own or that of another family member) did not appear to have an important influence on parents' perceptions of its value for their child. It is unlikely that parents' opinions about acceleration have been informed by the school-readiness literature. However, the recent spate of popular press articles and the increasing prevalence of advice from educational personnel and other parents may represent a secondhand influence. Parents of young boys are often cautioned to hold their children out of school to increase readiness. Thus, the initial concerns of parents or referring teachers about appropriate placement may become tempered by worries about adverse effects from schooling with older children. These fears may have certain logical grounds, though, as we have noted, an empirical basis for them has not been adequately established. Certainly such issues could be resolved for many students if schools were able to adjust curricular demands to the individual. Ironically, those schools with the strongest nativist beliefs are the ones with the most rigid curricular and scheduling prescriptions.

Coping With Difficulties

Smith and Shepard (1989) observed that schools that are apt to accommodate individual differences do not differ consistently with regard to teacher training, teachers' years of experience, or curriculum from more bureaucratic schools. They did, however, discover an unambiguous relationship between school structure and teachers' beliefs about school readiness and their willingness to address the individual needs of gifted students as well as students with learning difficulties. The most important factor appeared to be the degree to which the teachers and administrators are, as a matter of policy, committed to two beliefs: (1) What a child learns depends more on opportunities to learn, quality of instruction, and encouragement to persevere than on innate mental faculties, and (2) teachers can accommodate diversity. Smith and Shepard (1989) found that, in schools that were characterized by rigid formal routines, teachers were inclined to express nativist beliefs about achievement and development and afford little attention to students' individual instructional needs. In the more bureaucratic schools, teachers in higher grades tended to exert significant informal pressures on teachers in lower grades not to promote students who either lacked mastery of basic skills or appeared to be immature. In schools in which instruction was not driven by strictly interpreted performance objectives or compromised by unyielding daily schedules, teachers expressed beliefs that were more environmentalist. They were observed to be more responsive to individual needs of both high-achieving students and students with learning difficulties. Instead of practicing grade-level segregation, teachers cooperated across grade levels to meet students' needs. Guidance and support from administrative and instructional leaders are important in developing schools that work for children rather than schools that process students in batches.

Even so, efforts to provide appropriate levels of challenge and support in age-level classrooms will not result in the elimination of grade-level acceleration in primary grades. There will always be some students whose rate and level of achievement will be so discrepant from those of their peers that acceleration is necessary. The process of deciding who should be provided early admission or skipped in grade should become more rational so that placements may proceed with greater assurance that necessary support will be provided to precocious students—whether they remain with age-level peers or are accelerated. On the other hand, public education's current drift toward increased rigidity in its emphasis on (1) preschool readiness, (2) age-level grouping, and (3) specification of skills for mastery within grade levels offers bleak prospects for precocious young children. Parents consider acceleration in the first place because it is apparent that highly bureaucratic schools will not provide appropriate levels of academic challenge in classes with age-level peers. Such primary schools, however, are apt to block grade-level acceleration or fail to provide support for those students who do accelerate.

The decision about whom and when to accelerate should be based on rational, defensible concerns. Certainly more even-handed consideration must be given to the companion issues of appropriate academic placement and the potential social difficulties occasioned by acceleration. The decision, minimally, must concern itself with the overall demonstrated achievement of the student, the ability of the school to adjust curriculum to the needs of the individual student, the motivation and maturity of the student, and the level of acceptance the school has for such interventions. Rigid age guidelines and assertions of unwarranted developmental constraints are theoretically unsupported and empirically unjustified.

REFERENCES

Baer, C. J. (1958). The school progress and adjustment of underage and overage students. *Elementary School Journal, 55*, 331–336.

Bigelow, E. B. (1934). School progress of underage children. *Elementary School Journal, 35*, 186–192.

Boyer, H. L. (1983). *High school: A report on secondary education in America*. New York: Harper and Row.

Braga, J. L. (1971). Early admission: Opinion versus evidence. *Elementary School Journal, 72*, 35–46.

Colangelo, N., & Fleuridas, C. (1986). The abdication of childhood. *Journal of Counseling and Development, 64*, 561–563.

Carroll, J. B. (1963). A model for school learning. *Teachers College Record, 64*, 723–733.

Carroll, M. L. (1963). Academic achievement and adjustment of underage and over-age third graders. Chicago: Rand McNally.

Carter, L. B. (1956). The effect of early school entrance on the scholastic achievement of elementary school children in the Austin public schools. *Journal of Educational Research, 50*, 91–103.

Cook, T. D. & Campbell, D. T. (1979). *Quasi-experimentation design and analysis issues for field settings*. Chicago: Rand McNally.

Daurio, S. P. (1979). Educational enrichment versus acceleration: A review of the literature. In W. C. George, S. J. Cohn, & J. Stanley (Eds.), *Educating the gifted: Acceleration and enrichment* (pp. 13–63). Baltimore: Johns Hopkins University Press.

Diamond, G. H. (1983). The birthdate effect—A maturational effect? *Journal of Learning Disabilities, 16*, 161–164.

Deitz, C., & Wilson, B. J. (1985). Beginning school age and academic achievement. *Psychology in the Schools, 22*, 93–94.

DiPasquale, G. W., Moule, A. D., & Flewelling, R. W. (1980). The birthdate effect. *Journal of Learning Disabilities, 13*, 234–238.

Donofrio, A. F. (1977). Grade repetition—Therapy of choice. *Journal of Learning Disabilities, 10*, 349–351.

Elkind, D. (1981). *The hurried child: Growing up too fast too soon*. Newton, MA. Addison Wesley.

Elkind, D. (1986). Mental acceleration. *Journal for the Education of the Gifted, 11*(4), 19–31.

Forester, J. J. (1955). At what age should a child start school? *School Executive, 74*, 80–81.

Frick, R. (1986). In support of academic redshirting. *Young Children, 412*, 9–10.

Goodlad, J. L. (1984). *A place called school*. New York: McGraw-Hill.

Gredler, G. R. (1978). A look at some important factors in assessing readiness for school. *Journal of Learning Disabilities, 11*, 25–31.

Green, D. R., & Simmons, S. V. (1967). Chronological age and school entrance. *Elementary School Journal, 63*, 41–47.

Hall, R. V. (1963). Does entrance age affect achievement? *Elementary School Journal, 63*, 391–396.

Halliwell, J. W., & Stein, B. W. (1964). A comparison of the achievement of early and late starters in reading related and non-reading related areas in fourth and fifth grades. *Elementary English, 41*, 631–639.

Huff, S. (1984). *The pre-kindergarten assessment. A predictor of success of early and late starters.* Unpublished Ed.S. research project at Wright State University, Dayton, OH.

Ilg, F. L., & Ames, L. G. (1965). *School readiness: Behavior tests used at the Gesell Institute.* New York: Harper & Row.

Jackson, N. E., Famiglietti, J., & Robinson, H. B. (1981). Kindergarten and first grade teachers' attitudes toward early entrants, intellectually advanced students, and average students. *Journal for the Education of the Gifted, 4,* 132–142.

Kazdin, A. E. (1978). *The history of behavior modification.* Baltimore: University Park Press.

King, I. B. (1955). Effect of age of entrance into grade 1 upon achievement in elementary school. *Elementary School Journal, 55,* 331–336.

Kulik, J. A., & Kulik, C. C. (1984). Effects of accelerated instruction on students. *Review of Educational Research, 54,* 409–425.

Langer, P., Kalk, J. H., & Searls, D. T. (1984). Age of admission and trends in achievement: A comparison of blacks and Caucasian. *American Educational Research Journal, 21,* 61–78.

Maddux, C. D. (1983). Early school entry for the gifted: New evidence and concerns. *Roeper Review, 5*(4), 15–17.

Maddux, C. D., Stacy, D., & Scott, M. (1981). School entry age in a group of gifted children. *Gifted Child Quarterly, 4,* 180–183.

Mawhinney, P. E. (1964). We gave up on early entrance. *Education Digest, 30,* 8–9.

May, D. C., & Welch, E. L. (1984). The effects of developmental placement and early retention on children's later scores on standardized tests. *Psychology in the Schools, 21,* 381–385.

Miller, W., & Norris, R. C. (1967). Entrance age and school success. *Journal of School Psychology, 6,* 47–60.

Mischel, W. (1968). *Personality and assessment.* New York: Wiley.

National Commission on Excellence in Education. (1983). *A nation at risk: The imperative for educational reform.* Washington D.C.: Author.

Northwest Regional Educational Laboratory. (1979). *Annual report to the National Institute of Education on services provided to school districts by Title I Technical Assistance Center.* Portland, OR.

Obrzut, A., Nelson, R. B., & Obrzut, J. E. (1984). Early school entrance for intellectually superior children: An analysis. *Psychology in the Schools, 21,* 71–77.

Ohio School Psychologists' Association. (1989). *Early entrance testing and guidelines: An overview of procedures currently practiced in some Ohio school districts.* (Available from A. E. Ellenwood, Bowling Green State University, Bowling Green, OH 43403).

Partington, H. M. (1937). The relationship between first grade entrance age and success in the first three grades. *National Elementary Principal, 16,* 298–302.

Pennau, J. E. (1981). The relationship between early entrance and subsequent educational progress in the elementary school. *Dissertation Abstracts, 42,* 1478 (4A).

Pollins, L. D. (1983). The effects of acceleration on the social and emotional development of gifted students. In C. P. Benbow & J. C. Stanley (Eds.), *Academic precocity: Aspects of its development* (pp. 160–179). Baltimore: Johns Hopkins University Press.

Proctor, T. B., Black, K. N., & Feldhusen, J. F. (1986). Early admission of selected children to elementary school: A review of the research literature. *Journal of Educational Research, 80,* 70–76.

Shepard, L. A., & Smith, M. L. (1986). Synthesis on school readiness and kindergarten retention. *Educational Leadership, 44,* 78–86.

Smith, M. L., & Shepard, L. A. (1988). Kindergarten readiness and retention: A qualitative study of teachers' beliefs and practices. *American Educational Research Journal, 25,* 307–333.

Southern, W. T., Jones, E. D., & Fiscus, E. D. (1989a). *Academic acceleration: Concerns of gifted students and their parents.* Paper presented at the annual meeting of the National Association for Gifted Children, Cincinnati, OH.

Southern, W. T., Jones, E. D., & Fiscus, E. D. (1989b). Practitioner objections to the academic acceleration of young gifted children. *Gifted Child Quarterly, 33,* 29–35.

Uphoff, J. K. (1985, March). *Pupil chronological age as a factor in school failure.* Paper presented at the annual meeting of the Association for Supervision and Curriculum Development, Chicago.

Uphoff, J. K., & Gilmore, J. (1985). Pupil age and school entrance—How many are ready for success? *Educational Leadership, 43*(1), 86–90.

Uphoff, J. K., & Gilmore, J. (1986). Pupil age and school entrance—How many are ready for success? *Young Children, 41*(2), 11–16.

Uphoff, J. K., & Gilmore, J. (1987). Pupil age and school entrance—How many are ready for success? *Dimensions, 8*(7), 3–5.

CHAPTER 4

Affective Development in Accelerated Students

Dewey G. Cornell, Carolyn M. Callahan, Laurie E. Bassin, and Shula G. Ramsay
University of Virginia

The purpose of this chapter is to provide a critical review of the research literature on the relationship between affective development and academic acceleration. Affective development is defined broadly to include nonintellective aspects of development bearing on social and emotional adjustment. There is far more literature on this topic than can be summarized in a single chapter; instead, we will concentrate on characterizing the general state of the field, describing some important studies in selected areas and identifying needs for future research.

Most reviewers begin by pointing out the long-standing bias against academic acceleration in American education (Daurio, 1979; Montour, 1977; Pollins, 1983; Robinson & Janos, 1986). They note that educators and parents alike fear that children who are placed with older students will suffer social and emotional adjustment problems. Southern, Jones and Fiscus (1989) have documented the consistent concerns among practitioners that acceleration will have adverse effects on the students' social and emotional adjustment.

There are, in fact, a few highly publicized cases of accelerated students who developed serious psychological problems (Montour, 1977). Nevertheless, most reviewers contend that these are exceptional cases and that the research literature does not support the negative attitude many hold toward academic acceleration (Southern et al., 1989). Many studies are cited as evidence of adequate or even superior affective adjustment among most accelerated students (see Daurio, 1979). In addition, reviewers conclude that acceleration yields clear advantages in academic achievement (Kulik & Kulik, 1984). Roedell, Jackson, and Robinson (1980) go so far as to assert, "All available research evidence indicates that shortening the period of schooling for students who are intellectually advanced and socially mature is a beneficial practice" (p. 86).

Despite the apparent weight of evidence in favor of acceleration, concerns about the socioemotional adjustment of accelerated students persist, and most authorities agree that acceleration continues to be a much underutilized educational strategy (George, Cohn, & Stanley, 1979; Horne & Dupuy, 1981; Southern et al., 1989). It may be worthwhile to consider why a long tradition of seemingly consistent research findings has had so little impact on educational policies and public attitudes.

At least three explanations are possible for educators' hesitance to use acceleration. First, they may be largely unaware of the available research evidence and its implications for the use of acceleration. Second, it may be that educational policies are determined more by tradition and personal sentiment than by empirical evidence. Third, it is possible that the conclusions that researchers have drawn about the positive effects of acceleration are not as justifiable as they may appear. The conclusions may have been drawn from studies that will not stand up to critical scrutiny.

Although the first two explanations certainly have merit, the focus of this chapter will be on the third. If research is to have a legitimate use to inform policy makers and educators, it must be technically sound and persuasive. We ask the question, How well does the available research hold up to critical scrutiny? Unless this question can be answered unequivocally in the affirmative, the case will not be closed on the supposedly harmful effects of academic acceleration on affective adjustment, and, thus, the persistent concerns of educators and parents will not be allayed. Our admittedly skeptical approach to reviewing the literature should not be interpreted as a bias against acceleration. The best possible case *for* acceleration can be made only when the evidence can withstand critical review. Thus, we advocate a thorough and rigorous examination of the available empirical literature on acceleration.

IMPORTANCE OF THE CHILD'S AGE AND
FORM OF ACCELERATION

It is likely that the psychological impact of acceleration differs according to the age level of the student and the form of acceleration (e.g., early entrance, grade skipping, advanced placement, etc.). For example, the significance of peer contact and the quality of peer relationships change markedly from early childhood to adolescence. The psychological effects of any given form of acceleration can reasonably be expected to differ across age levels. Likewise, the demands for adaptation are likely to differ according to the different forms of acceleration that may be used. Any generalization about the effects of acceleration on affective development across either age levels or forms of acceleration must be regarded with skepticism.

In this review the effects of various forms of acceleration will be examined by age group, beginning with early school entrance, followed by primary and secondary school acceleration, and ending with early college entrance and college acceleration. Even these categories are heterogeneous, but they provide a means of organizing the literature.

EARLY SCHOOL ENTRANCE

The question of early entry to kindergarten or first grade must be considered in the context of the larger issue of school readiness. There is long-standing controversy and debate over the appropriate age to begin formal education (Elkind, 1987; Kagan & Zigler, 1987; Wolf & Kessler, 1979), and this influences attitudes toward early entrance of high-ability children. On one side of the debate are those who recommend enhancing the child's cognitive development through early experiences. In what might be termed the opposing camp are a long line of educators and developmental psychologists, ranging from John Dewey, G. Stanley Hall, and Arnold Gesell to David Elkind and Louise Ames, who stress the need for age-appropriate readiness for learning and the dangers in "pushing" children beyond their developmental level. Critics contend that not only is accelerated early education ineffective, but also it has adverse effects on later attitudes toward learning as well as on general social and emotional development (Elkind, 1981, 1987; Hirsh-Pasek, Hyson, Rescorla, & Cone, 1989; Kagan & Zigler, 1987).

Some authors claim that many students in the United States are "overplaced" as a result of entering school too early (Hedges, 1977; Wolf & Kessler, 1987; for a contrasting view, see Gredler, 1980). Consistent with this concern, there is a national trend toward raising the age limit for entering kindergarten. Even though most states permit exceptions to these age limits in principle, local school districts often refuse to permit them in practice (Wolf & Kessler, 1987). Moreover, many kindergarten and first-grade teachers have negative attitudes toward early entrance, based primarily on reservations about the early entrant's socioemotional maturity (Jackson, Famiglietti, & Robinson, 1981). All of these factors may help explain why early entry is a little-used practice for high-ability children (Wolf & Kessler, 1987). The Richardson Study, a national survey, found that only about 28% of school districts offered any form of early entrance program (Cox, Daniel, & Boston, 1985; Karnes & Chauvin, 1982b).

Previous Research Reviews

There have been so many reviews of general research on early admission, it is a challenging task just to review the reviews (among the more noteworthy are Braga, 1971; Braymen & Piersel, 1987; Devault, Ellis, Vodicka, & Otto, 1957; Gredler, 1980; Hedges, 1977; Moore & Moore, 1975; Newland, 1976; Proctor, Black, & Feldhusen, 1986; Reynolds, Birch, & Tuseth, 1962; Worcester, 1956). However, reviews may be subject to errors of interpretation and a tendency to reach unjustified positive conclusions (Halliwell, 1966).

Some reviewers within the field of gifted education claim that early school admission does not adversely affect the student's socioemotional adjustment (Newland, 1976; Proctor et al., 1986; Worcester, 1956). For example, based on their review of 21 studies published between 1928 and 1984, Proctor et al. (1986) conclude:

> On objective measures of school outcome and personal adjustment early admission results in few negative effects and on measures of child and family satisfaction the outcomes for most early entrants are positive. (p. 72)

In contrast, other reviewers take a less favorable view of early entrance (Braymen & Piersel, 1987; Halliwell, 1966; Hedges, 1977). Braymen & Piersel (1987) conclude:

> Overall, the literature is pessimistic about the success young entrants will experience in school. Those children who have been screened and selected for early entrance have a somewhat better chance of succeeding. Additional research is needed to determine which variables add significantly to predicting future school success of young entrants. However, even children who have been selected for early entrance achieve at a lower level than would be anticipated for them at the same grade level if they had entered school a year later. Further, the effects of early entrance on social and emotional development need to be considered. (p. 188)

Hedges (1977) conducted the most extensive review, covering more than 250 articles. He is decidedly opposed to early admission and quite critical of previous research. He contends that authors of some studies selectively cite or misinterpret previous research to fit their own biases and is careful to document his claims with extensive use of quotations and specific page references. Furthermore, he points out studies in which researchers reached positive conclusions about the effects of early admission when in fact their results indicated the opposite. Unfortunately, such studies were often cited by others as supporting early admission (Hedges, 1977).

Selected Versus Unselected Early Entrants

It is critical to distinguish between selected and unselected early entrants (Newland, 1976; Wallis, 1984). Selected entrants are students who were screened for early admission based on an assessment of their academic aptitude, and usually their social maturity as well. Unselected entrants are merely the youngest members of a given class or grade level. Studies of selected and unselected early entrants often reach different conclusions (Newland, 1976; Wallis, 1984). Studies of carefully selected early entrants who display substantially superior academic aptitude as well as social maturity show that they often do well in school, or at least as well as their older, unaccelerated classmates (Ahr, 1965; Bigelow, 1934; Birch, 1954; Birch, Tisdall, & Barney, 1964; Hobson, 1948; Lincoln, 1929; Mueller, 1955; Pennau, 1981; Ramos, 1980; Reynolds, 1962).

As emphasized by Newland (1976), the distinction between selected and unselected early entrants may help explain some of the discrepancies in the literature, but some studies do report negative outcomes with selected early entrants. Obrzut, Nelson, and Obrzut (1984) conducted a four-year follow-up study of 25 early entrants who had been subject to extensive screening. All had Stanford-Binet (L-M) IQs above 132 and adequate performance on both visual-motor drawing tests and informal tests of academic readiness (e.g., general information, alphabet knowledge, and counting skills). In addition, applicants for early entrance were screened for social maturity by a school psychologist and corroborated with parent interviews. At the fifth-grade follow-up, the accelerants demonstrated superior academic achievement over nonaccelerated, older classmates, but no advantage was found in the area of social maturity. Strikingly, 7 out of the 25 early entrants were retained during the 4-year period, as contrasted with only 1 of 40 nonaccelerants. The reasons teachers gave for retention focused on social immaturity, including short attention span and need for excessive teacher attention. Obrzut et al. (1984) conclude: "The findings of this study suggest that early school admission for intellectually superior children may place them 'at risk' in the social-emotional area of development" (p. 76).

Of course, a natural question is whether the studies that found adjustment problems were less selective in their early admission policies. Selection procedures are so varied as to make direct comparisons extremely difficult, but it does not appear that degree of selectivity alone can explain differences in study findings. Probably a combination of student characteristics and educational factors (curriculum, teacher attitudes, instructional techniques, etc.) explains differences in early entrance outcomes for individual students.

Maddux (1983) is one of the more recent authors to challenge early entrance of high ability children, a practice he boldly compared to the notorious and obsolete medical practice of bleeding patients to cure them of illnesses! His rather extreme view is not, however, based upon students who had been selected for early entrance. He observed that a group of learning-disabled children contained relatively more children who were born later in the academic year (May through August), and that a group of gifted-program children contained disproportionately more children who entered first grade at ages 6 years 6 months through 6 years 11 months rather than 6 years through 6 years 5 months. Thus it appears that early entry is associated with learning disability whereas late entry is associated with being placed in a gifted program (Maddux, Stacy, & Scott, 1981).

An explanation of Maddux's finding may lie in recognizing that the relationship between age at school entry and school success may be neither linear nor uniform, and that it is subject to multiple confounding variables, including ability level. For example, with children of relatively comparable ability within a single year level, it may be advantageous to be a few months older than one's peers, because in the *average* case there will be slight advantages in social, intellectual, and physical maturity due to age. However, this simple relationship may not hold in the special case of highly advanced children who are screened for early school entrance. These children are by definition exceptions to the general correlation between chronological age and psychological maturity. The question is not whether it is frequently desirable to be a few months senior to one's classmates but how selected children of exceptional ability fare when placed with older classmates. Gredler (1980) offers additional criticisms of the relative-age argument.

Conclusions About Early School Entrance

In summary, the question of early admission to school is far from settled. If anything, controversy has increased rather than decreased in recent years (Kagan & Zigler, 1987). The most liberal conclusion justified by the literature is that early entrance can be considered *if the applicants are carefully screened for social and emotional maturity as well as academic aptitude.* Early admission should probably be restricted to children who are extremely advanced relative to their chronological age in both academic and socioemotional domains (Roedell et al., 1980). Some authors (e.g., Davis & Rimm, 1989; Proctor, Feldhusen, & Black, 1988) have proposed procedures for selecting students for early admission, but specific criteria or standards have not been established or validated by empirical research.

PRIMARY SCHOOL GRADE ADVANCEMENT

Grade advancement is accomplished by a family of related procedures. Outright grade skipping, also called double-promotion, usually raises concerns that students might miss critical skills or content from the grade they skip. Therefore, grade advancement is often accomplished through some form of telescoping or compression of the curriculum for a grade. Sometimes a single grade is condensed into a summer session or two or more grades are covered in a shorter than usual time.

Klausmeier and Ripple (1962) reported an exemplary study of grade advancement. The authors investigated 26 students who skipped the third grade by completing a 5-week summer course. One important methodological feature of this study was the use of random group assignment in comparing accelerated students to equally capable controls. Near the end of the fourth grade, there were no group differences in teacher ratings of social and emotional adjustment, but accelerants did rank lower than matched nonaccelerants on a peer sociogram. In a follow-up study (Klausmeier, 1963) at the end of the fifth grade, accelerants appeared as well-adjusted as controls on all measures. A second follow-up study in the ninth grade (Klausmeier, Goodwin, & Ronda, 1968) found few group differences in participation in social activities but did not include more extensive measures of socioemotional adjustment.

Mirman (1962) studied 64 high school seniors who had been double-promoted sometime during their education and compared them with a nonaccelerated group with generally comparable IQs (all above 120 on an unspecified test). There were few group differences on adjustment measures including the California Psychological Inventory and leadership ratings. Unlike the Klausmeier and Ripple (1962) study, this study has a major weakness. It uses a posttest design that fails to control for any preexisting group differences on the outcome measures. This makes inferences about program effects hazardous, particularly since students selected for double-promotion may well be systematically different from nonaccelerants.

In his follow-up study, Matlin (1965) examined a variety of academic and socioemotional measures of 59 ninth-grade students who had completed fourth, fifth, and sixth grades in 2 years. Compared with a matched sample of equally intelligent classmates, accelerants evidenced high motivation, better study habits, and more positive attitudes toward school. However, accelerants were generally less active in school activities and leadership positions, and accelerated boys were rated as less mature than nonaccelerants by counselors.

Other studies that found little or no evidence of adjustment problems in accelerants include Engle (1935), Robeck (1968), Rusch and Clark (1963), and Terman and Oden (1947).

Conclusions

Feldhusen, Proctor, and Black (1986) endorse the practice of grade advancement and state: "There is no empirical basis for the belief that grade advancement will result in either social-emotional maladjustment or gaps in learning" (p. 26). This statement might be qualified by recognition of the methodological limitations of previous studies and the restrictions they place on our available knowledge. Feldhusen et al. (1986) do caution that candidates for grade advancement should have a comprehensive psychological evaluation, with evidence of considerable intellectual, academic, and socio-emotional strengths.

The literature on grade advancement is considerably less extensive, and less controversial, than the literature on early school entrance, despite the similarities in procedures and results. There may be more concern with the initial year of school because of its importance in establishing a foundation for future learning. Developmentally, the difficulties of being placed with older classmates may diminish with age. Finally, and perhaps most importantly, it is far easier to assess a candidate for grade advancement than for early school entrance, since educators have the benefit of knowing how well the student actually performs in school. Grade-advancement studies may be more consistent in their findings because they employ better selected accelerants, students with a proven "track record" of high achievements as well as good socioemotional adjustment in the school setting.

SECONDARY SCHOOL ACCELERATION

A wide range of acceleration options are available to secondary school students, including fast-paced classes, continuous progress curricula, independent study, part-time college course work, and special classes or schools for high-ability youth (Benbow, Perkins, & Stanley, 1983; Cox et al., 1985). Based on responses from 1,172 school districts nationwide, the Richardson Study (Cox et al., 1985) found that only 46 (3.9%) districts provide for early admission of students to middle school or junior high, and only 51 (4.4%) provide for early admission to senior high school. Gallagher, Weiss, Oglesby, and Thomas (1983) report that the use of advanced classes is the preferred programming option selected by parents, teachers, and administrators for high school students. Accordingly, opportunity to take Advanced Placement classes is offered by 30% of school districts, whereas opportunity to take college courses while in high school is available in 21% of school districts (Cox et al., 1985).

It is difficult to draw firm conclusions about the socioemotional effects of secondary school acceleration because studies often do not distinguish among different acceleration options. Studies also differ in how students are selected for acceleration and the grade levels at which acceleration occurs. In addition, the criteria for judging adequate social and emotional adjustment have been far ranging and often highly subjective, frequently relying only on student self-report.

Advanced Placement

Advanced Placement (AP) courses are often considered an acceleration option because they involve the study of advanced, college-level content and allow students to earn credits that will accelerate completion of their baccalaureate degrees (Stanley & Benbow, 1983). However, when these classes are simply a scheduling option in the regular school setting, the student remains with age peers and is not singled out to nearly the same degree as students who skip grades or enter college early. It logically follows that this arrangement reduces the likelihood that issues of social and emotional development arise, and, therefore, they have not been a target of systematic research and evaluation efforts. Studies have been devoted largely to demonstrating the ability to identify and teach students who will do well on the AP exam, although some include a few questions assessing student attitudes toward the experience (Mezynski, Stanley, & McCoart, 1983).

Other Advanced Courses

An evaluation of the Minnesota Talented Youth Mathematics Project (MTYMP) revealed somewhat conflicting results about student reactions to 2 years of mathematics acceleration in junior high school (House, 1978). The students reported high levels of student satisfaction with the program. Nevertheless, on the basis of the Mathematics Attitudes Inventory, students demonstrated an overall increase in anxiety about mathematics and decreases in math self-concept and enjoyment of math.

Project Advance of Syracuse University offers students the opportunity to take college courses in high school (Mercurio, 1980). Two Project Advance reports (Mercurio, 1980; Mercurio, Schwartz, & Oesterle, 1982) surveyed students after completion of their undergraduate studies and concluded that they are "exceptionally stable and high achieving" (Mercurio et al., 1982, p. 17). However, "stability" refers to remaining in college rather than emotional stability. Further, the authors reported low response rates from their two questionnaires (52% and 61%). Mercurio (1980) acknowledged that those having less favorable college experiences might be less likely to respond, so that results might be biased in a positive direction. Overall, student reaction to the program was quite positive. Of those who responded to the survey, more than 90% recommend these courses to other students.

Survey data from the Advance College Project at Indiana University, Bloomington, did not directly assess socioemotional adjustment (Lave, 1984; Gudaitis, 1986). However, students did report favorable reactions to the program and felt more confident about attending college and doing college work. Wilbur (1982) reported positive reactions by students in comparable advanced courses.

Talent Search Programs

The Study of Mathematically Precocious Youth (SMPY) has encouraged students to enroll in a variety of accelerated courses. Reports of these efforts focused primarily on demonstrating the ability to teach highly selected students a considerable amount of course material very rapidly (Benbow, 1983; Benbow et al., 1983; Stanley & Benbow, 1983; Stanley & Stanley, 1986). Additional efforts have been devoted to examining acceleration effects on student attitudes toward mathematics, academic achievement, college attendance, and later career interests (Benbow, 1983; Fox, Benbow, & Perkins, 1983). The accomplishments of the SMPY program are substantial and have had major influence on gifted education. The focus of this review is limited to research on program effects on student social and emotional adjustment, which has not been a major component of SMPY research.

Assessment of social and emotional adjustment has often been limited to survey questions in which the students rate themselves on Likert-type scales. Self-report measures are vulnerable to subjective bias and defensiveness, and a few questions cannot begin to tap the multiple facets of social and emotional functioning. The survey approach needs careful validation.

In a study entitled "The Effects of Acceleration on the Social and Emotional Development of Gifted Students," all of the *standard* measures of social and emotional adjustment (California Psychological Inventory, Strong-Campbell Interest Inventory, Study of Values) were obtained *prior* to student acceleration (Pollins, 1983). Future accelerants and nonaccelerants did not differ on any of the scales. The only postacceleration adjustment measures were survey questions asking the student to assess issues such as "how SMPY had helped him, and how acceleration had affected his social and emotional development" (p. 174). Overall, accelerants thought that SMPY and acceleration had slightly positive effects on their social-emotional development.

Unfortunately, the Pollins study has been cited as evidence that acceleration has no adverse effects on adjustment (e.g., see Brody & Benbow, 1987). In fact, the study provides little information on the effects of acceleration on social and emotional development because it does not adequately assess these areas after acceleration. Instead, the strongest conclusion that can be drawn from the study is that the factors that distinguish students who later choose acceleration from students who do not choose acceleration are not tapped by the three standard instruments used in the study. More recent follow-up surveys (Swiatek & Benbow, in press; Richardson & Benbow, in press) have added more questions on self-esteem and locus of control.

Brody and Benbow (1987) retrospectively compared four groups who engaged in different degrees of acceleration (including no acceleration) while in high school. Making use of several items from the Cattell 16 Personality Factor Questionnaire, the Adjective Checklist, and other measures, they found few significant group differences. The most radically accelerated students engaged in fewer extracurricular activities than more moderately accelerated students, but otherwise there appeared to be no negative effects on student adjustment or attitudes.

Thomas (1989) conducted a 4-year follow-up survey of 100 students who had participated in the 1984 Academic Talent Search at California State University, Sacramento. The author concluded that the talent search had an "overwhelmingly positive" (p. 1) impact on students. This is a highly questionable conclusion, given the serious methodological problems of the study. Students had engaged in many forms of acceleration, ranging from skipping primary grades (before the talent search) to AP courses, so that the direct effect of the talent search is unclear. Without a control group, or at least measures of adjustment obtained prior to the talent search, it is not possible to make inferences about effects of the search. Moreover, affective adjustment was assessed in an inappropriate manner. For example, students were asked to rate themselves on how they believed that acceleration had affected them in areas such as "general emotional stability" and "social life in general."

Conclusions

Studies of acceleration at the secondary school level rely primarily on questionnaire data from follow-up surveys of program participants. Although results are generally interpreted as evidence that there are no negative effects of acceleration, the more conservative conclusion is that students who choose to respond to follow-up surveys typically do not report negative effects. Surveys may not be the most sensitive or appropriate method of detecting adjustment problems, if they exist. Of course, uncontrolled follow-up data alone lend little insight into program effects.

Some studies rely on only a single question or two to assess social and emotional adjustment. Evidence of reliability or validity for these questions are lacking. This very cursory approach may contribute to finding nonsignificant results, which are then interpreted to mean an absence of adverse effects of acceleration. A few studies have administered more extensive psychological test batteries to accelerants, but these measures were obtained *prior* to acceleration and thus lend no insight into program effects (e.g., Pollins, 1983).

Some studies report lower levels of social or extracurricular activity in accelerants. Although this is usually interpreted as an undesirable effect of acceleration, it should be noted that the amount of weight to give this effect is essentially a value judgment. A gifted young musician might practice so many hours a day that he or she has little time left for sports, but this may or may not be considered a serious problem. Similarly, a talented young mathematician may choose to spend time working on difficult problems rather than joining a social club.

Despite these problems, students who do report negative effects and the factors that might influence those outcomes are lacking, as are studies that systematically assess the specific relationship between socioemotional adjustment and degree, type, and timing of acceleration. More studies that assess student changes over the course of acceleration programs (as well as postacceleration) are needed. Only a few studies have gone beyond self-report surveys to include more in-depth assessment of social and emotional factors.

EARLY COLLEGE ENTRANCE

Early college entrance is a highly controversial form of acceleration and is perhaps the most dramatic and unequivocal sign of precocious academic ability. The young person's completion of high school and entry into college at age 18 is often the point of separation from family and home and is commonly viewed as a major milestone in the transition from childhood to adulthood. Therefore, the decision to enter college early represents a momentous act of social and psychological acceleration in addition to academic acceleration.

The Richardson Study (Cox et al., 1985) results indicate that approximately 28% of responding school districts permit students to graduate 1 or 2 years earlier than usual, and approximately 11% (an overlapping group) permit students to graduate even sooner. A national survey of 302 college institutions (Fluitt & Strickland, 1984) found that 87% admit students prior to the usual age of high school graduation. A smaller percentage (16%) admit students of pre-high school age. Despite the widespread willingness to admit early entrants, few institutions make use of any special screening procedures or formal methods to assess the young student's potential for successful adjustment to college. Moreover, only about half of these institutions offer special counselors or advisors for these students once they are admitted (Fluitt & Strickland, 1984). This section will concentrate on early entrance studies conducted since 1950; earlier studies, which are almost unanimously positive, are reviewed elsewhere (Daurio, 1979; Keys, 1938; Pressey, 1949).

Program Effects

The question of how well accelerants adjust during their college years is not easily answered. Early college entrants who are only 1 or 2 years younger than college age may have far less trouble adjusting than younger youth. Accelerants who live at home and commute to college classes may face a much less radical experience than those who leave home and reside on campus. In addition, accelerants who are in college more or less "on their own" may have a more stressful experience than those who benefit from the support of a special program or association with a group of accelerant peers. These are obvious and plausible ideas, but as hypotheses they have received little research attention.

A further complicating factor is the issue of self-selection. Students who choose early college entrance may differ systematically from equally capable students who choose to remain among their age-mates and/or live at home. Colleges may differ too in how selective they are in screening and admitting young students. Most institutions rely on standard academic credentials and letters of recommendation; few have special provision for evaluating the youth's maturity or level of adjustment (Fluitt & Strickland, 1986).

Fund for the Advancement of Education Project

One of the largest research efforts was sponsored by Fund for the Advancement of Education, an organization established by the Ford Foundation (Fund for the Advancement of Education, 1953, 1957). This project supported 1,350 early entrants who enrolled in 11 different colleges and universities from 1951 to 1954. The social and emotional adjustment of early entrants was assessed on the basis of involvement in extracurricular activities, opinions of college staff, a clinical appraisal of student essays, and psychiatric interviews. Among the study findings, the most positive and unequivocal result was the accelerants' high level of involvement in extracurricular activities.

Although this study is frequently cited as finding little evidence of adjustment problems among early entrants, careful reading of the report raises questions about this conclusion. Although the project's assessment methods were commonplace at the time of the study, by modern standards they are seriously deficient. Clinical evaluations and staff opinions must be scrupulously evaluated for reliability and validity before placing confidence in their results. No efforts in this direction are reported (Fund for the Advancement of Education, 1953, 1957). Moreover, the report of findings is highly selective and often anecdotal. There are frequent references to various unpublished findings reported by the psychiatric team, the essay reviewer, and college staff, but the full results are unavailable for reader review.

In addition, evidence of adjustment problems among the accelerants tended to be minimized (Fund for the Advancement of Education, 1957). For example, almost all of the schools acknowledged adjustment difficulties among the students but gave diverse and sometimes conflicting reasons for them. Yale and Columbia staff speculated that adjustment problems were due to the selection of accelerants from rural backgrounds. University of Louisville staff felt that adjustment problems resulted from social problems associated with placing young students in college dormitories, whereas University of Wisconsin staff attributed problems to placing students in rooming houses rather than dormitories.

A University of Chicago dean is quoted as saying, "I have not seen a single scholar who had serious psychological problems of whom I felt that they would *not* have occurred if he had remained at home another year or two" (Fund for the Advancement of Education, 1957, p. 41). His highly speculative opinion is accepted uncritically. Moreover, the acknowledgment that some Chicago accelerants experienced "serious psychological problems" is not elaborated.

The use of a psychiatric team is of great interest because it represents a concerted effort to examine student adjustment that is unusual in the literature (Fund for the Advancement of Education, 1957). Although the lack of standard diagnostic procedures and blind interviewing render the results equivocal by current standards of psychiatric research, three observations are noteworthy. First, the clinicians reported that 5% of the 1951 class dropped out because of psychiatric disorders. These included cases of schizophrenia, character disorder, and "simple maladjustment" (p. 56), but they felt that the incidence of these problems was not greater than among regular students. They noted that many adjustment problems were in evidence prior to early college entrance or that the students came from unstable family environments, so that the potential for adjustment problems in college might have been predicted. This raises clear implications for careful screening of acceleration applicants.

Second, the clinicians criticized some schools for placing excessive stress on students by isolating them from other students or in other ways stigmatizing them as early entrants. They felt that those students who could most easily blend into the general student body (physically as well as socially and emotionally) had the fewest problems.

Finally, there was considerable disagreement between the psychiatrists and college staff on students' reasons for college withdrawal. Almost all of the students reported as academic failures by the college staff were viewed as leaving for psychological reasons by the psychiatrists. This is an important methodological point, since college staff may underestimate the incidence of psychological adjustment problems in favor of viewing problems as strictly academic.

Study of Mathematically Precocious Youth (SMPY)

The SMPY program is also well known for assisting identified students in early college entrance. Reports have concentrated on the academic success and early career accomplishments of a number of mathematically precocious youth, as opposed to their socioemotional adjustment (Eisenberg & George, 1979; Stanley, 1985; Stanley & McGill, 1986). Although academic success may often suggest positive socioemotional adjustment, more direct assessment of affective variables is essential. One SMPY study that reported few adjustment problems among early college entrants was based only on telephone interviews (Brody, Lupkowski, & Stanley, 1988). Moreover, the study does not present evidence of the reliability and validity of this procedure.

University of Washington Program

Considerable research has been conducted on accelerants attending the Early Entrance Program (EEP) at the University of Washington (Janos, Sanfilippo, & Robinson, 1986; Janos & Robinson, 1985; Janos et al., 1988; Robinson & Janos, 1986). In general, accelerants adjust favorably to EEP, although results must be interpreted in the context of this specific type of program and the concerted efforts made to facilitate healthy adjustment. The Washington program admits very young students (ages 10 to 14), who live at home for at least 2 years and then may or may not elect to move onto campus (Janos & Robinson, 1985). Students receive special advising and counseling, participate in a support group with other accelerated peers, and attend a Transition School during the first year.

Janos and Robinson (1985) found that 24 accelerants made academic progress superior to that of average college students and comparable to that of National Merit Scholars at the same university. In a further report, Robinson and Janos (1986) found few significant differences between these same accelerants and equally capable students who did not choose acceleration on three standard personality measures (Minnesota Multiphasic Personality Inventory, California Psychological Inventory, and Tennessee Self-Concept Scale). It is not clear from these two reports whether students were assessed before or during their acceleration program. Unfortunately, this kind of cross-sectional study does not permit conclusions about the effects of the acceleration program, as distinguished from any preexisting differences between accelerant and comparison groups.

Janos et al. (1986) compared a dozen EEP students with relatively low GPAs (2.9 or below) to higher achieving accelerants. The groups were comparable in academic aptitude and verbal ability and did not differ on measures of personality adjustment (California Psychological Inventory) or family environment (Family Environment Scale). Anecdotally, the authors reported that lower achieving students procrastinated markedly in completing study materials and that males and females differed in adjustment. The males seemed more withdrawn or conflicted, whereas the lower achieving females seemed surprisingly well adjusted but more involved in extracurricular activities (e.g., sports, work).

Janos et al. (1988) surveyed 63 early entrants about their peer relations and found that they relied heavily on relationships with other accelerants, especially during the first 2 years of college. According to student self-report, there were relatively few problems, particularly after a period of adjustment to college life.

Other Studies

In response to the Fund for the Advancement of Education study, Kogan (1955) examined young entrants to Harvard. He found no evidence of academic or socioemotional adjustment problems in comparison with older classmates.

Gregory and March (1985) described the early entrance program at California State University, Los Angeles, and gave several brief case reports of successful student adjustment to the program. Gregory and Stevens-Long (1986) reported on the need to provide regular counseling and support for early college entrants, based on experiences with the Early Entrance Program at California State University, Los Angeles. Although their report is nonempirical, their approach is important: They concentrate on describing practical strategies to help students cope with early college entrance rather than debating whether problems exist.

Cornell, Callahan, and Loyd (in press) examined the adjustment of 44 adolescent females during 1 year of an early college entrance program. In contrast to most previous studies, they found considerable variation in student affective adjustment. Although many students manifested no evidence of adjustment difficulties, over half of the students experienced some degree of depression during the year and five engaged in suicidal behavior. Approximately half of the students saw a counselor or therapist for adjustment problems and 13 left the program for stress-related reasons. In addition, students varied in their adherence to program rules, their peer relations, and in their self-reported satisfaction with the program. Of course, the absolute levels of student problems are difficult to interpret by themselves, without comparable data on the general college population. The point of this study is that there is variation in student adjustment that must be recognized. A recent follow-up study (Cornell, Callahan, & Loyd, 1990) of the same program found that those students who remained in the program for a 1-year period demonstrated unequivocal and consistent gains in measures of psychological adjustment (based on the California Psychological Inventory) in comparison with a group of equally bright, unaccelerated high school students.

Cornell et al. (in press) concentrated on identifying predictors of affective adjustment from among a battery of personality and family environment measures administered at the beginning of the academic year. They found consistent evidence that healthy personality characteristics and positive family relationships were associated with more favorable adjustment, suggesting that it may be possible to improve selection of students appropriate for early college entrance.

The contrast between studies that find few adjustment problems among accelerants and the Cornell et al. (in press) study is striking. Can the discrepant results be attributed to differences in the kinds of students admitted to the college programs, to differences in the programs themselves, or to methodological differences in how studies assess student adjustment? All three possibilities are viable hypotheses that can be resolved only with further study.

Long-Term Outcome

Janos (1987) reviewed archival data on 19 of Terman's subjects who entered college before age 16 and compared them with those on similarly capable subjects who entered college closer to the usual age. There were no significant group differences on any of the adjustment measures obtained over the decades of the Terman project, although Janos (1987) notes that the sample size was small and data were not complete for all cases.

A 10-year follow-up of Ford Foundation accelerants (Pressey, 1967) found that most of the graduates from three selected institutions went on to advanced professional training, entering their careers about 2 years younger than a classmate comparison group. At follow-up, the majority were married and had about the same number of children as did those in the comparison group. In response to a mail survey, almost all expressed satisfaction with their accelerated education. A number of respondents commented that they experienced initial social adjustment problems, but few indicated continuing maladjustment.

Stanley and Benbow (1983) conducted a historical review of 32 individuals who graduated from Johns Hopkins University prior to age 19 between 1876 and 1982. They document the notable academic and career success of these students but do not provide more direct data on socioemotional adjustment.

Conclusion

The literature on socioemotional adjustment to early college entrance is extremely positive; however, there are problems. The enthusiasm of some authors may not be entirely justified (e.g., Karnes & Chauvin, 1982a). Few studies have examined socioemotional adjustment with adequate psychological measures. Few studies have employed designs that permit inferences about program effects over time. Case reports and expert opinion indicate that many highly able students *can* adjust and do well in college; unfortunately, there is no systematic body of information that can be used as a guide to identifying which students will fare well in early college entrance programs. Some well-established programs (e.g., Janos & Robinson, 1985) provide routine counseling and support services to early entrants; research on successful student support strategies and counseling techniques would be a welcome addition to the literature.

DIRECTIONS FOR FUTURE RESEARCH

A major theme of this chapter is that many previous studies have been too hasty in concluding that there are no adverse effects of acceleration, when in fact problems of research design and inference often make unequivocal conclusions impossible. If research is to have a greater impact on educational policy and promote greater use of acceleration, methodological problems should be eliminated. Several recurrent problems in the literature can be identified.

Improved Assessment of Social and Emotional Adjustment

Although there is no single definitive means of assessing socioemotional adjustment, several principles should guide future research. First, researchers must recognize that socioemotional adjustment is a complex construct. It is difficult to define and measure adequately. Therefore, multiple assessments of related aspects of development should be used. It is misleading to conclude that there is no evidence of adjustment problems, if adjustment is assessed in a very narrow sense. For example, a single measure of self-esteem is an inadequate basis for reaching conclusions about students' socioemotional adjustment to acceleration. Even if self-concept is of particular interest to the researcher, multiple aspects of self-concept should be assessed (Byrne, 1984).

A comprehensive assessment of socioemotional adjustment must move beyond self-concept to include other intrapersonal as well as interpersonal adjustment constructs, all framed in a developmental context (Knoff, 1986; Walker & Roberts, 1983). Although an analysis of such constructs is well beyond the scope of this chapter, several general areas can be described. In the intrapersonal realm, researchers may want to assess the student's freedom from emotional distress (e.g., anxiety, depression, anger) as well as chart the student's developing emotional maturity and judgment. Instruments ranging from the California Psychological Inventory to the Rorschach are useful here. In the interpersonal realm, researchers may want to gather data on the student's family and peer relations.

Second, studies should avoid relying excessively on self-report measures. Respondent defensiveness or lack of insight may result in an inaccurate portrayal of the student's adjustment. A thorough assessment of a student's adjustment will include data from sources other than the student, such as family, teachers, or peers (Achenbach & McConaughy, 1987; Knoff, 1986). In addition, there has been little use of behavioral observation methods, despite their widespread use in other educational research.

Third, studies should rely on standard measures of social and emotional adjustment rather than untried, newly devised measures. Although it is certainly reasonable for researchers to experiment with new instruments, conclusions based on such measures must be made cautiously. Researchers are advised to rely primarily on standard measures with established reliability and validity.

Finally, we want to acknowledge that accelerants face special adjustment challenges and potential sources of stress (e.g., separation from age-mates and placement with older classmates) that are not necessarily addressed by standard personality tests. Investigators must take care to apply adjustment measures that are well-suited to the adjustment problems that accelerants may experience. This may require adaptation of existing instruments or development of new ones (subject to the concerns noted above). Clinical interviews may be particularly appropriate for an individualized and in-depth assessment of student attitudes and concerns. However, open-ended interviews should be regarded as exploratory and therefore subject to follow-up confirmation with more rigorous techniques. Most structured interview techniques can be subject to the same standards of reliability and validity applied to traditional tests.

Important adjustment topics deserving specific attention are

1. Stress-related program attrition
2. Need for mental health or counseling services
3. Incidence of depression, loneliness, suicidality, or other signs of emotional distress
4. A level of social activity and friendship that is developmentally appropriate and satisfactory to the accelerant

Evaluation of these factors should take into consideration base rates for several comparison groups, including the general college population and students of comparable ability.

Cross-Sectional and Retrospective Comparisons

Cross-sectional studies that compare subjects at a single point in time produce interesting and potentially useful findings, but they have well-known limitations (Cook & Campbell, 1979). For example, a typical study administers a battery of adjustment measures to students who have been in an acceleration program and compares them with a control group of unaccelerated students. Regardless of the results, such a study cannot demonstrate effects of the acceleration program. At a minimum, it would be necessary to control for any preexisting differences between groups, either by random group assignment (often impractical and potentially unethical) or statistical control of confounding variables. In addition, it would be useful to assess the students before and after acceleration to document any change that might be associated with the program.

Failure to Recognize Selective Factors Within the High-Ability Population

In their review of research on early school entrance, Proctor et al. (1986) make the important observation that many studies examined students who were carefully screened or otherwise selected for acceleration. Children who begin school early may have not only exceptional academic aptitude but also behavioral and motivational characteristics that distinguish them from other academically capable age-mates who do not enter school early. Therefore, although these studies demonstrate that some children can be successful in entering school early, results cannot be generalized to the broader, unselected population of academically capable youth.

The Absence of Group Differences

The absence of group differences between accelerants and nonaccelerants should not be interpreted to mean an absence of adverse effects of acceleration. This is a questionable inference to make from the failure to reject a null hypothesis. A lack of statistical significance may be attributable to several methodological problems, including a lack of statistical power, the influence of confounding variables, or excessive measurement error. Equally important, the instruments chosen to measure adjustment may not be sensitive to the kinds of adverse effects caused by acceleration.

Drop-Out Bias

Follow-up studies may fail to report adjustment data on students who dropped out of the acceleration program. This is understandably difficult because dropouts are often unavailable or unwilling to participate in the study (Cornell et al., in press). However, dropouts are critical subjects to lose, because they may well represent the students who experienced the most severe socioemotional adjustment problems.

Janos and Robinson (1985) deserve credit for acknowledging the number of accelerated students missing from their study, including 10 students who took a few college courses and then dropped out before enrolling full-time in the accelerated program. A more dramatic example of the dropout problem is reported in a follow-up to some of the Fund for Advancement of Education early college entrance programs. Pressey (1967) comments that two-thirds of the students in one university program left after the first year. None of these students were surveyed, and only 20 of the 47 who stayed in the program returned responses. Nevertheless, Pressey concludes that the majority of the students were satisfied with the program and that any adverse effects were minor or transient. The original Ford Foundation report (Fund for the Advancement of Education, 1957) acknowledges that the absence of data from dropouts would skew later results in a positive direction, but this point has been lost in later reviews and citations of the work.

The Choice of Comparison Group

Accelerants may look more or less successful depending on the researcher's choice of comparison group. Accelerants often look best when compared with unselected children of the same age who did not enter school early. In many studies, they compare favorably with older children in their classrooms, too. However, it is difficult to attribute these differences to the effects of acceleration; as noted above, these comparisons are biased by whatever factors are used to select the accelerants, usually intelligence. For example, early school entrants compare less favorably with older classmates matched on IQ (Proctor et al., 1986).

How Can Future Research Promote the Value of Acceleration?

Advocates of acceleration may despair of efforts to convince skeptics that early school entrance, grade skipping, early college entrance, and other acceleration practices are not only safe but effective and desirable educational strategies. Here are some suggestions for future research that might make the case for acceleration more compelling.

1. Demonstrate that successful acceleration can be predicted, and good candidates for acceleration can be reliably distinguished from poor candidates. Advocates of acceleration may be so preoccupied with defending the practice as a whole that they have not conducted research on the variation among accelerants.
2. Establish reliable and valid standard screening procedures. This follows from research recommended above. Most acceleration programs use a mixture of formal and informal screening procedures, with little consistency between programs. Unfortunately, screening for social maturity and general emotional adjustment is often the least well specified and least standardized component.
3. Study the kinds of adjustment problems accelerated youth experience and demonstrate that there are effective interventions to ameliorate them. Established acceleration programs often make use of formal counseling and advising, transitional programs, peer support groups, and so on. Their existence reflects recognition of students' affective needs; their students' apparent success suggests they are generally effective. Research that documents the importance of counseling and other support procedures would provide a valuable model for future acceleration programs.
4. Some reviewers contend that failure to permit acceleration by otherwise capable youth can have detrimental effects (Proctor et al., 1988). This contention is not well supported by the available evidence because so few studies have directly addressed this question. Studies that indicate the beneficial effects of acceleration do not necessarily demonstrate negative effects of nonacceleration. There are, of course, many anecdotal observations of children who are bored and/or disruptive in school because they are not adequately challenged. It would be useful to study such cases systematically and demonstrate improvement in their behavior after placement in an appropriate program. This would provide a compelling basis for acceleration that has not received much research attention.

CONCLUSION

We are wary of closing this review of literature with the time-honored admonition that "more research is needed." Much research has been conducted and quantity is not a need. Rather, there are specific research questions that need to be addressed and in a rigorous manner.

In order to give maximum emphasis to the most important conclusion, we will forego repeating other points and close with one final suggestion. Perhaps, given the mixed results of various studies, it is no longer even useful to debate whether acceleration *does* or *does not* have an adverse effect on affective development. Instead, research would more profitably focus on determining for whom acceleration might be desirable, and for whom it might be detrimental.

REFERENCES

Achenbach, T. M., & McConaughy, S. H. (1987). Empirically based assessment of child and adolescent psychopathology. Beverly Hills, CA: Sage.

Ahr, A. E. (1965). Early school admission: One district's experiences. *Elementary School Journal, 67,* 231–236.

Benbow, C. P. (1983). Adolescence of the mathematically precocious: A five-year longitudinal study. In C. P. Benbow & J. C. Stanley (Eds.), *Academic precocity: Aspects of its development* (pp. 9–37). Baltimore: Johns Hopkins University Press.

Benbow, C. P., Perkins, S., & Stanley, J. C. (1983). Mathematics taught at a fast pace: A longitudinal evaluation of SMPY's first class. In C. P. Benbow & J. C Stanley (Eds.), *Academic precocity: Aspects of its development* (pp. 51–76). Baltimore: Johns Hopkins University Press.

Bigelow, E. (1934). School progress of under-age children. *Elementary School Journal, 35,* 186–192.

Birch, J. W. (1954). Early school admission for mentally advanced children. *Exceptional Children, 21,* 84–87.

Birch, J. W., Tisdale, W. J., & Barney, W. D. (1964). Early admission of able children to school: The Warren Demonstration Project. *Education Digest, 30,* 5–7.

Braga, J. L. (1971). Early admission: Opinion versus evidence. *Elementary School Journal, 72,* 35–46.

Braymen, R. K. F., & Piersel, W. C. (1987). The early entrance option: Academic and social/emotional outcomes. *Psychology in the Schools, 24,* 179–189.

Brody, L. E., & Benbow, C. P. (1987). Accelerative strategies: How effective are they for the gifted? *Gifted Child Quarterly, 31,* 105–110.

Brody, L. E., Lupkowski, A. E., & Stanley, J. C. (1988). Early entrance to college:

A study of academic and social adjustment during freshman year. *College and University, 63,* 347–359.

Byrne, D. (1984). The general/academic self concept nomological network: A review of construct validity research. *Review of Educational Research, 54,* 427–456.

Cook, T. D., & Campbell, D. T. (1979). *Quasi-experimentation: Design & analysis issues for field settings.* Boston: Houghton-Mifflin.

Cornell, D. G., Callahan, C. M., & Loyd, B. (in press). Socioemotional adjustment of adolescent girls enrolled in a residential acceleration program. *Gifted Child Quarterly.*

Cornell, D. G., Callahan, C. M., & Loyd, B. (1990). Personality growth of female early college entrants. Unpublished manuscript, University of Virginia, School of Education, Charlottesville.

Cox, J., Daniel, N., & Boston, B. A. (1985). *Educating able learners: Programs and promising practices.* Austin: University of Texas Press.

Daurio, S. P. (1979). Educational enrichment versus acceleration: A review of the literature. In W. C. George, S. J. Cohn, & J. C. Stanley (Eds.), *Educating the gifted: Acceleration and enrichment* (pp. 13–63). Baltimore: Johns Hopkins University Press.

Davis, G. A., & Rimm, S. B. (1989). *Education of the gifted and talented* (2nd ed.). Englewood Cliffs, NJ: Prentice-Hall.

Devault, M. V., Ellis, E. C., Vodicka, E. M., & Otto, H. J. (1957). *Underage first grade enrollees: Their achievement and personal and social adjustment.* Austin: University of Texas Press.

Eisenberg, A. R., & George, W. C. (1979). Early entrance to college: The Johns Hopkins experience, study of mathematically precocious youth (SMPY). *College and University, 54,* 109–118.

Elkind, D. (1981). *The hurried child: Growing up too fast too soon.* Newton, MA: Addison-Wesley.

Elkind, D. (1987). *Miseducation: Preschoolers at risk.* New York: Knopf.

Engle, T. L. (1935). Achievements of pupils who have had double promotions in elementary school. *Elementary School Journal, 36,* 185–189.

Feldhusen, J. F., Proctor, T. B., & Black, K. N. (1986). Guidelines for grade advancement of precocious children. *Roeper Review, 9*(1), 25–27.

Fluitt, J. L., & Strickland, M. S. (1984). A survey of early admission policies and procedures. *College and University, 59,* 129–135.

Fox, L. H., Benbow, C. P., & Perkins, S. (1983). An accelerated mathematics program for girls: A longitudinal evaluation. In C. P. Benbow & J. C. Stanley (Eds.), *Academic precocity: Aspects of its development* (pp. 113–138). Baltimore: Johns Hopkins University Press.

Fund for the Advancement of Education of the Ford Foundation. (1953). *Bridging the gap between school and college.* New York: Research Division of the Fund.

Fund for the Advancement of Education of the Ford Foundation. (1957). *They went to college early.* New York: Research Division of the Fund.

Gallagher, J. J., Weiss, P., Oglesby, K., & Thomas, T. (1983). *The status of gifted/*

talented education: United States surveys of needs, practices, and policies. Ventura County, CA: Ventura County Superintendent of Schools Office.

George, W. C., Cohn, S. J., & Stanley, J. C. (Eds.). (1979). *Educating the gifted: Acceleration and enrichment.* Baltimore: Johns Hopkins University Press.

Gredler, G. R. (1980). The birthdate effect: Fact or artifact? *Journal of Learning Disabilities, 13,* 9–12.

Gregory, E. H., & March, E. (1985). Early entrance program at California State University, Los Angeles. *Gifted Child Quarterly, 29,* 83–86.

Gregory, E. H., & Stevens-Long, J. (1986). Coping skills among highly gifted adolescents. *Journal for the Education of the Gifted, 9,* 147–155.

Gudaitis, J. L. (1986). *Advance College Project final evaluation report, 1984–1985 school year.* Bloomington: University of Indiana. (ERIC Document Reproduction Service No. ED 267–097)

Halliwell, J. W. (1966). Reviewing the reviews on entrance age and school success. *Journal of Educational Research, 59,* 395–401.

Hedges, W. D. (1977). *At what age should children enter first grade: A comprehensive review of research.* Ann Arbor, MI: University Microfilms International.

Hirsh-Pasek, K., Hyson, M., Rescorla, L., Cone, J. (April, 1989). *Hurrying children: How does it affect their academic, social, creative, and emotional development?* Paper presented at the Biennial Meeting of the Society for Research in Child Development, Kansas City, MO.

Hobson, J. R. (1948). Mental age as a workable criterion for school admission. *Elementary School Journal, 48,* 213–321.

Horne, D. L., & Dupuy, P. J. (1981). In favor of acceleration for gifted students. *The Personnel and Guidance Journal, 60,* 103–106.

House, P. A. (1978). *Minnesota Talented Youth Mathematics Project: Evaluation report 1977–78.* St. Paul: Minnesota State Department of Education.

Jackson, N. E., Famiglietti, J., & Robinson, H. B. (1981). Kindergarten and first grade teachers' attitudes toward early entrants, intellectually advanced students, and average students. *Journal for the Education of the Gifted, 4,* 132–142.

Janos, P. M. (1987). A fifty-year follow-up of Terman's youngest college students and IQ-matched comparison subjects. *Gifted Child Quarterly, 31,* 55–58.

Janos, P. M., & Robinson, N. M. (1985). The performance of students in a program of radical acceleration at the university level. *Gifted Child Quarterly, 29,* 175–179.

Janos, P. M., Robinson, N. M., Carter, C., Chapel, A., Cufley, R., Curland, M., Daily, M., Guilland, M., Heinzig, M., Kehl, H., Lu, S., Sherry, D., Stoloff, J., & Wise, A. (1988). A cross-sectional developmental study of the social relations of students who enter college early. *Gifted Child Quarterly, 32,* 210–215.

Janos, P. M., Sanfilippo, S. M., & Robinson, N. M. (1986). "Underachievement" among markedly accelerated college students. *Journal of Youth and Adolescence, 15,* 303–313.

Kagan, S. L., & Zigler, E. F. (1987). *Early schooling: The national debate.* New Haven, CT: Yale University Press.

Karnes, F. A., & Chauvin, J. C. (1982a). Almost everything that parents and teachers of gifted secondary school students should know about early college enrollment and college credit by examination. *G/C/T, 24*(5), 39–42.

Karnes, F. A., & Chauvin, J. C. (1982b). A survey of early admission policies for younger than average students: Implications for gifted youth. *Gifted Child Quarterly, 26,* 68–73.

Keys, N. (1938). The underage student in high school and college. *University of California Publications in Education, 7,* 147–241.

Klausmeier, H. J. (1963). Effects of accelerating bright older elementary pupils: A follow-up. *Journal of Educational Psychology, 54,* 165–171.

Klausmeier, H. J., Goodwin, W. L., & Ronda, T. (1968). Effects of accelerating bright older elementary pupils: A second follow-up. *Journal of Educational Psychology, 59,* 53–58.

Klausmeier, H. J., & Ripple, R. E. (1962). Effects of accelerating bright older elementary pupils from second to fourth grade. *Journal of Education Psychology, 53,* 93–100.

Knoff, H. M. (Ed.). (1986). *The assessment of child & adolescent personality.* NY: Guilford Press.

Kogan, N. (1955). Studies of college students. *Journal of Counseling Psychology, 2,* 129–136.

Kulik, J. A., & Kulik, C. C. (1984). Effects of accelerated instruction on students. *Review of Educational Research, 54*(3), 409–425.

Lave, J. (1984). *Advance College Project final evaluation report.* Bloomington: University of Indiana. (ERIC Document Reproduction Service No. ED 258–977)

Lincoln, E. A. (1929). The later performance of under-aged children admitted to school on the basis of mental age. *Journal of Educational Research, 19,* 22–30.

Maddux, C. D. (1983). Early school entry for the gifted: New evidence and concerns. *Roeper Review, 5*(4), 15–17.

Maddux, C. D., Stacy, D., Scott, M. (1981). School entry age in a group of gifted children. *Gifted Children Quarterly, 25,* 180–184.

Matlin, J. P. (1965). *Some effects of a planned program of acceleration upon elementary school children.* Unpublished doctoral dissertation, University of California, Berkeley.

Mercurio, J. (1980). College courses in the high school: A follow-up study. *College and University, 56,* 83–91.

Mercurio, J., Schwartz, S., & Oesterle, R. (1982). College courses in high school: A four-year follow-up of the Syracuse University Project Advance class of 1977. *College and University, 58,* 5–18.

Mezynski, K., Stanley, J. C., & McCoart, R. F. (1983). Helping youths score well on AP examinations in physics, chemistry, and calculus. In C. P. Benbow & J. C. Stanley (Eds.), *Academic precocity* (pp. 86–112). Baltimore: Johns Hopkins University Press.

Mirman, N. (1962). Are accelerated students socially maladjusted? *Elementary School Journal, 62,* 273–276.

Montour, K. M. (1977). William James Sidis, the broken twig. *American Psychologist, 32,* 265–279.

Moore, R. S., & Moore, D. N. (1975). *Better late than early: A new approach to your child's education.* New York: E. P. Dutton.

Mueller, K. J. (1955). Success of elementary students admitted to public schools under the requirements of the Nebraska Program of Early Entrance. Unpublished doctoral dissertation, University of Nebraska.

Newland, T. E. (1976). *The gifted in socioeconomic perspective.* Englewood Cliffs, NJ: Prentice-Hall.

Obrzut, A., Nelson, R. B., & Obrzut, J. E. (1984). Early school entrance for intellectually superior children: An analysis. *Psychology in the Schools, 21,* 71–77.

Pennau, J. E. E. (1981). *The relationship between early entrance and subsequent educational progress in the elementary school.* Unpublished doctoral dissertation, University of Minnesota.

Pollins, L. D. (1983). The effects of acceleration on the social and emotional development of gifted students. In C. P. Benbow & J. C. Stanley (Eds.), *Academic precocity* (pp. 160–178). Baltimore: Johns Hopkins University Press.

Pressey, S. L. (1949). *Educational acceleration: Appraisal and basic problems.* (Bureau of Educational Research Monographs, No. 31). Columbus: Ohio State University Press.

Pressey, S. L. (1967). "Fordling" accelerates ten years after. *Journal of Counseling Psychology, 14,* 73–80.

Proctor, T. B., Black, K. N., & Feldhusen, J. F. (1986). Early admission of selected children to elementary school: A review of the research literature. *Journal of Educational Research, 80,* 70–76.

Proctor, T. B., Feldhusen, J. F., & Black, K. N. (1988). Guidelines for early admission to elementary school. *Psychology in the Schools, 25,* 41–43.

Ramos, J. M. (1980). *A study of the overt classroom behavior of public and nonpublic seventh graders with early school entrance experiences in comparison with their older classmates.* Unpublished doctoral dissertation, Case Western Reserve University.

Reynolds, M. C. (Ed.). (1962). *Early school admission for mentally advanced children: A review of research and practice.* Reston, VA: Council for Exceptional Children.

Reynolds, M. C., Birch, J. W., & Tuseth, A. A. (1962). Review of research on early admissions. In M. C. Reynolds (Ed.), *Early school admission for mentally advanced children: A review of research and practice* (pp. 7–18). Washington, DC: Council for Exceptional Children.

Richardson, T. M., & Benbow, C. P. (in press). Long-term effects of acceleration on the social-emotional adjustment of mathematically precocious youth. *Journal of Educational Psychology.*

Robeck, M. C. (1968). *California Project Talent: Acceleration programs for intellectually gifted pupils.* Sacramento: California State Department of Education.

Robinson, N. M., & Janos, P. M. (1986). Psychological adjustment in a college-level program of marked academic acceleration. *Journal of Youth and Adolescence, 15,* 51–60.

Roedell, W. C., Jackson, N. E., & Robinson, H. B. (1980). *Gifted young children.* New York: Teachers College Press.

Rusch, R. R., & Clark, R. M. (1963). Four years in three: An evaluation. *Elementary School Journal, 63*, 281–285.

Southern, W. T., Jones, E. D., & Fiscus, E. D. (1989). Practitioners objections to the academic acceleration of gifted children. *Gifted Child Quarterly, 33*, 29–35.

Stanley, J. C. (1985). Young entrants to college: How did they fare? *College and University, 60*, 219–228.

Stanley, J. C., & Benbow, C. P. (1983). Extremely young college graduates: Evidence of their success. *College and University, 58*, 361–371.

Stanley, J. C., & McGill, A. M. (1986). More about young entrants to college: How did they fare? *Gifted Child Quarterly, 30*, 70–73.

Stanley, J. C., & Stanley, B. S. K. (1986). High school biology, chemistry, or physics learned well in three weeks. *Journal of Research in Science Teaching, 23*, 237–250.

Swiatek, M. A., & Benbow, C. P. (in press). Fast-paced mathematics class and the development of mathematically precocious students. *Journal for Research in Math Education*.

Terman, L. M., & Oden, M. H. (1947). *Genetic studies of genius: Vol. 4. The gifted child grows up: Twenty-five years follow-up of a superior group*. Stanford, CA: Stanford University Press.

Thomas, T. A. (1989). Acceleration for the academically talented: A follow-up of the Academic Talent Search class of 1984. Unpublished manuscript, California State University, Academic Talent Search Project. Sacramento.

Walker, C. E., & Roberts, M. C. (Eds.). (1983). *Handbook of clinical child psychology*. NY: Wiley Interscience.

Wallis, L. R. (1984). Selective early school entrance: Predicting school success. *Journal for the Education of the Gifted, 7*, 89–97.

Wilbur, F. P. (1982). College courses in the high school: New opportunities for the twelfth year. *The Practitioner, 9*, 1–12.

Wolf, J. M., & Kessler, A. L. (1987). *Entrance to kindergarten: What is the best age?* Arlington, VA: Educational Research Service.

Worcester, D. A. (1956). *The education of children of above-average mentality*. Lincoln, NE: University of Nebraska Press.

CHAPTER 5

Young College Students: Assessing Factors That Contribute to Success

Linda E. Brody and Julian C. Stanley
Johns Hopkins University

How do students fare who enter college 2 or more years earlier than is typical? Accelerative strategies employed throughout the elementary and high school years often lead inevitably to students' completing much or all of their high school course work before most of their chronological age peers do. The next logical step for them is to enroll in college full-time. In addition, highly gifted students who are bored with regular-paced instruction in high school may choose to bypass one or more years and enter college early. Thus, evaluating the college and professional achievements of students who were "young entrants" to college (defined for the purpose of this chapter as those who did not yet become 17 years old by December 31 of the year in whose fall they became full-time college students) and "young graduates" (i.e., those not yet 20 years old when they completed all requirements for the bachelor's degree) has important implications for the practice of accelerating students in various ways at all age levels. The term *radical accelerant* will be used for students who are *extremely* young when they enter college.

Of course, acceleration has become increasingly controversial in the United States because it contradicts the current practice of grouping students in classrooms primarily on the basis of age rather than ability or educational need. Making special arrangements for students with exceptional abilities is sometimes viewed as "elitist." There is also an underlying concern that social and emotional maladjustment might result from placing precocious students in classes with older students. This worry has been fueled by individual case studies of selected accelerated students who exhibited emotional problems. Even when numerous cases of well-adjusted radical accelerants can be cited as support for the practice, a lack of understanding of the factors that contribute to their successes or failures may make one wary of encouraging a given student to enter college at a young age. Certainly, the practice of skipping several years in grade placement to become an extremely young college freshman is appropriate for relatively few individuals. This chapter attempts to summarize the research on early entrants to college and to identify factors likely to contribute to successful academic and social adjustment for each students.

HISTORICAL CONTEXT

Grouping students by chronological age has been a common practice in classrooms in the United States for only the last century or so. It was instituted as part of the educational reform movement designed to accommodate large numbers of immigrants in a society that was becoming increasingly industrialized. Previously, "few educators found the association of boys of 12 with young men of 20 in academies or college anomalous" (Kett, 1974, p. 11). Young students were commonly found in American colleges during our nation's early history (Daurio, 1979; Montour, 1976a).

Even after age grouping was instituted in American schools, in the absence of enrichment opportunities for precocious students programs of flexible promotion were quite popular in the 19th and early 20th centuries. Among the cities adopting them were St. Louis, Elizabeth, New Jersey, Cambridge, Massachusetts, and New York City (Tannenbaum, 1983). In Terman's group of subjects identified in California in the 1920s, the mean age at high school graduation was 16.9 years for boys and 16.8 years for girls, suggesting that it was common for bright children in that time period to skip grades and enter college one or more years early (Oden, 1968). Keys (1938) reported that between 1922 and 1930, 238 students entered the University of California at Berkeley before the age of 16 ½.

Gradually, however, grade skipping and accelerative programs became less common as some enrichment classes for the gifted were introduced in the 1920s. Pressey (1949) noted that "social maladjustment was not adequately guarded against and became unduly feared" (p. 140). The 1930s and 1940s saw reduced interest in the gifted and few efforts at acceleration, but occasional efforts were made to include enrichment in the regular classroom (Tannenbaum, 1983). World War II did, however, spark efforts to get young men into and out of college faster so that they could help in the war effort. Colleges were encouraged to accept young entrants as freshmen. The University of Illinois, the University of Chicago, and Ohio State University are examples of universities that engaged in this practice, and there is considerable evidence that the early entrants in these programs were highly successful academically (Daurio, 1979).

Nonetheless, after the war there was concern that accelerating young students into college would result in placing them in classes with much older veterans (Pressey, 1949). Interest in early entrance programs thus diminished somewhat until the Korean War replicated the wartime demands for men to complete their education quickly. At that time the Ford Foundation provided funding for an Early Admission Program through its Fund for the Advancement of Education. Scholarships were made available for young men and women not older than 16 ½ to enter college at any of 12 universities for 2 years before entering the military. For the first time, special care was taken in a program of this kind to attend to the social and emotional needs of the participants (Daurio, 1979; Fund for the Advancement of Education, 1953).

Although programming for the gifted was at a particularly low point in the 1950s, the Ford Foundation experiment had some effects. Most of the participating colleges instituted early admission programs as part of their regular admissions even after the Ford Foundation funding ended, and the College Board reported that in 1955–1956, 29 of its 169 member colleges had early admission programs (Fund for the Advancement of Education, 1957). The College Board Advanced Placement Program was instituted in the 1950s as a replacement for the Early Admission Program sponsored by the Ford Foundation. Accelerated programs were found in a few large public school systems, notably New York and Baltimore. A gradual awareness of personnel shortages in key fields was emerging, and concern over *Sputnik* in particular raised a new level of consciousness that something was needed to help gifted children. More difficult course work was introduced, particularly in science and mathematics, and ability grouping became more common. Some accelerative programs were introduced. In the 1960s, however, the focus on egalitarianism and concern with the underprivileged that resulted from the Civil Rights movement led to the elimination of most programs for the gifted. It has taken much effort since then to renew interest in either accelerated or enriched programs for gifted students.

In 1971 the Study of Mathematically Precocious Youth (SMPY) was founded at Johns Hopkins University by Julian Stanley. The Scholastic Aptitude Test (SAT) (developed to predict the performance of high school seniors in academically selective colleges) was administered to junior high school students to identify those who reason exceptionally well mathematically. This project called attention to the advanced abilities of these students and the need to provide course work at a much higher level than they were receiving in junior high school. The first few students with whom SMPY worked chose radical acceleration into college as their method of obtaining advanced course work (Stanley, Keating, & Fox, 1974). Since then, many highly talented mathematical and verbal reasoners have been identified by Stanley and his associates and in regional talent searches throughout the United States (Van Tassel-Baska, 1986). Early entrance to college is only one of a "smorgasbord" of alternatives offered to such students as options for accelerating or augmenting their educational programs (Benbow, 1979, 1986; Fox, 1974, 1976, 1979; Stanley, 1979). The majority of SMPY students do not skip more than one grade, if any, but supplement their schoolwork with challenging summer programs, Advanced Placement (AP) courses, part-time college courses, and the like. Nonetheless, SMPY's work with those students who have selected grade skipping and early entrance to college as their vehicle for obtaining more advanced work has done much to validate the potential benefits of radical acceleration for extremely able, highly motivated youths. Most of SMPY's proteges who have entered college early have done exceptionally well (Brody, Lupkowski, & Stanley, 1988; Nevin, 1977; Stanley, 1985a).

In 1977, the late Halbert Robinson founded the Early Entrance Program (EEP) at the University of Washington, which continues today. That program is virtually unique in being designed for much younger students than most previous programs for young entrants (students are typically under the age of 14 when they enter) and in providing extensive social, emotional, and academic support for the participants:

> The essential elements of the EEP are careful selection of students, sufficient numbers of participants to provide a "peer group," structured and unstructured group meetings during at least the first year of full-time university involvement, a lounge to use as "home base," and continued support through the provision of counseling. Since 1980, entry has occurred through a one-year Transition School on the campus, which provided preparatory education in conjunction with which the students gradually increase their load of university work. EEPers live with their families for at least two years, and many do so until graduation, though others have moved into a variety of group living situations as juniors and seniors. (Janos & Robinson, 1985, p. 175)

The Early Entrance Program includes a research component, and the studies conducted by the Center for the Study of Capable Youth at the University of Washington provide support for the effectiveness of early entrance to college at an exceptionally young age for carefully selected individuals (e.g., see Janos, Robinson, & Lunnenborg, in press).

Currently, in addition to EEP at the University of Washington, Simon's Rock College and Mary Baldwin College offer organized programs for young entrants, Mary Baldwin's being for females only. The University of North Texas has initiated an accredited program (the Texas Academy of Mathematics and Sciences) for students to complete their last 2 years of high school while simultaneously earning 2 years of college credit by taking only college honors courses. Moreover, qualified early entrants are accepted as full-time students on an individual basis at most colleges and universities (Brody, Assouline, & Stanley, 1990; Brody et al., 1988; Stanley, 1985b). Fluitt and Strickland (1984) found that 87% of colleges and universities admit qualified students prior to high school graduation, and 16% of the colleges polled actively recruit such students. It is likely that an even greater percentage of colleges accept students who are young as a result of acceleration but will graduate from high school prior to matriculation.

Examples throughout history of individuals who have accelerated their educational progress, graduated from college at an unusually young age, and proceeded to live full, productive lives are plentiful (Daurio, 1979; Hollingworth, 1929; Montour, 1976a, 1976b, 1976c; Stanley, 1985a). Even during periods when acceleration was not favored and early entrance programs were uncommon, some prodigies managed to accelerate their educational progress on an individual basis, and most were extremely successful personally and professionally. Just a few examples of notable young entrants are Paul Dudley, who entered Harvard at age 10 and graduated at age 14 in 1690; Charles Homer Haskins, who received his A.B. degree from Johns Hopkins in 1887 at age 16 and his Ph.D. there 3 years later (and was followed by 46 others from 1916 through 1989 who graduated from this school aged 15 to 18—see Stanley & Benbow, 1983); Merrill Kenneth Wolf, who graduated from Yale College in 1945 the month he became 14 (see Keating, 1976); and Jay Luo, who received his B.S. in mathematics with high honors from Boise (Idaho) State University in 1982 at age 12 years 45 days, thereby qualifying as probably the youngest student up to that time to earn a baccalaureate degree at an American university (Newsmakers, 1982). (In 1988, an 11-year-old boy was awarded a bachelor's degree from a California university under circumstances that engendered considerable controversy and criticism, and it was reported by the Associated Press that the young man has since entered junior high school with his age-mates.)

In spite of numerous examples of highly successful accelerants, much anti-acceleration sentiment in the United States stems from the public's knowledge of the case of William James Sidis. His talents, achievements, and lack of achievements throughout his life attracted a great deal of media publicity and contributed to the myth of "early ripe, early rot" among the gifted (Montour, 1977).

SIDIS AND WEINER: A COMPARISON OF TWO RADICAL ACCELERANTS

William James Sidis entered Harvard as a special student at age 11 in 1909. A few months later he gained national attention by delivering a highly respected lecture in higher mathematics before the Harvard Mathematical

Club. Sidis's father, an immigrant who earned advanced degrees after coming to the United States, began teaching him before the age of 2. William proved to be an exceptional student, learning to read by age 3 and knowing several languages by age 6. At that time he entered public school and passed through all seven grades in 6 months' time. The family then educated him at home until he entered college, except for 3 months at the age of 8 when he attended high school, but subsequently withdrew to continue his education at home. By age 10 he had completed the entire high school curriculum and knew algebra, trigonometry, geometry, and calculus. It took several petitions before Harvard would admit him as a special student.

During all of this time, throughout his childhood, Sidis was the subject of much scrutiny and publicity. The mathematics lecture at age 11 brought him even more to the attention of the public. Although he successfully graduated from college at 16, there were signs that he may have been experiencing some emotional difficulties during this period. He entered graduate school but did not finish, then entered law school but again did not complete the degree. He took a teaching job at the Rice Institute (now Rice University) in Texas but continued to be hounded by reporters and finally attempted to drop out of sight. He worked the rest of his life at low-paying routine clerical jobs, specifically rejecting both his father and academia and trying to avoid publicity. Periodically, however, until his death at age 46, reporters would find him and report his lack of living up to earlier expectations (Montour, 1977; Wallace, 1986).

Striking similarities in their backgrounds, yet important differences that contributed to very different outcomes, have sparked comparisons between Sidis and mathematician Norbert Weiner. Weiner finished high school at age 11, graduated from college at 14, and earned his Ph.D. from Harvard at 18. He was a graduate student at Harvard during the same period that Sidis was an undergraduate there, and his autobiography commented on Sidis's upbringing (Weiner, 1953). Like Sidis, Weiner also had a dominating father who controlled his education, and he exhibited social awkwardness as a boy. But there were important differences. For one thing, Weiner did attend public school, so he had access to other children as he was growing up. Also, although Sidis's father enjoyed the publicity engendered by having a son who was a prodigy, Weiner's father was aware of the possible negative effects and avoided publicity as much as possible. Weiner's father chose to send his son to Tufts College instead of Harvard because he felt it would make him less conspicuous. Weiner, who also credits his wife with helping him achieve independence from his family, became an eminent mathematician and fathered two daughters (Montour, 1977; Weiner, 1953).

In comparing the backgrounds of these two examples of radical acceleration, Montour (1977) concluded that "it was not extreme educational acceleration that destroyed William James Sidis emotionally and mentally, but instead an interaction of paternal exploitation and emotional starvation. Norbert Weiner had to surmount some of the same obstacles Sidis faced as a prodigy from a society that shunned them because of their early brilliance, but Weiner survived, his life pattern not being oriented toward self-destruction like Sidis's" (p. 276).

OTHER SELECTED RADICAL ACCELERANTS

Many other examples could be cited to counterbalance the Sidis story. One notable early entrant, mentioned earlier, was Merrill Kenneth Wolf, who completed his B.A. in music at Yale in 1945 when barely 14. "Kenny" exhibited exceptional verbal and musical talent. As a young child, although several attempts were made to enroll him in school, he was so advanced that he could not fit in academically. As a result, he was educated at home until the age of 10. He then enrolled in several courses at Western Reserve University (now Case Western Reserve), but his real interest was in music. So he moved (with his mother) to New Haven, Connecticut, where he enrolled in Yale as a 12-year-old sophomore to study with Paul Hindemith. After graduation, he received private instruction in music for several years. Finally, at age 21, approximately the age most students graduate from college, he entered medical school and subsequently became a professor of neuroanatomy. Unlike in the case of Sidis, there is no evidence that home tutoring was damaging to Wolf socially or emotionally. The educational path he chose allowed him to study at a pace appropriate for his abilities and have the opportunity to pursue two career interests, music and medicine (Keating, 1976, p. 346; Montour, 1976c).

Another prodigy who was educated at home is Ruth Lawrence. She graduated from Oxford University at the age of 13, completed the requirements for her Ph.D. degree in mathematics there in 1989 at the age of 17, and received a 1-year appointment to the faculty of Harvard University as one of the youngest Ivy League faculty members ever. Educated at home by her parents, along with her younger sister, Ruth entered Oxford as a full-time student at the age of 11. She lived off-campus with her father, who accompanied her to all classes and social events. Her father has been criticized for his overprotective nature (Bowen, 1985). More time will be needed before the full effects of Ruth's unusual educational experiences can be evaluated. To date, however, her academic successes have been startling.

Possibly the youngest person to be appointed a full professor at an American University is Charles Louis Fefferman. Unlike the previous examples, he spent his early years in the age-appropriate classroom. However, he exhibited strong interest and precocity in mathematics and science when quite young and by the age of 12 was enrolled part-time in courses at the University of Maryland. At the urging of his mathematics professor, Fefferman skipped high school and entered the university full-time at age 14. As a college student, he lived at home and continued to have an active social life. He was awarded his high school diploma concurrently with his bachelor's degree in mathematics and physics from the University of Maryland. He subsequently earned his Ph.D. degree in mathematics from Princeton at age 20 and joined the faculty of the University of Chicago as an assistant professor. A year later he was promoted to the rank of full professor at age 22. Dr. Fefferman is now an eminent professor of mathematics at Princeton, having received numerous awards and honors including the Fields Medal in 1978 (Levy, 1978; Montour, 1976b).

Colin Camerer, an SMPY protege, also attended public school during his early years. In the early grades he was allowed to move ahead at his own pace, so that by second grade he was doing fourth- or fifth-grade work. The family then moved. In the fifth grade, the school released Colin to take computer courses at the Maryland Academy of Science. His success there led to testing by Julian Stanley that revealed exceptional mathematical and verbal reasoning abilities. Since Colin was relatively old-in-grade, it was suggested that he skip the seventh grade. He did so and also enrolled in SMPY's first fast-paced mathematics course, where he completed all precalculus mathematics quickly. Colin then decided to skip the ninth and tenth grades and become an eleventh grader. He enjoyed the one year of high school, participating in many activities and supplementing the academic work with part-time college courses. In 1973, at age 14, however, he entered Johns Hopkins University full-time with sophomore standing. Following graduation from Hopkins the month he became 17, he earned an M.B.A. degree at age 19 and a Ph.D. degree at 22, both from the University of Chicago, becoming an assistant professor at Northwestern University. Currently, Colin is a tenured associate professor on the faculty of the Wharton School of the University of Pennsylvania (see Holmes, Rin, Tremblay, & Zeldin, 1984).

Many more cases could be described, and there is great variability in the paths taken. For example, John Stuart Mill was educated entirely at home and can't really be considered an "early entrant," since he never matriculated full-time in college (Packe, 1954). Wolf, Lawrence, and Sidis are examples of individuals who were largely educated at home prior to college but then enrolled as full-time college students. Weiner, Fefferman, and Camerer spent most of their early years in public school with some provision for acceleration but enrolled in college at unusually young ages. Of these, only Fefferman skipped high school completely. Brody et al. (1988) noted a wide variety of grade-skipping patterns among an SMPY population of young entrants to college.

With regard to achievement, there is great variability as well. It is usually the *most* successful and *least* successful prodigies who are likely to be spotlighted in the literature and by the media. Actually, only a few become full professors in their early 20s, just as few encounter the extreme emotional difficulties of someone like Sidis. The majority of early entrants fall somewhere in between. Typically, they graduate successfully from college and find professional fulfillment in some area of endeavor but most probably will not become eminent in their fields. There is a substantial body of research on the achievements of groups of early entrants to college; selected studies will be summarized below.

RESEARCH ON GROUPS OF EARLY ENTRANTS

Terman and Oden (1947) studied the effects of acceleration as part of Terman's monumental study of gifted students in California during the 1920s. They found that the accelerated students in their study were more likely to graduate from college and to attend graduate school, and the accelerated men experienced greater vocational success than the nonaccelerants. They concluded that "the influence of school acceleration in causing social maladjustment has been greatly exaggerated. There is no doubt that maladjustment does result in individual cases, but our data indicate that in a majority of subjects the maladjustment consists of a temporary feeling of inferiority which is later overcome. The important thing is to consider each child as a special case" (p. 275). They recommended that children of IQ 135 or higher be accelerated to permit college entrance by the age of 17 at the latest, and that a majority in this group would be better off at 16.

Janos (1987) compared the 19 youngest college students in Terman's study, all of whom had entered college before the age of 15 years 4 months, with a group of subjects from the Terman study matched on age and IQ. The early entrants were more likely to be high achievers in college, to enter their professions earlier, and to be rated as high achievers in a 1940 follow-up, but career differences were not evident 20 years later. No psychosocial differences between the groups were found. Unfortunately, this study required that all of the matched nonaccelerants had graduated from college, whereas the accelerants may not have. This probably biased some of the comparisons, such as long-term career success, in favor of the nonaccelerants.

A review of studies of students at Harvard, Columbia, the University of Minnesota, Dartmouth, Northwestern, Barnard, the City College of New

York, and elsewhere led Pressey (1949) to conclude that "the evidence was practically unanimous that younger entrants were most likely to graduate, had the best academic records, won the most honors and presented the fewest disciplinary difficulties" (p. 7). Recognizing that the youngest students are often also the ablest, Pressey also reviewed studies where ability was allowed for and concluded that accelerated students "still turn out as well academically as average students, or even seem to have profited to some extent by acceleration" (p. 8). These findings were also confirmed in Pressey's own studies of underaged entrants at Ohio State University, where he found that students entering young were more likely to graduate and to have better academic records than older students. They also participated in campus activities to the same extent as students who entered at the typical age (Pressey, 1949).

A study was conducted of the students in the Early Admission Program sponsored by the Ford Foundation at 12 universities during the early 1950s. In all institutions except one the accelerated group outperformed their total classes academically, and in 9 of the 12 institutions they outperformed a comparison group of students matched on the basis of aptitude but who had finished high school and entered college at the regular age. In spite of some initial difficulties reported, especially by the boys, about dating, by senior year the majority of the accelerants had attained good social adjustment; they participated in extracurricular activities and were well assimilated into the social life of the campus. A few of the students were found to have serious adjustment problems, but the proportion was less than for the freshmen classes as a whole (Fund for the Advancement of Education, 1953). When support for the project ended, 11 of the 12 colleges immediately incorporated early admissions into their regular admissions policy (Fund for the Advancement of Education, 1957). A follow-up study of the students who participated in this program at three colleges, conducted 10 years later, revealed that a majority of the accelerated students went on to obtain advanced professional training, and many had already entered outstanding careers. The accelerants reported little or no harm from skipping the high school work, some initial social difficulty when they entered the program that soon passed, and the advantage of beginning their career at a younger age (Pressey, 1967).

In an effort to assess the effects of acceleration, Julian Stanley and his colleagues at Johns Hopkins University have studied the achievements of early entrants to and young graduates of Johns Hopkins. Eisenberg and George (1979) studied 59 students who left high school at least a year early to enter Johns Hopkins as full-time students in either the fall of 1976 or 1977 and found the majority to have performed at least as well as the average Johns Hopkins freshman academically. Stanley (1985b) and Stanley and McGill (1986) reported on the progress of 25 accelerated students who entered Johns

Hopkins in 1980 at least 2 years early. Twenty-four of the students received a bachelor's degree at Johns Hopkins or elsewhere no later than 4½ years after entry, and the other one, who had excellent academic standing and was lacking only one semester toward graduation, left because of illness. Grades and earned honors at graduation suggested that the group was highly successful academically. Attempts to predict success from antecedent variables were restricted by the small sample size and limited data.

Expanding on this study, Brody et al. (1990) investigated the achievements of the 65 students who entered Johns Hopkins 2 or more years early during the period 1980 to 1984. The results also suggest a high degree of academic success in the group. An analysis of antecedent variables showed that the number of Advanced Placement credits earned was the best predictor of cumulative grade-point average and honors in college.

Stanley and Benbow (1983) also studied 32 young graduates from Johns Hopkins, those who from 1887 until 1982 received their bachelor's degree before the age of 19, a group that somewhat overlaps the early entrants to Hopkins. They found a high degree of success among these young graduates, as undergraduates as well as after graduation. Stanley continues to follow young graduates from Hopkins. There were 47 such students as of the May 1989 graduation.

SMPY proteges who were not necessarily Johns Hopkins students have also been studied. Pollins (1983) assessed the social and emotional adjustment of 21 male radical accelerants and 21 nonaccelerants matched on age and ability at approximately age 13. No negative social or emotional effects of acceleration were found, and being accelerated was associated with higher educational aspirations and greater perceived use of educational opportunities. Brody et al. (1988) studied mathematically talented students who were early entrants at 17 different universities. The group as a whole was found to have experienced excellent academic and social adjustment during the freshman year in college. Students who had skipped at least a year of school prior to college entrance were included in a study by Brody and Benbow (1987), and again no negative social or emotional problems appeared to result from the accelerative experience.

The Center for the Study of Capable Youth at the University of Washington in Seattle has conducted extensive research related to the development of intellectual precocity in general as well as on the specific effects of acceleration on the students who have participated in the Early Entrance Program at that university. In general, the students in this program entered college at considerably younger ages than those represented in most other studies. A comparison of University of Washington Early Entrants with three groups (regular-aged university students, National Merit Scholars, and students who qualified for acceleration but declined to participate) assessed social and emotional adjustment and found few differences, except that the college-aged students were more assertive and the accelerated students less conforming. There were, however, no indications of special adjustment difficulties in the accelerated group (Robinson & Janos, 1986). Students in the Early Entrance Program were also compared to regular-aged college students (who were matched to the accelerants on preadmission aptitude test scores) and National Merit Scholars on academic performance. The accelerated students earned grade-point averages comparable with those of the National Merit Scholars and higher than those of the matched university sample (Janos & Robinson, 1985). A more recent follow-up of a larger pool of subjects (43 early entrants) compared the students with comparison groups of matched university students, National Merit Finalists, and students who qualified for the EEP but declined to participate. This study confirmed the academic success and psychosocial adjustment of the early entrants (Janos et al., in press).

In 1979, Daurio (1979) surveyed the literature on acceleration and enrichment, including the research on early entrants to college. He concluded that "accelerated students are shown to perform at least as well as, and often better than, 'normal-aged' control students, on both academic and nonacademic measures" (p. 53).

The research clearly shows that as a group young entrants to college have been extremely successful academically and professionally and have not experienced significant social or emotional problems. There is no justification for assuming that academic difficulties or social and emotional adjustment problems are likely to accompany early entrance to college. One must bear in mind, however, that what is true for the majority may not be true for individuals. Certainly, some individuals have encountered difficulties, and one should approach acceleration, especially radical acceleration, with caution and careful planning. Taking great care about social and emotional aspects seems essential.

ISSUES IN RADICAL ACCELERATION

Students considering entering college several years younger than is typical should carefully examine their own strengths, weaknesses, experiences, interests, personalities, physical and emotional maturity, and circumstances in order to make decisions about such issues as how much to accelerate, when to accelerate, the type of college to attend, where to live as a young college student, and how best to use the time saved from entering college early. No one path is appropriate for all young entrants to college. These issues are explored briefly below.

How Much to Accelerate

Using a minimum of 2 years' acceleration as the baseline for defining early entrance to college (we believe that 1 year of acceleration is a fairly easy adjustment for most extremely bright students), examples can be found of students who entered college only 2 years early and encountered academic and/or social difficulties, whereas others encountered few problems skipping many more grades than that. Although one might assume that there is greater risk associated with more radical acceleration, that is not necessarily true because many factors are involved. Brody et al. (1990) found the number of Advanced Placement credits, but not age, to be predictive of academic achievement among Johns Hopkins early entrants. This was also supported in a study of early entrants at 17 universities who skipped between 2 and 6 years of school; their amount of acceleration did not appear related to academic achievement, as long as the student was academically prepared for the particular college selected and had taken advanced course work prior to entering college. In this study, the one student who had the most serious academic problems had skipped 5 years of school, but the other four students studied who had skipped 5 or 6 years of school had freshman grade-point average ranging from 3.7 to 4.0. Social adjustment problems also did not appear to be specifically related to the number of years accelerated, although most of the radically accelerated students lived at home during most or all of their undergraduate years (Brody et al., 1988).

On the other hand, we are familiar with a young man who entered college at 11, graduated with high honors at age 15, completed his Ph.D. at a highly prestigious university by age 20, and subsequently received a faculty appointment at an excellent university. Nonetheless, several years later he reported being quite miserable socially and was apparently a poor teacher. There was no indication that he had been pushed by his parents to accelerate. Because of his young age when he entered college, however, he commuted from home and apparently gave up his neighborhood friends and made few college friends. Thus, he missed crucial socialization experiences, including athletic and musical ones, during his formative years from age 11 onward. Although he excelled academically, this lack of social growth is greatly restricting his personal and professional development as an adult.

This story contrasts strongly with that of one of SMPY's most outstanding proteges who also entered college at age 11 and commuted from home. He managed to maintain ties with his childhood friends as well as make friends in college. An important interest of his was basketball. As a 14-year-old college junior he received permission to play on the high school basketball team. This provided an additional social outlet for him. In college, he even joined a fraternity, and the whole study body cheered when he walked across the stage at graduation. Thus, his social development continued during the years he was in college. After graduating at the age of 15, he enrolled in a high-caliber graduate program in another state, excelling academically while also seemingly having a satisfactory social life.

Thus, one must weigh his or her individual circumstances when deciding how much to accelerate. The other issues described below, especially whether the early entrant plans to live at home and whether there is a program for young entrants on the campus under consideration, may be important if one is contemplating extremely radical acceleration of 4 or more years.

Optimal Times to Accelerate

It has been suggested that the best time for students to skip grades is at natural transition points, that is between schools rather than within schools (Benbow, 1979; Fox, 1979; Stanley, 1979). There are advantages socially when a student bypasses the last year(s) of a given school and enters the next school (whether elementary school, middle school, high school, or college) fresh with everyone else, rather than skipping grades within a school and having to leave his or her classmates behind in the same building.

Many early entrants to college leave high school several years early without graduating. The importance of taking advanced course work before entering college even if one is not officially a senior has already been cited (Brody et al., 1988; Brody et al., 1990). Of the 24 students in the Brody et al. (1988) study, only four had spent 4 years in high school, whereas the others deliberately made the decision either to leave high school early or not to attend high school at all. The pattern of grades skipped in the group varied enormously and did not appear to be related to academic success, as long as the student had experienced course work at a high level before entering college.

Students choosing to leave high school early should also consider whether both their verbal and mathematical SAT scores are at least above average for the particular college selected. We know of two students who were extremely talented mathematically but whose verbal abilities were not yet well developed enough because of their young ages. Nevertheless, they chose to enter two of the most selective and difficult universities in the country several years younger than the typical age. They encountered academic difficulties that might have been avoided if they had either selected less demanding institutions or postponed their college entrance for even 1 year while working hard to develop their verbal abilities.

The decision about when to accelerate must be affected by the academic opportunities in school for the individual involved and the willingness of school authorities to permit grade skipping. Skipping the last year or more of high school is facilitated by organized early entrance programs that provide transition opportunities or by the student's having accelerated in course work, if not in grade placement, so that he or she has had academic experiences similar to other incoming college freshmen.

SELECTING A COLLEGE AS AN EARLY ENTRANT:
ORGANIZED PROGRAMS VERSUS INDIVIDUAL ACCELERATION

As was reported earlier, organized programs for early entrants currently exist at such colleges as the University of Washington, Simon's Rock College, Mary Baldwin College, and the University of North Texas. Typically, these offer the advantages of a peer group of early entrants as well as counseling and other services. The Transition School for early entrants at the University of Washington ensures that students have the academic skills necessary to compete in college courses. Also, Janos et al. (1988) found that the early entrants in the program tended to socialize with each other at first and gradually made friends among the older university students. For some individuals, this may make the transition to college easier. Of course, students in this program are unusually young; the advantages of an organized program may be less important for students who enter college "only" 2 or 3 years younger than usual.

In fact, the research literature and SMPY's personal experiences with young students suggest that there is no clear-cut answer as to whether an organized program is necessary or helpful. Many young students have completed Johns Hopkins and other universities that do not provide special programs or any organized support for young students, and most of those students did extremely well. Nor is organized support a guarantee that all students in the program will succeed, as the Early Entrance Program has not been completely free of students with difficulties (Janos, Sanfilippo, & Robinson, 1986). It is likely, however, that a student who is exceptionally young, relatively immature, and/or less self-reliant than the average college student will benefit from the support provided in an organized program.

One participant in the University of Washington program, who excelled academically and is now a graduate student at a top Eastern university, said she didn't socialize with regular college students until the end of junior year, but socialized with the other early entrants. She noted that she has met young entrants from other colleges that do not have organized programs and suggested that for her it would have been hard socially not to have the support of the other young entrants. On the other hand, interviews with students at colleges that did not have organized programs revealed few social problems (Brody et al., 1988). Many of these students were somewhat older than the

University of Washington students, however, or commuted from home and kept childhood friends, or were exceptionally mature. A number of these students said they made a point of not telling people their age. The one student in that study with the most serious complaints socially returned to high school after a year of highly successful academic work as a 15-year-old university freshman. This intellectually brilliant boy felt that he needed more time to develop socially and missed his high school friends. Perhaps 15 was too young for him to enter a sophisticated, selective university. He might have felt more comfortable at a college with more young entrants like himself and a more personalized, supportive atmosphere.

Commuting Versus Living on Campus

In Stanley's early work with young entrants to college, which began in 1969, most of the young students lived at home and commuted. Since then, SMPY has known many young college students who have chosen this option, whereas others have preferred to attend a college or university away from home and live on campus. Often, but not always, it's the younger students who choose to commute. The Early Entrance Program at the University of Washington requires its young students to live at home for at least the first 2 years. On the other hand, the programs at Simon's Rock College, Mary Baldwin College, and the University of North Texas are designed to be residential. Students, however, are typically housed with other young entrants. Usually, students who enter most colleges or universities as early entrants on an individual basis and wish to live on campus are assigned to roommates without consideration of age.

A study of young entrants at a variety of colleges included 12 students who chose to live at home or with a relative for at least the first semester and 12 students who lived in a dormitory (Brody et al., 1988). Both groups were extremely successful academically, and few students had serious complaints about fitting in socially. There were, however, minor complaints from several of the commuters about being too young to drive and missing social activities by not living in the dorms. On the other hand, one student (mentioned earlier) who entered college directly from the ninth grade and lived in a dorm did not feel socially ready for that environment and returned to high school. Another student entered a highly competitive university at age 13, lived in a dorm, and felt well accepted socially but encountered serious academic problems. Presumably, his immaturity made it difficult for him to balance demanding academic course work with his social life. That student has since graduated and is attending graduate school, but he did encounter severe academic difficulties that might have been avoided.

Sometimes students do not live near an excellent college or university and yet feel unready to live in a dorm. Some creative solutions have been found. For example, a young woman came to Johns Hopkins at age 13 with sophomore standing and lived in a graduate residence hall with a female adult companion (not her mother) to look after her. Another highly successful young entrant attended a large state university and lived in a dorm with his older brother, who was also attending that university. The reports on Merrill Kenneth Wolf and Ruth Lawrence indicate that a parent accompanied each of them to college. Occasionally, a young student may choose to live with a family not his own or perhaps with a relative near campus for the first year or two. The presence of and support of an adult may be particularly important for extremely young early entrants who are not in organized programs. However, one student who lived with his grandmother while he attended Johns Hopkins felt extremely isolated socially because he did not have childhood friends in the community and was cut off from college classmates because of his living situation. After the freshman year he transferred to an academically less demanding university in his home town.

In general, it may be best for younger early entrants to consider commuting for awhile. A magna cum laude graduate of Princeton chose to commute from home for the first 2 years and then moved onto the campus; this is a common compromise for many young entrants. There are many factors to consider when deciding whether to enter college early and where to live during the first year. These include the student's age, physical and emotional maturity, proximity to a local college, social and academic alternatives in high school, and support for early entrants at the college under consideration. Students who want to attend a university that does not offer special support for early entrants, live in a dorm, and have a "normal" social life may choose to enter college somewhat later than students who plan to attend a local college, live at home, and continue to socialize with childhood friends who live in the community.

How to Use the Time Saved

Students who graduate several years early from college have gained considerable time that may be devoted to their career, extra study, or exploring diverse interests. Accelerants vary considerably in the way they use this time saved; that depends on the circumstances, needs, interests, and opportunities of the individuals. Most young graduates, however, seem aware of the advantages of having this extra time available to them.

Rarely does a student who graduates from college several years earlier than typical immediately go to work in a permanent career (although we know of a recent truly outstanding 19-year-old mathematics graduate of a top university who took a full-time position in finance far from home immediately after graduation). Most choose to enter some form of graduate study. Those who go directly to graduate school, however, typically earn their Ph.D., M.D., J.D., M.B.A., or other terminal degree several years earlier than most other students their age and begin careers in these fields younger than their age-mates. This may have the benefit of giving them more productive years at a young age and thus being more effective over the length of their career. Lehman's (1953) work suggests that peak creativity occurs rather early in one's career, especially in scientific fields, so one argument for acceleration is that it may give people more highly productive and creative years for their careers. Some examples of young entrants who have chosen the "fast" route to earn professorial ranks at unusually young ages include Charles Louis Fefferman and Colin Farrell Camerer, who were described earlier in this chapter. On the other hand, Merrill Kenneth Wolf used 7 of the 8 years he saved to explore music before going into medicine.

An intellectually brilliant girl with whom SMPY has worked who graduated from college at age 17 finished medical school at age 21. At 22 she became a student in one of the country's top law schools, hoping to combine the two fields in some way. She might not have felt she could afford the time to do this if she had not been so young when she completed medical school.

Another young entrant chose to spend 5 years in college so that he could graduate with three majors, and then worked a year in a research center before starting graduate school. Many young entrants feel free to take more time to explore alternatives, accept fellowships to study abroad before starting graduate study, and change fields because of the extra years saved by entering college early.

At age 11, one of SMPY's most exceptional participants scored 4 on the College Board Advanced Placement Program's Level BC calculus examination, the equivalent of earning "A's" in both semesters of freshman calculus at a highly selective college or university (Mezynski, Stanley, & McCoart, 1983). He graduated from an excellent independent high school at age 14; took his B.A. degree in humanities, Phi Beta Kappa, at Johns Hopkins when 18; graduated first in his class at one of the country's top law schools at age 21; and then spent a year studying international law in Sweden as a Fulbright Scholar. After that he served for a year as a law clerk to a Federal Circuit Court judge. Even then, he was still young enough to win a Marshall Scholarship to Oxford University to study whatever he wished for 3 years. Thus, those 3 years saved initially paid off handsomely. Another Marshal recipient entered Oxford after graduating first in her class from a large prestigious state university at age 19. She may eventually go to law school but meanwhile is enjoying the opportunity to broaden herself intellectually that the Marshall Scholarship provides.

ALTERNATIVES TO ENTERING COLLEGE AT A YOUNG AGE

Although colleges today seem relatively willing to accept students a year or two younger than is typical, radical acceleration such as skipping all of high school seems less common than in the past except at programs such as the University of Washington. This is partly because of the continued fear of social and emotional maladjustment, but it can also be attributed to increased opportunities for students to stay in high school longer and still finds ways to be challenged adequately.

An ideal educational program allows students the opportunity to move at a pace suitable for their abilities in each subject area. Since students are rarely equally talented in all areas, it may be most appropriate for them to be studying at different grade levels with different age students in various subjects. Students who are mathematically talented but less talented verbally, for example, may need provisions to move ahead fast in mathematics and science but not as much in languages, literature, or the social sciences. Even a student who is almost equally talented in all areas may still prefer to stay with her or his age-mates for at least part of the time and not enroll full-time in college at a young age. Numerous options are available that allow students to accelerate or enrich their school curriculum so that they will be challenged in their area(s) of strength and enter college with a broad background. Each student should consider his or her own interests and needs and the resources in the home community and design a uniquely appropriate program. Exceptionally talented individuals may still enter college somewhat earlier than is typical, but probably not as early as they might have if these options were not available.

Advanced Placement Courses

The Advanced Placement program offers students the opportunity to take college-level courses, but in their high school with high school students. A wide range of AP courses are available if the high school offers them, and students may take AP courses in areas of strength while perhaps enrolling in less challenging courses in other subjects. A successful score on the AP examination following completion of the course usually results in the awarding of college credit by the institution in which the student enrolls full-time and also exemption from the two-semester college course, or at least the latter. Often, students who earn enough AP credits can obtain sophomore status when they enroll in college and thereby complete college in 3 years, if they choose to do so. In 1988, more than 400,000 AP examinations were administered to almost 300,000 students (Advanced Placement Program, 1988). As of May 1989, there were 29 different tests available in 24 subjects.

Part-Time College Courses

Students who need advanced work beyond the AP curriculum in one or more subjects but are not ready to enroll full-time in college often find it appropriate to attend a local college on a part-time basis. These courses may transfer to the institution the student eventually attends, although that is not guaranteed. Usually one is not forced to repeat a course, however, even if credit is not given, so part-time college courses can be an excellent way of making high school much more challenging while also providing the opportunity for the student to stay in high school. It will also enhance one's preparation to do well in college. The able student should choose appropriately difficult courses at the best available local college(s). Some high school officials can be persuaded to let certain college courses "double-count," that is, give credit also at the high school level. Some states and school systems now offer students free tuition to attend college part-time if they need an advanced course the high school doesn't offer.

Summer Programs

A wide variety of summer programs is offered for gifted students. Those provided by the regional talent searches for students identified on the Scholastic Aptitude Test have been a particularly important mechanism for allowing students to move ahead in their area(s) of strength without necessarily changing their grade placement in school. Over 3,000 students annually attend the summer programs offered by the Johns Hopkins Center for the Advancement of Academically Talented Youth (CTY), and similar programs are offered by Arizona State University, California State University at Sacramento, Duke University, Iowa State University, Northwestern University, the University of Denver, the University of Washington, the University of Wisconsin at Eau Claire, and others. Outstanding summer mathematics programs for high school students include those at Ohio State University, Hampshire College, and Boston University. Numerous summer programs are also offered by many other colleges and universities, school systems, state departments of education, and private schools and camps. Students may choose to take academic courses that might offer accelerative opportunities when the student returns to school, or enrichment courses that offer exposure to new areas of study. A student might accelerate in a course through a summer program, so that he or she can take more challenging courses in school, including AP and part-time college courses (e.g., see Stanley & Stanley, 1986). This might eventually lead to early entrance to college as well. Enrichment courses offer students the opportunity to gain a broader background before starting college.

Correspondence Courses or Independent Study

Students whose high schools do not offer much advanced work or who do not live near a college might choose to work on advanced course work independently or through a correspondence course rather than enter college full-time early. This option requires considerable motivation but can be a useful alternative for those who are not ready academically to take college work in all subject areas or who do not feel ready socially for the atmosphere of a college.

It is probably desirable to have an adult "monitor" in the home town who will make sure the correspondence-study student sends his or her lessons, promptly and carefully done, and profits maximally from the instructor's comments on lesson assignments returned. Such a monitor need not be skilled in the subject itself. Typically, parents may not be ideal monitors for this purpose.

Correspondence courses are available through selected universities and private schools. Many selective colleges and universities where able students want to become freshmen will not give course credit for correspondence courses, but these may prepare students to score high on the corresponding AP exam or on an examination by the relevant department in the colleges or universities they later enter as full-time students. Another possibility is to take correspondence-study courses from the university one hopes to attend soon, if that school will give regular credit for them. The interested student should inquire around and "comparison shop." Consider, for example, whether the enrollees would be free to telephone the instructor for specific assistance.

Academic Fairs or Competitions

Students who seek greater academic challenges in high school should be aware that not all learning occurs in a classroom. They should take advantage of the opportunities to learn and participate in a variety of competitions, depending on their interests and areas of strength. In particular, in science and mathematics, students should be aware of the Westinghouse Science Talent Search and the International Mathematical, Chemistry, and Physics Olympiads. There are also opportunities to compete in debates, foreign language and writing competitions, and college-bowl-type competitions. These experiences offer challenge, recognition, the opportunity to interact with students who share similar interests and abilities, and often prizes, including attractive scholarships. For example, in 1989 the high school senior from Arkansas who ranked first in the Westinghouse Science Talent Search won a

$20,000 scholarship to be used at the college or university of his choice, and even the 10th-ranking person won $7,500.

Mentorship or Internship Opportunities

As students refine their career goals, they need opportunities to experience the world of work. They also need exposure to role models in fields related to their interests. Mentorships and internships can offer these experiences while also providing an opportunity for learning. Often these arrangements carry advanced credit. The Research Science Institute sponsored by the Center for Excellence in Education in McLean, Virginia, conducts a program each summer whereby students, most of whom recently completed the 11th grade, are paired with a mentor who is a scientist or mathematician. Those students have the opportunity to learn about the mentor's work while also developing a project of their own, perhaps suitable for submission to the Westinghouse Science Talent Search. Often, individual high schools offer mentorships with members of the community; if these are not available, enterprising students can usually arrange such an opportunity for themselves.

Study Abroad Opportunities

Students who find the level of high school course work unchallenging but are not anxious to enroll in college early may benefit from the opportunity to study abroad. Courses in a high school in another country, particularly if taught in a foreign language, may be extremely challenging, and the opportunities for personal growth that come from experiencing life in another country can be enormous. Well-motivated students might take a break from high school to study abroad and return to graduate with their class, or, with possible advanced credit, graduate early but delay college entrance. For example, an especially brilliant girl graduated from a public high school in Illinois at age 15, gained admittance to a top-flight university, got a leave of absence for a year, and then as an exchange student in Portugal "repeated" her senior year in high school there. After that, at age 16, she became a college freshman, fluent in the Portuguese language and ready to get the most out of her subsequent experiences.

Utilizing These Options to Meet Individual Needs

SMPY has worked with many students who have selectively used the above options as an alternative to entering college early. Often these students, many of whom undoubtedly could excel early in college, feel adequately challenged by the flexible program they have designed by moving ahead in some subjects and not in others. They may be committed to specific high school activities, such as representing the United States on the International Mathematical Olympiad (IMO) team, which would not be an option if they were full-time college students. Many plan to attend a highly selective college or university and want to be prepared to enjoy fully the academic and social benefits of being residential students at such an institution. One such student entered a prestigious college age-in-grade. He had attended a reasonably rigorous public high school that met most of his academic needs through honors and Advanced Placement courses, while he moved rapidly through mathematics in summer programs. He also represented the United States on the IMO team three times, winning one silver and two gold medals, and excelled in the Westinghouse competition. He began college with a broad background and valuable experiences that would have been missed if he had chosen to enter college early.

A different path was selected by a recent graduate of Johns Hopkins who chose to enroll simultaneously at Hopkins and a local private school from the ages of 13 to 17. The school gave him academic credit for the courses he completed at college, and he earned his high school diploma and baccalaureate degree simultaneously. He graduated from college at an unusually young age, but keeping one foot in high school allowed him to maintain a relationship with his age peers and be involved in school activities, especially athletics and social events. A boy from Guatemala did similarly in Baltimore, earning his high school diploma and college baccalaureate at age 17, but from a different independent high school and a Jesuit college.

Many talented students may still choose to enter college early but, because of the availability of the curricular options listed above, skip fewer grades than they might have otherwise and enter college extremely well prepared for the demanding academic and social environment they are likely to encounter there. An example of a spectacular student who has carefully chosen the latter route is Terry Tao of Australia.

Case Study: Terry Tao

Australian Terence (Terry) Tao is the most mathematically precocious youth SMPY has ever known (see Gross, 1986; Stanley, 1988, 1989). Winner of a gold medal in the IMO in 1988 the day before his 13th birthday, he had scored 760 on the mathematical portion of the Scholastic Aptitude Test at age 8. The oldest of three brothers, and the son of a pediatrician father and a mother who graduated with honors in physics and mathematics from the University of Hong Kong, Terry taught himself to read before the age of 2 by watching "Sesame Street." By age 5 he had completed all of the elementary school mathematics curriculum at home with guidance from his mother while he attended a neighborhood kindergarten with children of his own age.

He also attended a Saturday program for the gifted, giving him the opportunity to work and socialize with other gifted students. Meanwhile, by reading, talking with educators, and visiting local schools, Terry's parents realized that he needed a specialized educational program that would accommodate the discrepancies between his social and intellectual development as well as the fact that not in all subjects was his performance uniform.

They worked with the schools to allow Terry to attend classes in various grades for different subjects. For example, at age 6 he was attending different classes with third, fourth, fifth, and sixth graders while continuing his study of more advanced mathematics at home. At age 7 he began taking some classes at the local high school, while continuing to be enrolled in the elementary school for other subjects. By the time Terry had reached his 10th birthday he was taking math and physics at a university while also enrolled in Grade 12 chemistry, Grade 11 geography and Latin, Grade 10 French, and Grade 9 English and social studies (Gross, 1986). Although he probably will graduate from college no later than age 15 or 16, he and his parents have been careful not to rush him toward full-time college entrance, preferring to provide him instead with an optimal individualized schedule, thus ensuring that he will be well prepared for college socially and academically when he does matriculate full-time. When Terry was 10, his father noted that:

> There is no need for him to rush ahead now. If he were to enter [college] full-time now, just for the sake of being the youngest child to graduate, or indeed for the sake of doing anything 'first,' that would be simply a stunt. Much more important is the opportunity to consolidate his education, to build a broader base. Attending part-time, as he is now, more emphasis can be placed on creativity, original thinking and broader knowledge. He may be a few years older when he graduates but he will be much better prepared for the more rigorous graduate and post-doctoral work. (Gross, 1986, p. 7)

Terry has also used his summers to supplement his course work, having served on Australia's IMO team three summers and in a mentorship experience with a prominent mathematician one summer through the Research Science Institute. He has combined accelerative and enrichment experiences to design a program that meets his own unique needs and provides for maximum intellectual and social development.

APPARENT POSITIVE AND NEGATIVE EFFECTS OF ACCELERATION

The many case studies in the literature suggest that one should be careful about stereotyping the effects of acceleration on individuals. Although the overwhelming majority of early entrants are successful, there is great variability in the influences on the individual's development, achievement, and personal happiness. We suggest that the following positive and negative effects are possible.

Possible Positive Effects:

1. Because early entrants are younger when graduating from college, they may be more likely to pursue graduate studies.
2. Early entrants may feel they have more time to pursue several interests by earning degrees in several fields, thus feeling more fulfilled personally and bringing a broader background to their careers.
3. Early entrants may be more motivated throughout their school years because acceleration has provided greater challenges.
4. Peer relationships may actually be better because early entrants are exposed to intellectual peers, if not age peers.
5. Early entrants may be more productive in their career, since they will begin work at a younger age when productivity and perhaps also creativity are likely to be highest.

Possible Negative Effects:

1. Early entrants may experience difficulties in peer relations if they have trouble relating to older students or if they are excluded from parties and other social events because of their age.
2. Early entrants may have difficulty competing in extracurricular activities such as sports or music because of smaller physical stature due to their younger age or because they had fewer years prior to college to develop skills.
3. Early entrants may be forced to attend a less selective college than they might have attended if they had entered college at the typical time, either because they wish to live at or near home or because fewer years in high school prevented the student from developing the necessary background and credentials to be accepted at a top college.
4. Early entrants may regret missed experiences in high school if they spent less than 4 years there (e.g., attending the prom, being elected to a position of leadership, being on an athletic team, etc.).
5. Early entrants may experience discrimination at the next level after college because of age, such as getting admitted to medical or law school or finding a job. This does not seem to be a problem where studying toward a Ph.D. degree in mathematics, science, or engineering or working in those fields thereafter is concerned.

6. Acceleration may encourage early entrants to focus on a major field at too young an age for them to have had enough experiences to make a wise decision.

RECOMMENDATIONS FOR MAKING EARLY ENTRANCE TO COLLEGE MORE EFFECTIVE

The research literature and SMPY's personal experiences with a fairly large number of students who have entered college early suggest that the following recommendations may facilitate greater success, both academically and socially, among students who elect to enter college 2 or more years younger than is typical:

1. Students are encouraged to complete successfully some college or advanced high school level course work (Advanced Placement courses, 12th-grade honors courses, or rigorous part-time college courses) before enrolling in college full-time so they will have academic experiences similar to other college freshmen. (High scores on College Board Achievement Tests are another indicator of an excellent educational background.)
2. Mathematical and verbal reasoning abilities (as measured by scores on the Scholastic Aptitude Test) should be at least average for the particular college or university the student chooses to attend. Thus, early entrants should be aware that their scores should be higher if they aspire to highly selective institutions, and mathematically talented students should be sure that their verbal abilities are well developed before they apply to college early.
3. Early entrants should take advantage of whatever challenging opportunities their high school has to offer before moving on to college.
4. Students who enter college early should be highly motivated to do so, that is, they themselves should *eagerly* choose to do it, not be pushed into it.
5. Early entrants to college who are leaving high school prior to graduation should consider the impact on extracurricular activities, and also whether they will regret missing any particularly important high school experiences.
6. Radical accelerants may want to commute to college, at least at first, in order to minimize adjustment difficulties.
7. Early entrants should consider whether they will have any regrets if their early entrance to college forces them to attend a less selective institution than they might have attended otherwise or to commute instead of living in a dorm.
8. Early entrants are encouraged to seek opportunities to interact with older

students while still in high school through advanced course work, summer programs, and the like, so they will be comfortable socializing in college with students several years older.

9. Students should be encouraged to develop outside interests and hobbies such as athletics and performing arts that will give them something in common with their chronological age peers who are not likely to be able to relate to them on an academic or intellectual level.

10. Early entrants are advised to avoid publicity so that unreasonable expectations don't foster emotional difficulties.

CONCLUSION

Acceleration in subject matter and/or grade level is a vital component of the package of special educational provisions that should be available for youths who reason extremely well mathematically and/or verbally. Specifically, the literature shows that early entrance to college has been a successful and rewarding experience for the majority of students who have used this vehicle to enhance their educational progress.

Nonetheless, this paper should not be viewed as a paean of praise for educational acceleration per se. One must, developmental psychologists insist, care for the "whole child," not *just* his or her cerebral cortex. Proper social and emotional nurturing should fit hand in glove with academic and intellectual facilitation. Only if a child gets a full, broad education across the curricular and extracurricular board, including attention to physical and aesthetic development, is that person likely to become an effective, creative, happy adult.

Being able to participate in some form of athletics well enough not to be embarrassed, and preferably considerably better than that, gives the intellectually talented child desirable contacts with athletic peers who may not be his or her intellectual peers. Similar benefits can be gained by attaining proficiency in at least one performing art, such as some aspect of music, dance, drama, or art.

It is not advisable to pursue specialized academic subjects without attending to the important need that precocious students become individuals who are interesting not only to others but also to themselves. A superb liberal arts education can help one do this. The math-talented youth needs to pursue mathematics and related subjects vigorously and, for many such youths, professionally. This is crucial, but effective only in the context of also getting a good education, in the broadest sense of that word. From infancy onward, parents of intellectually talented children and those children themselves need to strive for balance and integration while also using the youths' greatest intellectual strengths to become effective specialists. For example, parents must devote as much care and attention to educational, athletic, aesthetic, social, and emotional considerations as they do to mathematics itself and its close relatives, if mathematics is their child's area of strength. Appropriate educational acceleration can help provide the extra time and leeway to develop the child into a liberally educated, humane, self-actualizing adult who can contribute creatively and productively to a technical field while being a fine person, parent, spouse, relative, neighbor, friend, and civic improver.

This is a tall order, of course, but a goal toward which the talented youth and his or her parents and educators must strive in order not to produce "only" a mathematician, physicist, computer scientist, electrical engineer, physician, lawyer, architect, scholar, financial analyst, or politician. When viewed in this framework, both educational acceleration and educational enrichment constitute powerful tools in the inevitably eclectic plan that should be tailored specially for each precocious child and revised continually to accord with developing abilities, potentialities, and achievements. Eventually, the results will usually repay the parents and the able youths amply for their efforts.

REFERENCES

Advanced Placement Program. (1988). *AP yearbook 1988*. New York: The College Board.

Benbow, C. P. (1979). The components of SMPY's smorgasbord of accelerative options. *Intellectually Talented Youth Bulletin (ITYB)*, 5(10), 21–23.

Benbow, C. P. (1986). SMPY's model for teaching mathematically precocious students. In J. S. Renzulli (Ed.), *Systems and models for developing programs for the gifted and talented* (pp. 1–26). Mansfield Center, CT: Creative Learning Press.

Bowen, E. (1985, August). Oxford's amazing adolescent. *Time*, p. 55.

Brody, L. E., & Benbow, C. P. (1987). Accelerative strategies: How effective are they for the gifted? *Gifted Child Quarterly, 3*, 105–110.

Brody, L. E., Assouline, S. G., & Stanley, J. C. (in press). Five years of early entrants: Predicting successful achievement in college. *Gifted Child Quarterly*.

Brody, L. E., Lupkowski, A. E., & Stanley, J. C. (1988). Early entrance to college: A study of academic and social adjustment during freshman year. *College and University, 63*, 347–359.

Daurio, S. P. (1979). Educational enrichment versus acceleration: A review of the literature. In W. C. George, S. J. Cohn, & J. C. Stanley (Eds.), *Educating the gifted: Acceleration and enrichment* (pp. 13–63). Baltimore: Johns Hopkins University Press.

Eisenberg, A. R., & George, W. C. (1979). Early entrance to college: The Johns Hopkins experience, study of mathematically precocious youth (SMPY). *College and University, 54*, 109–118.

Fluitt, J. L., & Strickland, M. S. (1984). A survey of early admission policies and procedures. *College and University, 59,* 129–135.

Fox, L. H. (1974). Facilitating educational development of mathematically precocious youth. In J. C. Stanley, D. P. Keating, & L. H. Fox (Eds.), *Mathematical talent: Discovery, description, and development* (pp. 47–69). Baltimore: Johns Hopkins University Press.

Fox, L. H. (1976). Identification and program planning: Models and methods. In D. P. Keating (Ed.), *Intellectual talent: Research and development* (pp. 32–54). Baltimore: Johns Hopkins University Press.

Fox, L. H. (1979). Programs for the gifted and talented: An overview. In A. H. Passow (Ed.), *The gifted and the talented: Their education and development, 78th Yearbook of the National Society for the Study of Education* (pp. 104–126). Chicago: University of Chicago Press.

Fund for the Advancement of Education of the Ford Foundation. (1953). *Bridging the gap between school and college.* New York: Research Division of the Fund.

Fund for the Advancement of Education of the Ford Foundation. (1957). *They went to college early.* New York: Research Division of the Fund.

Gross, M. (1986). Terence Tao. *G/C/T, 9*(4), 2–9.

Hollingworth, L. S. (1926). *Gifted children: Their nature and nurture.* New York: Macmillan.

Holmes, J. S., Rin, L., Tremblay, J. M., & Zeldin, R. K. (1984). Colin Camerer: Radical educational accelerant, now well along professionally. *G/C/T, 33*(3), 33–35.

Janos, P. M. (1987). A fifty-year follow-up of Terman's youngest college students and IQ-matched agemates. *Gifted Child Quarterly, 31,* 55–58.

Janos, P. M., & Robinson, N. M. (1985). The performance of students in a program of radical acceleration at the university level. *Gifted Child Quarterly, 29,* 175–179.

Janos, P. M., Robinson, N. M., & Lunnenborg, C. E. (in press). Academic performances and adjustment status of early college entrants, non-accelerated peers, and college classmates. *Journal of Higher Education.*

Janos, P. M., Robinson, N. M., Carter, C., Chapel, A., Cufley, R., Curland, M., Daily, M., Guilland, M., Heinzig, M., Kehl, H., Lu, S., Sherry, D., Stoloff, J., & Wise, A. (1988). A cross-sectional developmental study of the social relations of students who enter college early. *Gifted Child Quarterly, 32,* 210–215.

Janos, P. M., Sanfilippo, S. M., & Robinson, N. M. (1986). "Underachievement" among markedly accelerated college students. *Journal of Youth and Adolescence, 15,* 303–313.

Keating, D. P. (1976). *Intellectual talent: Research and development.* Baltimore: Johns Hopkins University Press.

Kett, J. (1974). History of age grouping in America. In J. S. Coleman et al. (Eds.), *Youth: Transition to adulthood, a report to the panel of youth of the President's Science Advisory Committee* (pp. 6–29). (Publication No. 4106–00037). Washington, DC: U.S. Government Printing Office.

Keys, N. (1938). The underage student in high school and college. *University of California Publications in Education, 7,* 145–271.

Lehman, H. C. (1953). *Age and achievement.* Princeton: Princeton University Press.

Levy, J. C. (1978). Fefferman receives Fields medal. *Intellectually Talented Youth Bulletin (ITYB), 5*(4), 3.

Mezynski, K., Stanley, J. C., & McCoart, R. F. (1983). Helping youths score well on AP examinations in physics, chemistry, and calculus. In C. P. Benbow & J. C. Stanley (Eds.), *Academic precocity* (pp. 86–112). Baltimore: Johns Hopkins University Press.

Montour, K. (1976a). American pre-revolutionary prodigies. *Intellectually Talented Youth Bulletin (ITYB), 2*(9), 1.

Montour, K. (1976b). Charles Louis Fefferman: Youngest American full professor. *Intellectually Talented Youth Bulletin (ITYB), 2*(7), 1.

Montour, K. (1976c). Merrill Kenneth Wolf: A bachelor's degree at 14. *Intellectually Talented Youth Bulletin (ITYB), 2*(7), 1.

Montour, K. (1977). William James Sidis, the broken twig. *American Psychologist, 32*(4), 265–279.

Nevin, D. (1977). Young prodigies take off under special program. *Smithsonian, 8*(7), 76–82.

Newsmakers. (1982, May 31). *Newsweek,* p. 57.

Oden, M. H. (1968). The fulfillment of promise: 40-year follow-up of the Terman gifted group. *Genetic Psychology Monographs, 77,* 3–93.

Packe, M. S. (1954). *The life of John Stuart Mill.* New York: Macmillan.

Pollins, L. D. (1983). The effects of acceleration on the social and emotional development of gifted students. In C. P. Benbow & J. C. Stanley (Eds.), *Academy precocity* (pp. 160–178). Baltimore: Johns Hopkins University Press.

Pressey, S. L. (1949). *Educational acceleration: Appraisal and basic problems.* (Bureau of Educational Research Monographs, No. 31). Columbus: Ohio State University Press.

Pressey, S. L. (1967). "Fordling" accelerates ten years after. *Journal of Counseling Psychology, 14,* 73–80.

Robinson, N. M., & Janos, P. M. (1986). Psychological adjustment in a college-level program of marked academic acceleration. *Journal of Youth and Adolescence, 15,* 51–60.

Stanley, J. C. (1979). The study and facilitation of talent for mathematics. In A. H. Passow (Ed.), *The gifted and the talented: Their education and development, 78th yearbook of the National Society for the Study of Education* (pp. 169–185). Chicago: University of Chicago Press.

Stanley, J. C. (1985a). How did six highly accelerated gifted students fare in graduate school? *Gifted Child Quarterly 29,* 180.

Stanley, J. C. (1985b). Young entrants to college: How did they fare? *College and University, 60,* 219–228.

Stanley, J. C. (1988). Triple threat Terry Tao tallies twice thus far. *G/C/T, 11*(2), 39.

Stanley, J. C. (1989). He did it! *G/C/T, 12*(3), 40.

Stanley, J. C., & Benbow, C. P. (1983). Extremely young college graduates: Evidence of their success. *College and University, 58,* 361–372.

Stanley, J. C., Keating, D. P., & Fox, L. H. (1974). *Mathematical talent: Discovery, description, and development.* Baltimore: Johns Hopkins University Press.

Stanley, J. C., & McGill, A. M. (1986). More about "Young entrants to college: How did they fare?" *Gifted Child Quarterly, 30,* 70–73.

Stanley, J. C., & Stanley, B. S. K. (1986). High-school biology, chemistry, or physics learned well in three weeks. *Journal of Research in Science Teaching, 23,* 237–250.

Tannenbaum, A. J. (1983). *Gifted children.* New York: Macmillan.

Terman, L. M., & Oden, M. H. (1947). *Genetic studies of genius: Vol. 4. The gifted child grows up: Twenty-five years' follow-up of a superior group.* Stanford, CA: Stanford University Press.

VanTassel-Baska, J. (1986). The use of aptitude tests for identifying the gifted: The talent search concept. *Roeper Review, 8,* 185–189.

Wallace, A. (1986). *The prodigy.* New York: Dutton.

Weiner, N. (1953). *Ex-prodigy.* Cambridge, MA: MIT Press.

CHAPTER 6

Effects of Programs for the Gifted: A Search for Evidence

John F. Feldhusen
Purdue University

There are many questions that should be asked about the effects of gifted programs. Do programs for gifted students have significant effects on their achievement in school? Do children in these programs learn to be better thinkers? Does their motivation to learn increase? Do they develop more positive and stable self-concepts? Do they clarify their career goals? These are among the most salient questions about the effects of programs for gifted students.

Such questions indicate something about the intended nature of the benefits from the special programming. Each of the questions listed above suggests an expectation that programs for gifted students should contribute to qualitative differences between the gifted students and their less capable peers. It is also appropriate to ask whether acceleration is more effective than enrichment services in meeting the needs of the gifted. The programs reviewed in this chapter illustrate both types of service.

Acceleration options vary, but all are based on the assumption that gifted students will learn more in less time than is allowed for the instruction of students in the general program. Thus, the assumed effect of the various forms of acceleration is a quantitative difference—more or further in less time. The differences between the options of enrichment and acceleration are important. Should the goal be to learn more in less time, or should the goal be to proceed through the educational curricula and to higher levels more quickly than is ordinarily granted? By *acceleration* we mean raising the level and/or pace of instruction to be commensurate with students' achievement levels and capacity or rate of learning. The second grader who is advanced to third grade during the school year, the high school student who takes a correspondence course for college credit, and students who complete an algebra course in 3 weeks in a summer program have all been accelerated. Enrichment, on the other hand, refers to qualitatively different sorts of programs and effects on achievement. The following are examples of students involved in enrichment activities: a student who does an in-depth study of Galileo in fifth grade, another who is writing a collection of short stories, and a third who is reading biographies of great mathematicians. As the distinction is frequently made, acceleration elevates the level and pace of instruction whereas enrichment exposes students to more and in greater depth.

Of course, it may be difficult to determine if "programs" for the gifted have significant effects, since programs vary a great deal in goals and in the amount of time that gifted children receive special services. Perhaps the more reasonable question is whether or not current popular program models and programs have significant effects on learning outcomes among gifted children. At a local level, one might ask if a particular program is meeting its goals.

AN ANALYSIS OF PROGRAM MODELS

Major program models are presented in detail in Renzulli's (1986) *Systems and Models for Developing Programs for the Gifted and Talented* and in Maker's (1982) *Teaching Models in Education of the Gifted.* Juntune (1986) also presented descriptions of a wide variety of operating programs in *Successful Programs for the Gifted and Talented* along with some informal evaluation of each model. These reports are valuable contributions in that they offer specific details about the organization and operations of the models and programs that currently dominate the field of gifted education in the United States. (See Table 6.1.)

Renzulli (1986) presents several operational models (see Table 6.1). He uses the term *operational* to mean that the models are being implemented in school programs more or less in the format by which they are described in the chapters. All are described in general form, and evaluation evidence of a positive nature is presented for several of the models.

In contrast, the programs described by Juntune (1986) are specific local implementations of program designs. They include preschool, elementary, junior high, and senior high school programs and a wide variety of specialized programs such as future studies, computer technology, independent study, cluster grouping, mentorships, leadership development, visual arts, and thinking skills development. For all of these programs, a description of how evaluation is carried out is provided. In each case, the assertion or implication is given that evaluation is positive. Rarely, however, are any hard data presented to support the summative evaluation statements.

Maker (1982) presents 11 instructional models, but only 2 are explicit models for education of the gifted. These are Renzulli's (1977) Enrichment Triad and Treffinger's (1975) self-directed learning. The other 9 models pre-

Table 6.1 Operational Models for Gifted Education Programs

1. The Study of Mathematically Precocious Youth, Camilla Person Benbow
2. The Autonomous Learner Model for the Gifted and Talented, George T. Betts
3. The Integrative Education Model, Barbara Clark
4. The Learning Enrichment Service (LES): A Participatory Model for Gifted Adolescents, Jerry Ann Clifford, Ted Runious and Elizabeth Smyth
5. The Purdue Three-Stage Enrichment Model for Gifted Education at the Elementary Level, John Feldhusen and Penny Britton Kolloff
6. The Purdue Secondary Model for Gifted and Talented Youth, John Feldhusen and Ann Robinson
7. The Grid: A Model to Construct Differentiated Curriculum for the Gifted, Sandra N. Kaplan
8. The SOI System for Gifted Education, Mary Meeker and Robert Meeker
9. The Enrichment Triad/Revolving Door Model: A Schoolwide Plan for the Development of Creative Productivity, Joseph S. Renzulli and Sally M. Reis
10. The Secondary Triad Model, Sally M. Reis and Joseph S. Renzulli
11. Cultivating Simultaneous Student Growth in Both Multiple Creative Talents and Knowledge, Calvin W. Taylor
12. Talents Unlimited: Applying the Multiple Talent Approach in Mainstream and Gifted Programs, Carol Schlichter
13. The Enrichment Matrix Model, Abraham J. Tannenbaum
14. Fostering Effective, Independent Learning Through Individualized Programming, Donald J. Treffinger
15. The Cognitive-Affective Interaction Model for Enriching Gifted Programs, Frank E. Williams.

Adapted from Renzulli (1976)

sented are Bloom's (1956) concerning the cognitive domain; Krathwohl, Bloom, and Meisia's (1964) concerning the affective domain; Bruner's (1960) Structure of a Discipline; Guilford's (1967) Structure of Intellect; Kohlberg's (1966) Stages of Moral Development; Parnes's (1977) Creative Problem Solving; Taba's (1962) Teaching Strategies Program; Taylor's (1968) Multiple Talents Approach; and Williams's (1970) Teaching Strategies for Thinking and Feeling. These are all theoretical models for instructional design and evaluation, not explicit designs for gifted education programs. However, all of the models have cognitive and affective underpinnings that program developers have seen as appropriate for gifted programs. Several of the models such as those of Bloom (1956), Krathwohl et al. (1964), Kohlberg (1966), Parnes (1977), Taba (1962), and Taylor (1968) have been evaluated extensively in applications other than gifted education. It should also be noted that Taylor's (1968) Multiple Talents and Guilford's (1967) Structure of Intellect models have undergone extensive development efforts in gifted education. Schlichter (1986) adapted Taylor's model in the form of Talents Unlimited, whereas the

Structure of Intellect has been applied by Meeker and Meeker (e.g., 1986). Each applied model has developmental evaluation.

All the instructional models can serve as theoretical paradigms for the design of programs and curriculum in gifted education. All are cognitively oriented and facilitate nigher level thinking activities in gifted programs.

Evidence From Comprehensive Reviews

Daurio (1979) did an extensive review of the literature on enrichment and acceleration. Following a paradigm that delineates irrelevant and relevant academic enrichment, he concluded that irrelevant enrichment activities that are not linked to gifted youths' talents or abilities (e.g., a special unit on ancient Egypt for the mathematically gifted) have not been shown of value. However, he concluded that relevant academic enrichment, or classes designed to provide instruction suitable for the talents of gifted youth (e.g., foreign language study for verbally gifted youth), does provide significant benefits for the gifted. Both approaches are contrasted with acceleration, a process that allows gifted youth to move to higher level classes ahead of the conventional age-grade schedule. Acceleration includes a variety of practices, such as early admission to school, grade advancement, early entrance to college, accelerated completion of the baccalaureate degree, and acceleration within subject matter strands. Daurio concluded that the evidence for acceleration is generally positive and "acceleration appears to be the more feasible method for meeting the needs of gifted students" (p. 53).

Feldhusen, Proctor, and Black (1986), Proctor, Black, and Feldhusen (1986), and Proctor, Feldhusen, and Black (1988) did comprehensive reviews on grade advancement and early admission of gifted children. They concluded that early entrants gained a year in achievement and suffered few personal adjustment problems. For grade advancement they noted that the research literature is almost totally supportive of advancement for precocious children, and there is little basis for the belief that it will cause social or emotional adjustment problems. In their reports they propose guidelines, based on results from the research, for the decision-making process among school personnel to select youth for grade advancement.

Brody and Benbow (1987) reviewed the research and evaluation evidence concerning the SMPY program (Stanley & Benbow, 1982) with particular attention to long-range effects. Their report is a review of data and results on accelerated and nonaccelerated youth at four levels of acceleration: (Group 1) high acceleration with grade skipping; (Group 2) Advanced Placement courses but no grade skipping; (Group 3) subject matter acceleration in class, special classes, or by tutoring; and (Group 4) no acceleration. They found *no* harmful effects from acceleration and a number of positive effects. Group 1 earned more awards and attended more selective colleges. Group 2 participated most in extracurricular activities, whereas members of Group 1 often limited themselves to clubs. More students in Groups 1 and 2 planned to earn Ph.D.s or degrees in law or medicine than in Groups 3 and 4. There were no differences among groups on indices of social and emotional adjustment.

Kulik and Kulik (1984) carried out a meta-analysis of 26 studies of the effects of accelerating gifted students. Achievement of gifted students was significantly higher in accelerated classes. The average effect size was 0.88 standard deviations higher than for same-age nonaccelerates. The results for noncognitive outcomes were "sketchy" because few studies investigated these effects. Those studies that did investigate noncognitive outcomes considered various traits and, thus, were difficult to compare with each other. Kulik and Kulik (1984) cautioned that their results do not speak to long-range effects.

Kulik and Kulik (1987) reported a meta-analysis of 49 studies on grouping gifted students in special classes or programs. They concluded that general ability grouping of all students is not very effective in improving achievement, but grouping the gifted together in special classes produces much higher achievement for gifted and talented students. They also found that when gifted and talented students are grouped within an otherwise regular heterogeneous classroom and given special enriched or accelerated activities, their achievements also are significantly higher than nongrouped gifted students.

Feldhusen and Treffinger (1985) reviewed research on full-time, self-contained classes for the gifted. The review included five original data-based studies and one meta-analysis of 52 studies on grouping. They summarized their review as follows:

> We conclude from this review that the needs of highly able children are not fully satisfied in regular classrooms, that special classes with well trained teachers can produce superior achievement, the gifted and talented children will develop superior thinking skills and broader interests in special classes, and that social adjustment and learning will not be impaired for any children when special classes are organized. (p. 35)

No research was found on comprehensive high school programs. However, as noted earlier, there are numerous reports on specific components of secondary programs, and they provide descriptions of secondary programs that have been carefully developed and evaluated (e.g., Betts, 1986; Clifford, Runion, & Smyth, 1986; Feldhusen & Robinson, 1986; Reis & Renzulli, 1986; Silverman, 1980).

Global Program Evaluations

Feldhusen and Clinkenbeard (1986) reviewed 87 studies on teaching creativity and creative problem solving and concluded that it is possible to increase children's creative-thinking and problem-solving abilities using well-established educational programs such as the Productive Thinking Program (Covington, Crutchfield, Davis, & Oton, 1972), the Purdue Creative Thinking Program (Feldhusen, 1988a), and New Directions in Creativity (Renzulli & Callahan, 1986). These programs appear especially effective in increasing children's fluency, the ability to produce a greater number of ideas.

Gallagher, Weiss, Oglesby, and Thomas (1983) reviewed evaluation research on general programmatic approaches to education of the gifted and talented, notably creative enrichment, cognitive skills training, independent study, and leadership programs. They drew the following conclusions:

> Current studies on the training of creativity or productive thinking skills suggest that specific improvements can be made in such dimensions as fluency, flexibility, originality, etc., under a program of systematic training. There remains a lack of evidence on the transfer of such specific skills to other academic assignments. The subjective testimony of students, parents, and teachers indicates a positive feeling about independent study programs and programs to improve leadership skills. (p. 57)

These results suggest that training in creativity can bring about immediate gains for students. That is, students can produce a greater quantity of ideas. However, it is not clear that they then apply the new creative thinking skill in other areas of study. Results also indicate students, parents, and teachers like programs that stress thinking skills, independent study, and leadership training.

Gallagher et al. (1983) also conducted three national surveys directed to teachers, parents, and administrators; state directors of gifted education; and a sample of local gifted education program directors to assess attitudes toward and current practices in teaching the gifted and talented. There were 1,200 respondents to the first survey, from which data the researchers drew the following conclusions:

1. At the elementary school level, the preferred strategy is the resource room/pullout program, where the gifted child spends about an hour a day with a specially trained teacher and the rest of the day in the regular classroom. Special classes are the second choice, with special schools and regular program enrichment viewed as much less desirable.
2. The preferred program strategy at the secondary level is that of advanced

special classes, with independent study as a second preference. Here, special schools, resource rooms, and enrichment are not considered strong candidates.

3. Overall, there was a call for more programs, better trained personnel, and the integration of regular and special programs in elementary and secondary schools.

From the second survey, completed by state directors, they reported that the following were seen as essential elements for good program development:

In-service education for GT teachers	95%
In-service education for classroom teachers	90%
Specially trained teachers	83%
In-service education for support personnel	60%
A program director	50%
Special teaching materials	50%

Several other needs were noted but none were identified by over 50% of respondents.

The third part of the project was the local program survey, which focused on evaluation of essential program components by program directors and specified program models used. The most highly rated components were in-service education for GT teachers and classroom teachers, and having specialized teachers, a program director, and special teaching materials. Researchers also found that the resource room/pullout model was the most popular in use, followed by a consultant teacher model, enrichment in the classroom, independent study, and mentoring. Gallagher et al. (1983) conclude as follows:

> Our program evaluation data, though sparse, is consistent with survey findings. It appears that almost every special program yields positive results. Attempts to teach complex materials succeed. Attempts to strengthen creative and productive thinking skills also succeed. Attempts to help students produce more sophisticated intellectual products succeed. And attempts to improve attitudes and interest levels also tend to succeed. (p. 65)

The results of the Gallagher et al. (1983) survey suggest that directors see their programs as successful. They feel that

1. They are teaching complex ideas to gifted students
2. They are helping gifted students become creative thinkers

3. Students are doing sophisticated projects
4. The emerging attitudes and interests of students are positive

Cox, Daniel, and Boston (1985) also carried out a major survey of the status and efficacy of gifted education in the United States by questionnaire to school districts and by on-site observation of a number of gifted programs. They found all of the following program options in operation in some location:

Enrichment in the Regular Classroom	25%
Part-Time Special Class	65%
Full-Time Special Class	73%
Independent Study	44%
Itinerant Teacher	79%
Mentorships	31%
Resource Rooms	47%
Special Schools	75%
Early Entrance	94%
Continuous Progress	83%
Nongraded School	Not Rated
Moderate Acceleration	16%
Radical Acceleration	9%
College Board Advanced Placement	20%
Fast-Paced Courses	Not Rated
Concurrent or Dual Enrollment	24%

The most widely used options were enrichment in the regular classroom, part-time special classes, independent study, resource rooms, and full-time special classes. Cox et al. (1985) also asked questions about the programs to make possible a judgment about how substantial they were (e.g., number of students, time allotted, differentiated materials, and content related). Of the 16 options the percentage of each type rated as substantial according to these criteria is shown in the list above. Two options, nongraded schools and fast-paced courses, were not rated because appropriate criteria were not available.

These results show that the most substantial models were judged to be early entrance, concurrent or dual enrollment, continuous progress, itinerant teacher, special schools, full-time special class, and part-time special class. Nearly all these options give gifted and talented youth an opportunity to advance to higher level subject matter and to be placed with gifted and talented peers. Cox et al. (1985) also noted that strong programs had a special supervisory staff, written goals and philosophy, and a special budget. Weak programs offered enrichment activities less than 3 hours a week. Full-time special classes were most cost effective. They drew the following conclusions:

1. From a national perspective the efforts to improve education for our most capable students look fragmented and discontinuous. There is no national consensus, not even a common pattern or generally accepted approach to meeting the special needs of this population. (p. 42)
2. Programming for the gifted or for superior students is likely to be hit-or-miss, more often characterized by zeal than informed by systematic planning. (p. 43)
3. Symptomatic of the patchwork approach to programming for able learners is the widespread use of the part-time special class, the "pull-out" program, which our survey shows is the nation's most prevalent practice for enriching the education of able learners. Of all the districts responding . . . over 70 percent reported they have a pull-out program. (p. 43)
4. It is a part-time solution to a full-time problem. Able learners need a program that matches their abilities every hour of the school day not just once or twice a week. (p. 43)

Evaluation reports are available on other types of programs for the gifted such as summer programs, Saturday programs, and special enrichment efforts. However, each program model is typically a unique configuration of activities and time allotment to the program. Thus, it is difficult to get a composite picture of the effects of programs in general.

The large evaluation efforts of Gallagher et al. (1983) and Cox et al. (1985) are useful in giving us a general status report. However, they are of limited value in telling us about specific program models.

EVALUATION OF SPECIFIC MODELS

Feldhusen and Treffinger (1985) reviewed the basic characteristics of several major program models, including creative enrichment; the Purdue Three-Stage Model (Feldhusen & Kolloff, 1979); the Enrichment Triad Model (Renzulli, 1977; Renzulli & Smith, 1978); Treffinger's (1980) Creative Learning Model; individualized educational programs (IEP); special full-time classes for the gifted; and secondary programs for the gifted. For most of the enrichment models the research or evaluation evidence is quite limited.

Purdue Creative Thinking Program

Huber, Treffinger, Tracy, and Rand (1979) evaluated the Purdue Creative Thinking Program (Feldhusen & Clinkenbeard, 1986) with gifted and regular students in grades 4 to 6. The program was used by students on an individual basis with students directing themselves through the material. The program produced significant gains in creative-thinking skills for both gifted and regular students.

The Purdue Three-Stage Model (PACE)

Nielsen (1985) conducted a comprehensive evaluation of the Purdue Three-Stage Model (PACE) in a consolidated school district in Indiana using an experimental-control group design with 40 gifted students in grades 3 through 8 in the experimental group and 34 gifted students at the same grade levels as controls. The dependent variables were critical-thinking skill and self-concept. Self-concept was measured with two scales, one a measure of general self-concept, the Piers-Harris (Piers, 1984), and the other of self-concept as a gifted person, the ME Scale (Feldhusen & Kolloff, 1981). For experimental students in grades 3 to 6 there were significant gains in critical-thinking skills and in self-concept related to giftedness. Attitudinal assessment showed the program to be viewed favorably for grades 3 to 6 but significantly less positive in grades 7 to 8. Nielsen speculated that the latter might be due to students' perception of the programs as more appropriate for elementary school children.

Kolloff and Feldhusen (1984) carried out an evaluation of the Purdue Three-Stage Model with children in grades 3 to 6 using an experimental-control group design. The dependent variables were self-concept and creative thinking. They concluded that gifted students in the special program, the three-stage model, made significantly greater gains in creative thinking than controls, but there were no differences in self-concept. However, this later was interpreted positively in view of the fact that several other evaluation reports indicated that gifted students' self-concepts became less positive after experience in a gifted program. Gifted students sometimes hold very positive self-concepts because of their superior status in regular classrooms. When they enter a special or new program and are suddenly surrounded by other gifted youth, their sense of superiority disappears and self-concept declines (Coleman & Fults, 1982, 1985).

The Renzulli Enrichment Triad

Renzulli (1988) has assembled several technical reports of research and evaluation projects related to the Enrichment Triad and the Revolving Door Identification models. Two studies report positive effects on gifted children's project development skills (Olenchak & Renzulli, 1989; Starko, 1988). However, two other studies reported positive learning effects from gifted student participation in an Enrichment Triad type of program on creative productivity, research interest, and project development skill. That is, gifted children who participated improved in their ability to produce creative ideas, became more interested in doing research, and developed skill in doing independent research projects.

CONCLUSION AND DISCUSSION

This discussion of a broad range of the research and evaluation reports on the effects of educational programs for gifted and talented youth suggests that there is reason to both rejoice and lament. The evidence in favor of all modes of acceleration and grouping of gifted and talented youth is positive, although evidence of long-range effects is quite limited. On the other hand, evidence of effects of enrichment services is quite limited, and practically none of its speaks to long-range effects. This is indeed a paradox because enrichment-type programs seem to dominate the field of services currently offered in American schools and the schools of several foreign countries (Fetterman, 1988).

The positive effects of gifted programs, and especially of acceleration and grouping, are generally documented for academic concerns. Gifted children in such programs learn more subject matter and/or develop skills in creative thinking, independent study, and research. Generally social and emotional adjustment does not change, and self-concept might even decline slightly. Attitudes toward learning and program activity grow more positive.

School personnel are perennially worried that special grouping and acceleration of gifted students may contribute to problems in social and emotional adjustment or the development of a sense of elitism. They often consider enrichment programs as a way of avoiding those effects. Yet the research does not indicate that such problems actually result from grouping and acceleration services.

A number of researchers and evaluators conclude that the major needs of gifted and talented youth are

1. Instruction in the basic subject matters at levels and pace that fit their precocity
2. Interaction with peers of like ability
3. Intellectual challenges that develop sound thinking skills

Feldhusen (1988b) reviewed a number of theoretical and research-based systems for teaching thinking skills and concluded that a broad range of thinking and metacognitive skills can and should be taught to gifted children. It also seems likely that early experience in research and other investigative activities may be profitable in the long-range development of gifted youth. Full-time, self-contained classes at the elementary level and special, accelerated classes at the secondary level such as honors and Advanced Placement courses can probably best meet the academic needs of the gifted and talented. Reviews by Brody and Benbow (1987), Feldhusen et al. (1986), and Kulik and Kulik (1984) indicate that participation in nonacademic activities and social-emotional adjustment are not likely to suffer as a result of acceleration.

The overall impression one may also derive from this review is that there has been a wide variety of research on educational programming and services for the gifted. However, because few funds have been available from federal or state agencies or foundations, the research has often been poorly funded. Thus, the research rarely consists of reports from large, well-designed studies. Much of it is graduate student research or reports of unfunded studies. However, several major reports included in this review were both well funded and well designed. The greatest current need is for more long-range follow-up studies to determine the effects of programs and services on gifted students' success in college and graduate school and their achievements in adulthood.

REFERENCES

Betts, G. T. (1986). The autonomous learner model for the gifted and talented. In J. S. Renzulli (Ed.), *Systems and models for developing programs for the gifted and talented* (pp. 27–56). Mansfield Center, CT: Creative Learning Press.

Bloom, B. S. (1956). *Taxonomy of educational objectives. Handbook I, Cognitive domain.* New York: Longman, Green.

Brody, L. E., & Benbow, C. P. (1987). Accelerative strategies: How effective are they for the gifted? *Gifted Child Quarterly, 31*(3), 105–109.

Bruner, J. S. (1960). *The process of education.* Cambridge, MA: Harvard University Press.

Clifford, J. A., Runion, T., & Smyth, E. (1986). The learning enrichment service: A participatory model for gifted adolescents. In J. S. Renzulli (Ed.), *Systems and models for developing programs for the gifted and talented* (pp. 92–125). Mansfield Center, CT: Creative Learning Press.

Coleman, J. M., & Fults, B. A. (1982). Self-concept and the gifted classroom: The role of social comparisons. *Gifted Child Quarterly, 26,* 116–120.

Coleman, J. M., & Fults, B. A. (1985). Special class placement, level of intelligence, and the self-concepts of gifted children: A social comparison perspective. *Remedial and Special Education, 6,* 7–12.

Covington, M. V., Crutchfield, R. S., Davis, L. V., & Oton R. M. (1972). *The productive thinking program.* Columbus, OH: Charles E. Merrill.

Cox, J., Daniel, N., & Boston, B. A. (1985). *Educating able learners*. Austin: University of Texas Press.

Daurio, S. P. (1979). Educational enrichment versus acceleration: A review of the literature. In W. C. George, S. J. Cohn, & J. C. Stanley (Eds.), *Educating the gifted: Acceleration and enrichment* (pp. 13–63). Baltimore: Johns Hopkins University Press.

Feldhusen, J. F. (1988a). *The Purdue creative thinking program*. West Layayette, IN: Purdue University Media-Based Services.

Feldhusen, J. F. (1988b). Thinking skills and curriculum development. In J. Van Tassel-Baska, J. F. Feldhusen, K. Seeley, G. Wheatley, L. Silverman, & W. Foster (Eds.), *Comprehensive curriculum for gifted learners* (pp. 314–334). Boston: Allyn and Bacon.

Feldhusen, J. F., & Clinkenbeard, P. R. (1986). Creativity instructional materials: A review of research. *The Journal of Creative Behavior, 20*(3), 153–182.

Feldhusen, J. F., & Kolloff, P. B. (1979). A three-stage model for gifted education. *Gifted Child Today, 44*, 15–18.

Feldhusen, J. F., & Kolloff, M. B. (1981). ME: A self-concept scale for gifted students. *Perceptual and Motor Skills, 53*, 319–323.

Feldhusen, J. F., Proctor, T. B., & Black, K. N. (1986). Guidelines for grade advancement of precocious children. *Roeper Review, 9*(1), 25–27.

Feldhusen, J. F., & Robinson, A. R. (1986). The Purdue secondary model for gifted and talented youth. In J. S. Renzulli (Ed.), *Systems and models for developing programs for the gifted and talented* (pp. 155–178). Mansfield Center, CT: Creative Learning Press.

Feldhusen, J. F., & Treffinger, D. J. (1985). *Creative thinking and problem solving in gifted education*. Dubuque, IA: Kendall-Hunt.

Fetterman, D. M. (1988). *Excellence and equality: A qualitatively different perspective on gifted and talented education*. Albany: State University of New York Press.

Gallagher, J. J., Weiss, P., Oglesby, K., & Thomas, T. (1983). *The status of gifted/talented education: United States survey of needs, practices and policies*. Los Angeles: Leadership Training Institute.

Guilford, J. P. (1967). *The nature of human intelligence*. New York: McGraw-Hill.

Huber, J., Treffinger, D. J., Tracy, T., & Rand, D. (1979). Self-instructional use of programmed creativity-training materials with gifted and regular students. *Journal of Educational Psychology, 71*(3), 303–309.

Juntune, J. J. (1986). *Successful programs for the gifted and talented*. St. Paul, MN: National Association for Gifted Children.

Kohlberg, L. (1966). Moral education in the schools: A developmental view. *School Review, 74*, 1–29.

Kolloff, P. B., & Feldhusen, J. F. (1984). The effects of enrichment on self-concept and creative thinking. *Gifted Child Quarterly, 28*(2), 53–57.

Krathwohl, D. R., Bloom B. S., & Masia, B. B. (1964). *Taxonomy of educational objectives, Handbook II, Affective domain*. New York: David McKay.

Kulik, J. A., & Kulik, C. C. (1984). Synthesis of research on effects of accelerated instruction. *Educational Leadership, 42*, 84–89.

Kulik, J. A., & Kulik, C. C. (1987). Effects of ability grouping on student achievement. *Equity and Excellence, 23*(1–2), 22–30.

Maker, C. J. (1982). *Teaching models in education of the gifted.* Rockville, MD: Aspen Publications.

Meeker, M., & Meeker, R. (1986). The SOI system for gifted education. In J. S. Renzulli (Ed.), *Systems and models for developing programs for the gifted and talented* (pp. 194–215). Mansfield Center, CT: Creative Learning Press.

Nielsen, M. E. (1985). Evaluation of a rural gifted program: Assessment of attitudes, self concepts, and critical thinking skills of high-ability students in grades 3 to 12. (Doctoral dissertation, Purdue University, 1984). *Dissertation Abstracts International, 45,* 3114 A.

Olenchak, F. R., & Renzulli, J. S. (1989). The effectiveness of the schoolwide enrichment model on selected aspects of elementary school change. *Gifted Child Quarterly, 33*(1), 36–46.

Parnes, S. J. (1977). Guiding creative action. *Gifted Child Quarterly, 21,* 460–472.

Piers, E. V. (1984). *Piers-Harris children's self-concept scale.* Los Angeles: Western Psychological Services.

Proctor, T. B., Black, K. N., & Feldhusen, J. F. (1986). Early admission of selected children to elementary school: A review of the literature. *Journal of Educational Research, 80*(2), 70–76.

Proctor, T. B., Feldhusen, J. F., & Black, K. N. (1988). Guidelines for early admission to elementary school. *Psychology in the Schools, 25,* 41–43.

Reis, S. M., & Renzulli, J. S. (1986). The secondary triad model. In J. S. Renzulli (Ed.), *Systems and models for developing programs for the gifted and talented* (pp. 267–305). Mansfield Center, CT: Creative Learning Press.

Renzulli, J. S. (1977). *The enrichment triad model: A guide for developing defensible programs for the gifted.* Mansfield Center, CT: Creative Learning Press.

Renzulli, J. S. (Ed.). (1986). *Systems and models for developing programs for the gifted and talented.* Mansfield Center, CT: Creative Learning Press.

Renzulli, J. S. (1988). *Technical report of research studies related to the revolving door identification model.* Storrs: Bureau of Educational Research, University of Connecticut.

Renzulli, J. S., & Callahan, C. M. (1986). *New directions in creativity.* Mansfield Center, CT: Creative Learning Press.

Renzulli, J. S., & Smith, L. H. (1978). Developing defensible programs for the gifted and talented. *Journal of Creative Behavior, 12,* 21–29.

Schlichter, C. (1986). Talents unlimited: Applying the multiple talent approach in mainstream and gifted programs. In J. S. Renzulli (Ed.), *Systems and models for developing programs for the gifted and talented* (pp. 352–390). Mansfield Center, CT: Creative Learning Press.

Silverman, L. (1980). Secondary programs for gifted students. *Journal for the Education of the Gifted, 4*(1), 30–42.

Stanley, J. C., & Benbow, C. P. (1982). Educating mathematically precocious youth: Twelve policy recommendations. *Educational Researcher, 11*(5), 4–9.

Starko, A. J. (1988). Effects of the revolving door identification model on creative productivity and self-efficacy. *Gifted Child Quarterly, 32,* 291–297.

Taba, H. (1962). *Curriculum development, theory and practice.* New York: Harcourt, Brace & World.

Taylor, C. W. (1968). The multiple talents approach. *The Instructor, 77,* 142, 144, 146.

Treffinger, D. J. (1975). Teaching for self directed learning: A priority for the gifted and talented. *Gifted Child Quarterly, 19,* 46–59.

Treffinger, D. J. (1980). *Encouraging creative learning for the gifted and talented.* Ventura, CA: Ventura County Superintendent of Schools.

Williams, F. E. (1970). *Classroom ideas for encouraging thinking and feeling.* Buffalo, NY: DOK.

CHAPTER 7

Identification of Candidates for Acceleration: Issues and Concerns

Joyce VanTassel-Baska
College of William and Mary

Over the past 50 years academic acceleration has resurfaced in discussions of the education of gifted children. Major reviews of the literature (e.g., Daurio, 1980; Gallagher, 1969; Kulik & Kulik, 1984; Reynolds, Birch, & Tuseth, 1962; VanTassel-Baska, 1986) have carefully noted the overall positive impacts of acceleration on the development of gifted individuals at various stages of their lives. Regrettably, many educational practitioners appear not to be aware of the results of this research (Southern, Jones, & Fiscus, 1989b).

Rather than embracing the concept and attempting to devise ways to effectively employ the various forms of acceleration, educators still shun this approach to serving gifted students, even after five decades of largely positive research results. VanTassel-Baska, Patton, and Prillaman (1989) found that among program interventions for the disadvantaged gifted, acceleration ranked ahead of nontraditional placements but behind such approaches as independent study and college course work. This relatively low status continues to lend credence to the belief that acceleration is neither a routinely practiced nor a highly valued strategy in gifted education. Consequently, it is important to review the major issues regarding acceleration to determine why there is such a discrepancy between research findings and educational practice.

Basing their opinion on "common sense" and their admittedly limited personal experience, many practitioners report being philosophically opposed to the practice (Southern et al., 1989b). Because acceleration options are used so infrequently, it is not likely that many educators have actually had direct experience with accelerated students. Instead, they apparently hesitate to endorse acceleration partly because of traditional negative characterizations of its effects, two of the most notable being (1) the hurried child and (2) the maladaptive child.

THE EFFECTS OF ACCELERATION

The Hurried Child

Elkind's (1981) book *The Hurried Child* described hazards that confront the child who is forced to grow up too soon and too fast. Unfortunately, the title of his book has, however, stuck in the public consciousness as a metaphor for a gifted child who moves more rapidly through education than age-level peers. Although Elkind did not address academic acceleration for gifted students, it is clear that he regards the lockstep, assembly-line processing of children as too often characteristic of American education and a major threat to the healthy development of young children. In this point, he shares the concerns that have led parents and educators to consider academic acceleration. Elkind has since hedged on either accepting or rejecting the option, leaving the impression that he is ambivalent (e.g., Elkind, 1986). The image of the "hurried child" has, nevertheless, had a powerful effect on the development and rational evaluation of options for acceleration. This image conjures up the notion that the gifted child is being rushed through school—at the risk of his or her emotional well-being—in an effort to beat the clock before checking in as a bonafide "natural resource." Childhood is a precious time of innocence and discovery. Popular wisdom seems to ask, What's the rush? For example, to the casual observer it seems that allowing capable children to take algebra at age 10 or at age 14 amounts to speeding their education. Because this fast pace is considered a risk to the social-emotional development of the accelerants, and because they will eventually take the higher level courses, it is difficult to justify the use of acceleration within the limits of commonsense notions.

The validity of the hurried child metaphor is limited by the correctness of two basic assumptions. First, it is assumed that the learner is actually hurried through school and childhood relationships. Second, it is also assumed that virtually all children who are capable of superior performances in advanced curricula will still be around and interested if they are forced to either wait for, or plod through, instruction along with their age-level peers. Neither assumption has ever been supported. Thus, educators and parents who have squarely confronted the problems of meeting the needs of demonstrated precocity should not have to defend hurrying a child. More rapidly paced instruction and advanced placements can be legitimately regarded recognitions and accommodations of the abilities, achievements, and needs of capable learners.

The Maladaptive Child

Much debate has also arisen with respect to potential risks to the social and emotional development of students as a result of acceleration (e.g., Maddux, Stacy, & Scott, 1981; Obrzut, Nelson, & Obrzut, 1984). Examples of poorly adjusted adults are "exhibited" as case studies of the ravages of acceleration over time (Daurio, 1979; Pressey, 1949). Some gifted children who have been accelerated will complain about such problems as being isolated in the classroom, being the last to drive, or feeling odd about being one of the last to go through puberty. Parents may perceive that their child is immature and, in hindsight, regret accelerating the child. Southern, Jones, and Fiscus (1989a) observed that although gifted adolescents did not consider that acceleration necessarily posed clear dangers, they were nevertheless skeptical about the effects it would have had on their own social relationships.

The effect of acceleration on social and emotional development has not been well researched. There exists a strong belief among educators and the general society that children's social and emotional adjustment is inextricably linked to associating with children born within 6 months of their own ages for 13 years of schooling. Even though many studies have shown that factors such as family nurturance, the roles of significant others, and self-perception are more important in determining good social and emotional development than mere association with chronological age peers (see VanTassel-Baska & Olszewski-Kubilius, 1988), there persists a specious assumption that instructional placement with same-age peers will contribute substantially to reducing the development of maladaptive behavior among gifted students.

ACCELERATION AND THE CONCEPT OF GIFTEDNESS

Precocious students, by definition, demonstrate accelerated development and learning compared with their same-age peers. What we provide in the name of acceleration are curricula and services that are appropriately paced and/or at an appropriate level to meet the needs of children who have demonstrated, compared with their peers, advanced learning and development. Thus, those who deny the fundamental role of acceleration in a program delivery system for the gifted are denying that advanced intellectual development in one or more areas defines giftedness.

The fact that acceleration receives such little attention and acceptance among educators—including principals, school psychologists, and a fair proportion of coordinators of gifted education programs (cf. Southern et al., 1989b)—speaks strongly to their rejection of the defining attributes of giftedness. Their rejection of acceleration also points to their lack of knowledge of the functional aspects of instructional options for gifted students. Enrichment activities are often preferred to acceleration by educators, parents, and students (Jackson, Famiglietti, & Robinson, 1981). Enrichment programs may have greater appeal because they appear to be more conservative departures from the traditional age-measured curriculum.

According to the usual distinction between acceleration and enrichment, acceleration gives precocious students the chance to proceed through the curriculum at a more rapid pace than age-level peers of more average aptitude, whereas enrichment provides elaborated instructional experiences but not at either a more rapid pace or a higher level. The logic of such a distinction between acceleration and enrichment is, however, indefensible. It ignores the fact that gifted students learn at a more rapid pace than do their age-mates. By the time they appear as candidates for acceleration, they are already achieving at higher levels. Enrichment activities seek to reduce emphasis on speed of learning in favor of emphasizing elaborated study. Through the use of enrichment techniques, students are kept at work in grade level on grade-level appropriate tasks. Enrichment may concentrate on group problem solving and peer interaction, often including projects that are connected with social responsibility, for example, environmental concerns or community service efforts. These activities are beneficial and appropriate for many students. Yet when they delay a student's academic progress or when their sole purpose is to maintain grade-level placement, they are indefensible. To the extent that enrichment activities are devoid of advanced levels of instruction and study, they contribute to the general ambivalence about accommodating precocious students. Programs based solely on enrichment do not present sufficient challenge to highly able students. These students cannot be adequately served until schools are willing to accelerate the pace of instruction as needed by individuals and groups of gifted children.

Characteristics of Potential Accelerants

The question of who should participate in acceleration options cannot at this time be adequately determined from the existing literature. The ranges of abilities, ages, and options are too broad for quick summary. It is, however, helpful to examine illustrative cases. Such descriptions illuminate important considerations regarding the process of acceleration. The following section will review several issues that are consistently important to the selection of successful candidates for acceleration and offer a case in point.

Cognitive ability and performance. Students with superior intellectual abilities are able to manipulate abstract symbol systems much better than their average age-mates. They are also able to learn complex new skills and process large amounts of information at faster rates. Many gifted students are early readers who are achieving 2 to 6 years above their age-level peers (Gallagher, 1985). Proceeding along in a lockstep instructional program with their peers is not appropriate for many highly capable learners. Acceleration could reasonably be considered if it appears that classroom instruction is characterized by (1) a dearth of new skills and knowledge being presented, (2) incremental progression through a repetitive series of developmental-skills exercises, and (3) the precocious student's rapidly gaining the given objective and then being required or allowed to mill about until the rest of the class catches up. Such situations become extremely problematic for capable learners. If students who learn at an exceptionally rapid pace are required to sit out of appropriate instruction, they will almost certainly fail to come close to their potential for academic achievement.

Students in the upper 2% of the general population of measured intelligence have been considered good candidates for acceleration. For an acceleration of 2 years, Gallagher (1985) advocated that students have IQs of 130 or above. Terman and Oden (1947) chose a cutoff of 135 to recommend 2 or more years' acceleration. In addition to general measures of intellect, performances on specific achievement and aptitude tests are frequently used to make decisions about particular subject-matter acceleration (Benbow & Stanley, 1983). Subject-matter acceleration would be advisable for students whose exceptional achievements are limited to certain areas and are so pronounced that they would need instruction at a significantly higher level than is provided to their age-mates.

Affective characteristics. Many gifted learners will exhibit boredom and impatience if they are forced to be schooled at the level of their same-aged peers (Clark, 1988). The disparity between the pacing of instruction and their demonstrated abilities to learn can contribute to inattention, boredom, frustration, and inappropriate social and emotional behavior in highly capable learners. Concern is frequently expressed over the possibility that students will experience difficulties if they are separated from their same-age peers or schooled with older classmates. Concern is also in order if they lack interaction with intellectual peers (Gallagher, 1985). The only satisfactory situation for the gifted child who has been neglected in the regular classroom is to find "learning mates." Such peers may be obtained through the formation of advanced instructional programs or through placement in grades or classes one or more levels ahead of the student's current placement.

Interest and motivation to be accelerated. The interest of a student in participating in different acceleration options is a crucial variable for consideration. Students must want to be accelerated. They must understand the needs and implications of acceleration regardless of the type employed. Not all students who are able to handle accelerated programs may wish to participate in them. Students should be consulted about such program opportunities, with a competent adult explaining the relative advantages of the programs. Potential drawbacks should also be noted. For example, it may mean leaving friends who are age-mates in a given classroom, doing more work, and being presented with a greater challenge. For some students, acceleration would not be an acceptable option. As long as the case is made, it seems prudent to allow students to decide for themselves. Success in accelerative programs depends on the motivation and commitment of students to succeed as well as their ability. Parents and educators must, however, encourage gifted learners to participate in challenging learning situations that may include accelerative aspects, such as classes at museums or planetariums, summer courses at universities, special interest clubs for adults in computers or rocketry, and dozens of similar opportunities. On the other hand, it should not be an option for gifted students to avoid difficult or challenging work. The lack of appropriate levels of instruction and expectations for performance may bring about intellectual laziness in gifted students—a problem that may be very difficult to overcome.

John: A Case Study

John is a 6-year-old boy who shows extraordinary ability and interest in mathematics, topping out on in-grade achievement measures and scoring at the level of fifth graders on the Peabody Individual Achievement Test (PIAT) in the Math Concepts section. He enjoys doing mathematics at home on Saturdays. His father is an engineer and his mother is a teacher. They support his interest in mathematics. John also enjoys playing around with mechanical objects in his spare time. His reading abilities are at the level of a second grader. His record in other first-grade subjects is excellent. His kindergarten and first-grade teachers perceive John to be very able, and each has commented on her inability to challenge him sufficiently in mathematics. John, however, is small for his age and has displayed inappropriate social behavior in the classroom. His organizational skills are not remarkable, and he is frequently inattentive.

The following data suggest that some accelerative option would be appropriate:

1. John is highly advanced in one academic area (mathematics).
2. John's other academic performances are above average.
3. John's interests are in the direction of his apparent strengths.

4. John's parents are supportive of his learning, particularly in mathematics.

On the other hand, some factors suggest that some acceleration options may not be appropriate.

1. John has not managed to develop socially appropriate responses to the classroom demands for compliance and self-discipline.
2. Although he is a good student, John's precocity in mathematics is not evenly matched by his performance in other academic areas.
3. John is only 6 years old. He has only just begun first grade, so his adjustment to the school routines and demands is only beginning to develop.
4. John is small for his age.

After an examination of the evidence both for and against accelerating John, it may be useful to raise related issues concerning his candidacy for acceleration. As reasonable questions, one could pose the following:

1. Which acceleration options would be most profitable for John? Although a case could be made for grade skipping, the evidence clearly indicates that acceleration in mathematics is a more appropriate option.
2. Does it appear likely that John would progress rapidly in all academic areas if given a program that would allow such opportunities? Perhaps a telescoped option is preferable. John would be able to move through second- and third-grade curriculum skills in all areas based on his capacity to do so.
3. What should be reasonable expectations for performance and achievement? If acceleration is limited to instruction in mathematics, then a more radical departure from the performances of age-level peers would be a reasonable expectation. On the other hand, if the instructional program provides for accelerated learning in all academic areas, then perhaps more modest goals should be expected.

Given the facts of this case report, it is justifiable to provide some form of acceleration for John. It would be unconscionable to ignore his abilities and achievements.

Organizational Necessities to Meet the Needs of the Gifted

An important problem in accommodating the needs of gifted students becomes apparent: The current organizational structure of our schools does not provide sufficient flexibility to readily allow a broad range of options to accommodate the various needs of accelerants. Schools should allow for the following types of curriculum flexibility.

- Younger students placed in advanced-level courses, including early entrance, grade skipping, telescoping, and subject-matter acceleration
- Credit and/or placement given for achievement completed outside the school program
- Substitutions for required courses
- College credit and high school credit earned simultaneously
- Flexible time for demonstrating subject-matter proficiency
- Opportunities to explore specific topics of interest

If such flexibility were prevalent, addressing the needs of the gifted might become everyday practice in schools across the country.

Table 7.1 indicates some features of various typical candidates for acceleration and suggests reasonable paths of academic development. Ideally the practice of acceleration is the act of providing optimal learning situations with an appropriately matched curriculum. The setting in which the acceleration is facilitated should be a secondary consideration. Excellent classroom teachers can accommodate such needs in their own classrooms with individualized educational planning. If the teacher lacks either the skills, resources, or confidence to address the gifted child's need for accelerated learning, an advanced placement or a separate class grouping may be in order.

WHAT CONSTITUTES A CURRICULUM FOR ACCELERATED LEARNING

A basic principle of instruction for gifted students is that many gifted learners need content acceleration at a number of stages in their development. Although a district's programs may include elaborations on basic materials and activities that enrich, expand, and enhance learning opportunities, it must be recognized that a student's aptitude for accelerated learning is fundamental to the operation of the program and its benefits. It may be difficult to obtain a program that is consistently fast paced, enriching, and well organized. Yet such goals must be targeted if the student's needs are to be met. As an example, in a program for primary-grade students reading at advanced levels, the following program attributes would be appropriate:

- Work out of a basal materials program for advanced grade levels
- Participate in an inquiry-based study of appropriate children's literature (e.g., Junior Great Books)
- Have a writing program that encourages elaboration and incorporation of ideas from literature into stories
- Use supplementary materials for the development of vocabulary skills
- Read selected biographies and books in the content areas (including subjects dealing with multicultural issues)
- Include experiences in foreign language in the curriculum
- Emphasize the development and use of logic and critical thinking
- Derive spelling work from both basal and literary reading selections
- Tell stories and read one's own stories
- Encourage and provide time to pursue free reading based on children's interests

Although the overall emphasis of the program is whole language experience with a strong emphasis on enrichment of the basic curriculum, the underlying issue of appropriate level of instruction is stressed through careful assessment of reading-skill levels at various stages during the year, access to advanced reading materials—including basal and literature programs, and a vocabulary and spelling program that corresponds with the level of reading instruction. This list of interventions for gifted learners in the primary school shows the scope of activities that acceleration should provide in setting the curricular pattern in every content area.

Subject-matter acceleration in other content areas also has importance for students in the primary grades. In math, for example, there is also the need to consider the following matters beyond the assessment:

1. A focus on developing spatial skills and concepts through geometry and other media
2. A focus on problem-solving skills with appropriately challenging problems
3. An emphasis on the use of calculators and computers as tools in the problem-solving process
4. More emphasis on mathematical concepts and less on computational skills
5. Focus on logic problems that require deductive thinking skills and inference
6. Emphasis on applications of mathematics in the real world through creation of projects that provide experience
7. Emphasis on algebraic manipulations
8. Work with statistics and probability

Table 7.1 Archetypal Features of Candidates for Acceleration Matched With Intervention

EARLY ADMISSION
Developmentally advanced in all academic areas by at least 2 years; identified by parents and confirmed by a psychologist.
Suggested Intervention: Early entrance to kindergarten with appropriately advanced curriculum, careful monitoring of progress throughout early elementary years. Additional acceleration will probably be warranted by junior high school. Early graduation from high school may also be considered (Proctor, Black, & Feldhusen, 1986).

CONTENT ACCELERATION
Precocity in verbal areas; above average in other academic endeavors; identified by teachers during the primary years of schooling.
Suggested Intervention: Content acceleration to appropriately challenging levels in reading; early application of verbal abilities to writing, dramatics, and debate; formation of literary discussion group that provides a peer-group context (Davis & Rimm, 1988).

GRADE ADVANCEMENT
Developmentally advanced child in all academic areas with above average (not outstanding) grades, is bored by the school regular and gifted program; identified by parents/self through talent search participation at junior high level.
Suggested Intervention: Grade acceleration to high school; course selection and program guided by academic strengths and interests; careful monitoring of performance in advanced classes to ensure both challenge and success (Stanley, 1979).

EARLY EXIT FROM HIGH SCHOOL
Highly motivated student who is excelling in all areas at the high school level; identified by teachers and awards.
Suggested Intervention: Early graduation from high school with emphasis on career counseling and college selection of liberal arts study (Stanley, 1979).

Again the accelerated mathematics curriculum is balanced with a strong enrichment element, but at the same time it allows for skills, concepts, and requisite materials to be at a challenging level for the child rather than geared to grade-level considerations.

Who Can Work With Accelerated Learners?

Good teachers can accommodate the placement of a precocious child in their classes. If, however, an instructional option is seriously intended to provide an opportunity to accelerate a capable child's learning, it will take an exceptional teacher. Several ideal qualities that should be sought in teachers of accelerated students are:

1. *Eager backing of acceleration options for able learners.* The attitude of the teacher toward acceleration will have a critical influence on the adaptation and progress of accelerated students. Whereas accelerants are likely to have difficulties in classrooms where resistant teachers attribute most problems to their young age, neither can it be expected that they will fare well in classrooms where their advanced placements are merely tolerated. A teacher should be able to rise to the challenge of accelerating the learning of capable students. Such a teacher will furnish educational activities, plan and follow strategies, and set expectations that will promote and maintain accelerated achievement. Teachers need to carry out frequent assessments of the accelerant's achievement and adjustment. If difficulties appear, they should be analyzed and dealt with promptly and rationally.

2. *Capability to adapt and modify a curriculum to provide accelerative experiences.* Teachers chosen to work with these students need to understand how to compress material, select key concepts for emphasis, and share knowledge systems with their students. They should not double the homework amount or "cover" more material in class (VanTassel-Baska & Olszewski-Kubilius, 1988).

3. *Adequate training and competence for teaching in the content area of the program.* Capable learners should have teachers who are eminently prepared to teach subject matter. This is especially true of accelerated learners. Their exceptional aptitudes will allow them to acquire new skills and knowledge rapidly and also to explore issues that students in the regular class programs will not have time to address. Teachers need to prepare for incorporating appropriate content expertise (Gallagher, 1985), arranging mentorships (Boston, 1976), and arranging alternate learning placements, such as laboratories, clinics, and internships (VanTassel-Baska & Olszewski-Kubilius, 1988).

4. *Preparation in organizing and managing classroom activities.* A teacher of an accelerated program of study must be very conscious of the differences within an accelerated group of learners. Some will be capable of moving very rapidly; others may wish to explore an area of interest in depth. Classroom environments should be flexible enough to accommodate such individual differences. Skill in the use of cluster grouping and regrouping within an accelerated program is highly desirable for such teachers. Teachers of accelerated students can use student contracts, academic centers in the room, independent reading time, and library-based study to assure integration of the range of students needs.

Making Acceleration a Useful Option

School districts will need to plan and prepare carefully to assure that accelerative experiences will have beneficial effects for students. Networks of content area experts, artists, and educators from all levels and sectors of the community should be developed to discuss acceleration issues, produce cooperative plans, and identify mentors and resource persons. Preschool educators and university experts in early childhood should be involved from the beginning, because early referral is an important aspect of any acceleration plan. Such a task force should, for example, address the need to devise appropriate curricula and to examine logistical issues regarding early entrance and early exit options.

In order to maximize curriculum and program flexibility, it may be appropriate to develop written policy statements regarding acceleration. Indefensible restrictions should be removed to assure that capable students will have maximum opportunities in the educational system—not be merely confined in it. Provisions need to be considered for at least the following opportunities:

1. Continuous progress based on ability and performance, not age or grade, in individual curriculum areas
2. Early entrance to school
3. Appropriate credit and/or placement for advanced course work taken off campus, given validation of proficiency
4. Early involvement in college work through the College Board Advanced Placement Program or local arrangements with institutions of higher education.

CONCLUSION

Although educators have every reason to show concern about the practice of acceleration, there is little basis in either research or effective practice not to utilize it with selected individuals or groups of gifted leaners. Candidates for acceleration vary among themselves, and the nature of the acceleration practice should be responsive to those individual variations. Schools, however, need to ensure that support structures for accelerative practice are in place and that competent teachers are available to carry out such programs. Only then will the gifted learner be well served in our schools.

REFERENCES

Benbow, C. P., & Stanley, J. C. (Eds.). (1983). *Academic precocity: Aspects of its development.* Baltimore: Johns Hopkins University Press.

Boston, B. (1976). *The sorcerer's apprentice: A case study for the role of the mentor.* Reston, VA: Council for Exceptional Children.

Clark, B. (1988). *Growing up gifted* (3rd ed.). Columbus, OH: Merrill.

Daurio, S. P. (1979). Educational enrichment versus acceleration: A review of the literature. In W. C. George, S. J. Cohn, & J. C. Stanley (Eds.), *Educating the gifted: Acceleration and enrichment* (pp. 13–63). Baltimore: Johns Hopkins University Press.

Davis, G. A., & Rimm, S. B. (1988). *Education of the gifted and talented* (3rd ed.). Englewood Cliffs, NJ: Prentice-Hall.

Elkind, D. (1981). *The hurried child: Growing up too fast too soon.* Newton, MA: Addison Wesley.

Elkind, D. (1986). Mental acceleration. *Journal for the Education of the Gifted, 11*(4), 19–31.

Gallagher, J. (1969). Gifted children. In R. L. Ebel (Ed.), *Encyclopedia of education research* (4th ed., pp. 537–544). New York: Macmillan.

Gallagher, J. J. (1985). *Teaching the gifted child* (3rd ed.). Boston: Allyn and Bacon.

Jackson, N. E., Famiglietti, J., & Robinson, H. B. (1981). Kindergarten and first grade teachers' attitudes toward early entrants, intellectually advanced students, and average students. *Journal for the Education of the Gifted, 4*, 132–142.

Kulik, J. A., & Kulik, C. C. (1984). Synthesis of research on effects of accelerated instruction. *Educational Leadership, 42*(2), 84–89.

Maddux, C. D., Stacy, D., & Scott, M. (1981). School entry age in a group of gifted children. *Gifted Child Quarterly, 4*, 180–183.

Obrzut, A., Nelson, R. B., & Obrzut, J. E. (1984). Early school entrance for intellectually superior children: An analysis. *Psychology in the Schools, 21*, 71–77.

Pressey, S. L. (1949). *Educational acceleration: Appraisal of basic problems.* (Bureau of Educational Research Monographs, No 31). Columbus: Ohio State University Press.

Proctor, T. B., Black, K. N., & Feldhusen, J. F. (1986). Early admission of selected children to elementary school: A review of the literature. *Journal of Educational Research, 80*(2), 70–76.

Reynolds, M., Birch, J., & Tuseth, A. (1962). Review of research on early admission. In M. Reynolds (Ed.), *Early school admission for mentally advanced children.* Reston, VA: Council for Exceptional Children.

Southern, W. T., Jones, E. D., & Fiscus, E. D. (1989a). *Academic acceleration: Concerns of gifted students and their parents.* Paper presented at the annual meeting of the National Association for Gifted Children, Cincinnati, OH.

Southern, W. T., Jones, E. D., & Fiscus, E. D. (1989b). Practitioner objections to the academic acceleration of young gifted children. *Gifted Child Quarterly, 33*, 29–35.

Stanley, J. C. (1979). The study and facilitation of talent for mathematics. In A. H. Passow (Ed.), *The gifted and talented: Their education and development, 78th Yearbook of the National Society for the Study of Education* (pp. 169–185). Chicago: University of Chicago Press.

Terman, L. M., & Oden, M. H. (1947). *Genetic studies of genius: Vol. 4. The gifted child grows up: Twenty-five years' follow-up of a superior group*. Stanford, CA: Stanford University Press.

VanTassel-Baska, J. (1986). *Acceleration*. In J. Maker (Ed.), *Critical issues in gifted education*. Rockville, MD: Aspen.

VanTassel-Baska, J., & Olszewski-Kubilius, P. (Eds.). (1988). *Pattern of influence on gifted learners*. New York: Teachers College Press.

VanTassel-Baska, J., Patton, J., & Prillaman, D. (1989). Disadvantaged gifted learners: At risk for educational attention. *Focus on Exceptional Children, 22*(3), 1–15.

CHAPTER 8

Practical Concerns in Assessment and Placement in Academic Acceleration

Sylvia Piper and Karen Creps
Wood County Office of Education
Bowling Green, Ohio

Mark returns from kindergarten with an assignment to find pictures of objects beginning with the letter *m*. A self-taught reader, he uses the index from a mail-order catalog and rapidly completes the task.

Sara, who is capable of rapid mental computation of three-digit sums, is faced with several pages of second-grade math facts drill.

John, having exhausted the school library fund of software, now writes programs for his sixth-grade classmates as they develop computer literacy.

Carol expands her two-page theme for sophomore English into a short story that merits publication in an adult literary magazine.

These students, and many others like them who seem to learn much faster than their same-age peers, illustrate the difficulty inherent in matching gifted students and curriculum. These students often enter school or a particular grade level possessing skills equivalent to those held by much older children. Teachers faced with this situation soon become aware that the scope and sequence of grade-level instruction is inappropriate. Parents may notice that the enthusiasm their child shows for school and learning begins to wane. The student quickly realizes that the expectations in the classroom represent at best only practice of skills learned long ago and at worst meaningless repetition.

Materials and procedures identified in this paper were developed under the auspices of the superintendent and staff of the Wood County Board of Education. The authors gratefully acknowledge their help and support.

Some students, like John, will engage in activities and behaviors that provide additional experiences and challenges. For most, however, the opportunity to do so is limited by narrowness of curriculum and the pressure placed upon classroom teachers to structure activities for a large number of students with widely diverse abilities. Yet experts, from Elkind (1988) to Sisk (1988), agree that the responsibility for constructing a "good fit" between curriculum and student ability belongs to the school. Finding the fit for students who achieve, or could potentially achieve, at levels comparable to those of older students may suggest interventions that move students through the academic curriculum at a more rapid than normal pace. Interventions of this nature would place gifted students with chronologically older students. These sorts of options are identified as academic acceleration, and schools often face the prospect of deciding when and for whom such interventions are warranted.

The school setting and the levels of concern or resistance shown by those involved in making academic acceleration decisions create other issues that must be addressed. Parents, teachers, and students may express concern about the student's ability to cope with the academic and social demands of advanced placement. Teachers express reluctance to deviate from age-normal placements (Southern, Jones, & Fiscus, 1989b). Parents worry that such placements will deprive the student of age-appropriate experiences or will place demands so great as to deny the student time for normal recreation and social relationships. Students often express concern about leaving friends and familiar settings. It is, however, important to note that each of these groups also foresees major difficulties in failure to intervene (Southern, Jones, & Fiscus, 1989a).

The age of the student under consideration raises other issues. It is unlikely that the types of concerns expressed, or the importance given to the concerns, will be the same for children being considered for early admission to kindergarten as for those students being considered for early college entrance. The age of the individual limits the choice of assessment instruments that can be used, the timing of the move, and the range of placements available.

Researchers, too, have indicated some reservations about the universal appropriateness of acceleration. Despite generally positive findings, Cornell, Callahan, Bassin and Ramsay (Chapter 4) have noted, there is evidence that not all children may benefit from acceleration. For some, the process may result in difficulty adjusting to the new settings. For others, the desire to compete in interscholastic athletics or other extracurricular activities may represent an obstacle to acceptance of accelerative options. Some may experience problems in the transition to post-secondary school or adult life.

Even when decision makers are convinced that some form of acceleration is desirable, they face a series of assessment decisions concerning the most appropriate placement for the student under consideration. Which of the available options provides the best "fit" between student and academic demand? Many choices, ranging from grade advancement of one or more years to advanced placement in only some content areas, are available. Early admission, concurrent enrollment, and faster pacing through compacted curriculum are other intervention strategies available to decision makers. Determining the appropriateness of a given acceleration option is a complex process that requires attention to (1) the ability of the student, (2) the feasibility of various acceleration options at different grade levels, and (3) the availability of resources.

School districts must explore the many issues that have an impact on accelerative options before selecting the option appropriate for a particular student. School districts should design and implement procedures that will

1. Accurately assess the level of performance and potential of gifted students
2. Determine appropriate placements for students
3. Ensure support for placement decisions from all constituents of the decision-making process
4. Monitor and evaluate the suitability of those decisions

Furthermore, a district should outline a reasonable and clearly articulated policy for the application of these procedures.

A process for examining questions of academic acceleration will contain an element of informal as well as formal procedures. For example, teachers, administrators, or parents might make a preliminary exploration into difficulties individual students are experiencing. In doing so the potential benefits of accelerative options could be considered without initiating the formal referral process. It is beneficial to have an individual who can act as agent for informal explorations, and who can later coordinate any formal assessments. In many districts, this might be the coordinator or teacher of the gifted. Alternately, it could be a member of the administration or school psychology staff responsible for disseminating information about gifted education programs in the district. In any case, it should be an individual who can make an initial assessment of the level of need in individual cases and provide interim assistance in meeting the needs of students while waiting for more formal assessment.

ACCELERATION PROCESS PROCEDURES

The procedures used for evaluation, assessment, and decision making should be formalized and standardized. A standard procedure is more likely to ensure that adequate information will be collected for every case to be considered and that final decisions will be consistent. The complexity and demands of these decisions make it desirable to assign the tasks to a group comprised of professionals as well as parents and, where practicable, the student. The decision-making process should include participation from individuals with appropriate expertise and from those affected by the results of the decision. Lastly, the procedure should avert problems of personal bias and assist school personnel in finding wider acceptance of potential placements.

Even the most carefully constructed process is fallible. The dynamics of personnel resources, school settings, and the development of children themselves may invalidate placement decisions and, thus, threaten the "goodness of fit" that was targeted. It is essential, therefore, that placement decisions be flexible, subject to periodic evaluation, and undergo change as needed.

The following process for addressing academic acceleration was developed and has been implemented in several school districts in northwestern Ohio. It provides consistency in the referral process as well as written documentation of the action taken in individual cases. A flowchart of the process is shown in Figure 8.1.

REFERRAL-ACTION PROCESS

Informal Referral

The informal referral process begins when the gifted education professional is made aware of a student who may benefit from an accelerative option. Teachers, administrators, or parents may contact the gifted education professional with a query about ways to meet the needs of a bright student. An expression of concern for the adjustment of a student in the current grade placement or even an explicit suggestion that acceleration be considered in a particular case may alert the trained professional to the possible existence of a mismatch between student and school placement. Parents and teachers can provide valuable information as they seek advice about a student's placement.

> The curriculum seems like review for Suzie. She masters new concepts almost as quickly as they are introduced.
> I really have to work to keep up with Jenny. She is always asking what she can do next while others are still working on the assignment.
> Andy sees connections and relationships other second graders cannot see. When the principal asked him if he knew when women received the right to vote, Andy replied that he didn't know, but if

Figure 8.1   Referral-Acceleration Process

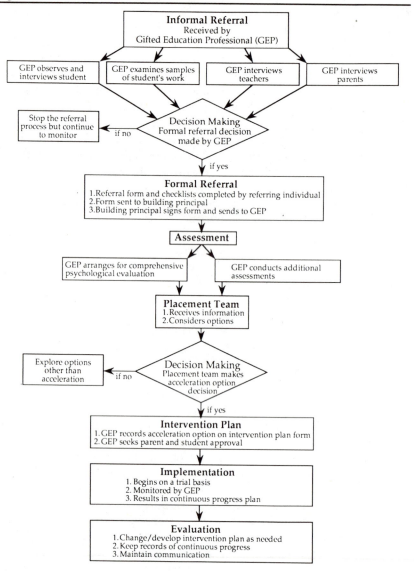

the principal looked it up in the encyclopedia under constitution he could probably find it "because that is where the amendments would be."

My daughter frequently asks me why she finds things funny that other kids do not. It seems that she understands and uses humor that escapes other children her age.

Comments of this kind may trigger suspicion that the student might benefit from an accelerative option. Such a suspicion suggests that further information should be gathered. A follow-up should include observations of the student in a variety of academic and social settings. While observing, the gifted education professional should note how the student uses structured and free time, responds to classroom questions, structures thinking, interacts with age-mates, attends to a task, and works independently.

Information gathered through observations should be supplemented with information obtained from interviews with the student. The interview should be structured in a way that will permit the gifted education professional to determine what the student

- Likes and dislikes about school
- Would change about school
- Finds challenging in school
- Likes to do with free time, both in and outside of school (hobbies and pastimes)
- Looks for in friends
- Views as an ideal school day

Another source of information would be samples of the student's academic work. These samples should be examined for overall quality of production, depth of insight, vocabulary usage and sophistication, and relative sophistication of the work compared with that expected in the grade level being considered.

Interviews with teachers and parents should be utilized to determine whether their views substantiate other findings. Teacher responses to inquiries about student behaviors can provide fruitful information about a student's potential suitability for academic acceleration. The following areas might be explored:

- Classroom behavior
- Ability to work independently
- Acceptance of authority
- Quality of classroom response

- Frequency and appropriateness of responses
- Decision-making skills in comparison with those of age-mates
- Evaluation of own work
- Ability to express agreement/disagreement with teacher and/or peers
- Self-selected activity choices
- Relationships with peers, older children, adults

Teachers should also be asked if they feel a more formal referral procedure is warranted.

Parent interviews can provide anecdotal information about the student as well as insight into parental attitudes regarding accelerative options. Some areas that should be explored include

- Kinds of activities the child engages in at home
- Degree to which the child reports attitudes toward school
- Potential changes in the child's behavior or attitude toward school
- Child's level of maturity and emotional stability
- Parents' view of accelerative options in general
- Parents' view of an accelerative option for their child

Parents should also be asked if they feel accelerative options should be pursued.

Informal referral procedures generate a wealth of information. The gifted education professional should use the results to determine if a particular case merits the more intensive (and more costly) formal referral. Does the profile of the student generated by the process suggest that the student may benefit from acceleration? Certainly, if the informal assessments of parents and teachers lead them to feel strongly that such a step is merited, the gifted education professional should regard this information of major significance.

In cases where disagreement exists, professional judgment must be exercised. Teachers are often reluctant to recommend acceleration options. Some are conservative in their approach to acceleration because they feel the process may result in social or emotional harm. Others regard the recommendation that a student be moved out of their classroom as a sign of failure on their part. Parents, too, may be conservative about the acceleration of their children. Although they may feel strongly that the curriculum is inappropriate for their child, this feeling may be contradicted by school personnel. Subsequent stages of the assessment become increasingly more formal and technical, so parents may be increasingly more apt to acquiesce to professional judgments.

It is the job of the gifted education professional to sort through these disagreements. Although the actual performance of the student in the school setting ought to be the single most important factor to be considered, the feelings of teachers, parents, and students are also important. If any of these parties express strong resistance to further assessment, the gifted education professional must clarify the purpose of a formal referral. Those resisting a formal referral must understand that it is not equivalent to a final decision. It can be viewed as a needs assessment, providing data that will lead to an informed decision regarding the most appropriate option for the student.

Formal Referral

Formal referral should supply pertinent information without being cumbersome and time consuming. The time required to collect information will vary depending upon the age of the student, the extent of formal testing to be undertaken, and the number of content areas to be assessed. Very young children may require more time for assessment and more individual application of instruments.

Much of the information needed in a formal referral can be obtained from school records. It is readily available and quickly collected. If district policy requires individual rather than group test information, the time required for data collection increases greatly. Individual assessment of ability, generally assigned to a school psychologist, could require 2 or more days for testing and compiling the results.

The items listed below indicate the type of information that would be appropriate in a formal referral:

1. General student information
   Name, age, expected year of graduation, and so on
   Type of abilities prompting referral
   Reason(s) for referral
   Scores on recent standardized tests
   Current grades and classroom achievement
   Any available psychological reports
2. Appropriate checklists and qualitative information
   Rating of behavioral characteristics
   Attendance patterns
   Summaries and pertinent information extracted from interviews
   with parents, teachers, and the student
   Results of structured and/or informal observations

The first section above calls for information from permanent records and standardized test results. The second section requires information that is more qualitative in nature. Results of interviews and observations collected through any phase of referral will be useful. In addition, the gifted education professional will need to make a determination of the types of behavioral checklists that will be needed. A large variety of these forms are available. Most forms of this type are designed to be filled out by teachers; however, some may be used by administrators and parents. Some checklists are designed to be filled out by the students themselves. Information from checklists of this latter type can provide additional sources of information and help compensate for data provided from a single, potentially biased source.

A referral form and packet should be organized to assist decision makers. Figure 8.2 provides a form designed to present available data in a standardized format.

Assessment

The gifted education professional reviews the informal and formal referral data and makes arrangements for the comprehensive psychological evaluation to accompany each formal referral. The most valuable information for decisions involved with accelerative options will come from the norm-referenced data of individual ability and achievement tests administered by a trained individual during the comprehensive psychological evaluation. This information is needed because the available test data for most students are the result of group ability and achievement tests. Group test results are subject to many threats to the validity of the information provided. Accurate assessment of the student may not have occurred during group testing if the student was suffering from illness, test anxiety, or distractions in the test environment. On the other hand, individual tests, administered by trained professionals, allow assessment of the student's physical and emotional response to the testing situation. From the one-on-one individual psychological evaluation, an informal assessment of the student's attention, tolerance for frustration, problem-solving skills, and creativity can be made. Grades, observations, and interviews may be subject to individual bias in application or interpretation and cannot provide norm-referenced measurement. Instruments that will minimally be included in such an evaluation are

1. An individual intelligence test such as the Wechsler Intelligence Scale for Children, Revised (Wechsler, 1974) or the Kaufman Assessment Battery for Children (Kaufman & Kaufman, 1983)
2. An individual achievement test such as the Kaufman Test of Educational Achievement (Kaufman & Kaufman, 1985) or the Woodcock-Johnson Psycho-Educational Battery, Revised (Woodcock & Johnson, 1989)

Figure 8.2 Referral Form for Gifted Education

Student _____ Birthdate _____ Class of _____
School District _____ Building _____ Current Grade _____
Parents

Home Address _____ Home Telephone _____
_____ Work Telephone _____

Referred by: _____
                signature   ·   date

                position

Referral received by _____
                      building principal   date

Referral received by _____
                      coordinator of gifted education   date

1. INDICATE TYPE OF ABILITY PROMPTING REFERRAL.
   _____ superior cognitive ability
   _____ superior academic ability (specify) _____
   _____ creative thinking ability
   _____ visual and/or performing arts ability (specify) _____

2. STATE REASON(S) FOR REFERRAL.

3. ATTACH A PHOTOCOPY OF THE LAST 24 MONTHS. Results should be available in student's permanent record folder.

4. PROVIDE STUDENT'S MOST RECENT SEMESTER GRADE IN EACH OF THE APPROPRIATE SUBJECT AREAS.

_____ READING	_____MATH	_____SOCIAL STUDIES	_____ENGLISH/LANGUAGE ARTS
_____SCIENCE	_____MUSIC	_____ART	_____DRAMA
_____OTHER _____			

5. Has this student been evaluated for giftedness and/or special programming previously?
   _____yes   _____no
   If yes, attach a photocopy of all previous evaluation reports. Psychological reports are not always filed in a student's permanent record folder. Please check with the building principal and/or school psychologist to determine whether a psychological evaluation was completed for this student.

6. Please provide/attach any additional data/items which will be useful when evaluating this student's ability. (Examples: personal characteristics, awards won, anecdotes, hobbies, etc.)

3. An assessment of social maturity and/or adaptive behavior such as the Vineland Social Maturity Scale (Doll, 1965)
4. For young children, assessments of basic academic skills

Most of the instruments listed are standard for all educational assessments. In the case of referrals for academic acceleration, the following should also be considered:

1. Subject-specific achievement tests and skill checklists such as Key Math–Revised (Connoly, Nachtman, & Pritchett, 1971) and informal reading inventories
2. Creativity tests such as Torrance Test of Creative Thinking (Torrance, 1966)
3. Higher level thinking tests such as the Ross Test of Higher Cognitive Abilities (Ross & Ross, 1966)
4. Self-concept instruments such as the ME Scale (Feldhusen & Kolloff, 1986)
5. Interest inventories such as the Interest-A-Lyzer (Renzulli, 1977)

The evaluation of specific academic skills is of particular value when considering grade advancement. Many teachers, as well as parents, are concerned that students who are advanced will miss valuable basic skills. Direct assessment of basic skills will provide decision makers with important information of the current functioning of the candidate for acceleration and on the possible need for instruction of specific skills.

Placement Team

The gifted education professional assembles a placement team that has the responsibility for reviewing data and developing a recommendation for placement. The core group of the team should include the gifted education professional, building principal, guidance counselor, and school psychologist. Additional members of the team would be those school personnel who are directly involved in the particular placement. These personnel would usually include (1) the teacher in the current placement, (2) the referring teacher (if different), and (3) the teacher(s) who might be receiving the new placement. The gifted education professional will generally be responsible for coordinating the team.

The major task of the placement team is to determine an appropriate accelerative option for the student under consideration. To this end, the team reviews existing data, may invite other professionals or the parents to assist in the process, and requests that additional data be collected if necessary.

Decision Making

The placement team conducts a review process that results in a recommendation for or against acceleration. During the review process, team members share their concerns and consider the following:

1. The needs of the student
2. The demands of any new placements
3. The acceptability of possible placements to the parents, teachers, and the student
4. Any evidence of potential difficulties in adjustment

The placement team must also assess the availability of various support services in a receiving placement, the existence of natural support systems in the form of friends and acquaintances in the new setting, and the timing and salience of the placement. Counseling services, a supportive teacher, and the presence of friends and acquaintances in the new setting would all help ensure the success of a placement, especially for children who express hesitancy or fear about the move. The team must consider whether or not the placement will require motor skills or organizational skills that the candidate for acceleration has not yet developed to the extent older classmates have (Hultgen, 1989). For example, if the receiving setting assumes the ability to work independently, this may be a difficulty for children who have never been required to set time lines and meet deadlines independently. They may fail despite high ability and achievement.

The receiving setting is also an important consideration. At the very least, the teacher must be in favor of the placement and be willing to monitor academic and social growth throughout the initial placement period. Teachers who are skeptical about the benefits of acceleration in general may launch a self-fulfilling prophecy of failure for accelerants. For example, teachers may attribute all problems to immaturity, or they may assume that the student should independently learn skills that were skipped during the process of the acceleration.

The placement team has responsibility for examining two major areas. The first is the level of aptitude and achievement of the candidate. Various authors have provided guidelines for accelerative decisions. Davis and Rimm (1988), for example, recommend that students considered for grade advancement should have an IQ of at least 135. Feldhusen, Proctor, and Black (1986), on the other hand, suggest 125. Clearly, candidates for acceleration should show evidence of ability that is in the superior range. Achievement should be at least at the upper range of the receiving setting (Feldhusen et al., 1986; Robinson & Weimer, Chapter 2). It is not necessary that students have mastered all the skills taught before the projected placement, merely that they show evidence of being able to acquire them rapidly. Excessive deficits, however, may lead to frustration on the part of the student and teacher and threaten the success of the placement before the student has a chance to acquire requisite skills.

The second area for scrutiny involves the adjustment and maturity of the student. A primary concern for the team is the extent to which the new placement is desired by the student. As students approach the latter stages of their school careers, they may express increasing reluctance to be separated from peers and current school settings (Southern et al., 1989a). Any reluctance endangers the potential success of the placement. In addition, deficits in social or emotional adaptation may be cause for concern. It is important to keep in mind, however, that some of the difficulties observed in candidates for acceleration may arise from the inappropriateness of the current placement (Robinson & Weimer, Chapter 2; Feldhusen et al., 1986). In these cases, the team must exercise clinical judgment as to whether acceleration options would be more likely to lessen these problems or make them worse.

Placement

For a student who is deemed a likely candidate for acceleration, the various accelerative options can be placed generally into two categories: grade skipping and subject-matter acceleration. The former involves the placement of a student in a higher grade for all instruction. Grade skipping is simpler and less expensive to administer compared with various other program options for gifted students. Compared with other options, grade skipping requires no special materials or facilities and can reduce the need for special programs and schedules.

Subject-matter acceleration involves receiving instruction or taking classes in particular subject-matter areas at higher grade levels. It is especially appropriate in reading, mathematics, and languages where instruction is more or less sequential. It is most appropriate for students with advanced abilities that are not generalized across the curriculum.

From the student's perspective, it is generally conceded that skipping a grade or multiple grades is the more drastic option. It is also true, however, that subject-matter acceleration can create logistical problems that may affect student adjustment and create administrative difficulties. Dual attendance at different schools, for example, can remove the student from a great deal of contact with chronological peers and opportunities for socialization in either setting. Scheduling, transportation, record keeping, and the necessity for maintaining flexibility in programming options all serve to make this option

difficult to implement. Both strategies have potentially negative consequences for the adjustment of the student to the new placement as well as
the adjustment of school administration to the student.

For the placement team, consideration of any accelerative option requires an assessment of the breadth of the student's abilities, the degree to
which the student exceeds current grade-level achievement, and the salience
of adjustment problems. Students who may reasonably be recommended for
subject-matter acceleration are those who exhibit

1. A narrow range of exceptional abilities
2. Achievement that is superior, but not radically so
3. Evidence of problems in social or emotional development
4. Reluctance for more radical placements

Davis and Rimm (1988) caution that no matter how capable the student may
be, no more than one grade should be skipped at a time. After a period of
adjustment and observation, further intervention may be warranted.

Every attempt should be made to reach a consensus decision by the
placement team. Sharply divided recommendations that result from forced
votes are likely to cause difficulties later. In the event that a consensus cannot
be reached, it would be wise to gather additional information and meet again
when it is available.

Students who are not considered likely candidates for acceleration in
this phase may be recommended for interventions that do not include placement with older peers or more rapid pacing in current placements. The
teachers of such students may be provided with supplemental resources and
guidance for developing enrichment strategies. Additional extracurricular
and summer programs might also be recommended as appropriate.

Intervention Plan

Following the placement team meeting, the gifted education professional should record the results of the team's recommendation on an Intervention Plan form. The Intervention Plan is a concise record of the results of
the team's deliberation, the recommended placement, when the placement
will take place, schedules for implementation and evaluation, and so on. A
sample of a form used for this purpose is presented in Figure 8.3.

Student/Parent Notification

Students and parents must be informed of the disposition of the placement team. This is normally done in a meeting with the gifted education

Figure 8.3   Intervention Plan for Gifted Education

Student _____ Birthdate _____ Class of _____
School District _____ Building _____ Current Grade _____
Parents _____
Home Address _____ Home Phone _____
_____ Work Phone _____

CONFERENCE PARTICIPANTS

I agree with this plan and give permission for the recommended option.

Parent	Date	Student	Date
Principal	Date	Gifted Education Profession	Date
Teacher	Date	Teacher	Date
Psychologist	Date	Guidance Counselor	Date
Other/Title	Date	Other/Title	Date
Other/Title	Date	Other/Title	Date

Check Recommended Option
____ Grade Skipping
Subject Matter Acceleration—Specify Subject(s) _____

Briefly Explain Why this acceleration option was recommended and how it will be implemented.

_____
_____
_____
_____
_____
_____
_____

When will the acceleration begin and what will be the duration?

_____

How and on what schedule will the placement be monitored?

_____
_____

How and when will reevaluation take place?

_____
_____

professional, psychologist, administrator, and other members of the team appropriate for a particular placement. The team should detail and clarify the rationale for the recommended placement and provide responses to parent and student questions. If the decision of the team is to maintain the current placement, the student and parents should be informed as to the concerns the team had in reaching its decision. It is essential that the decision not be given the appearance of a final judgment upon the student's ability. Students who are considered for acceleration are almost invariably high achievers and capable learners. Moreover, the basis for conservatism in placement often rests on developmental concerns that may change as students mature.

If accelerative options are recommended, parents and students should both concur in the plan. Although parental consent is legally required, it is unlikely that a placement will be successful if the student is opposed. Should the placement decision be rejected, other options for meeting the student's needs should be explored.

Implementation of Acceleration Options

Acceleration should begin on a trial basis. What constitutes an adequate length of time for the trial period can vary from a single grading period to a whole semester. It is important to give the student adequate time to adjust to new demands, acquire and display requisite skills, and meet and interact with classmates in the new placement. In cases where adjustment seems delayed, it is possible to extend the trial period before a final disposition is given.

During this period, the gifted education professional and the receiving teacher have major responsibility for keeping communication open among all the constituents of the process. It is essential that the placement be monitored and evaluated during this period. The teacher must assess the quality of the work, keeping in mind that it need not be perfect. The teacher should also be cognizant of the social needs of the student during the trial period. Occasions for social interaction with other students should be engineered and observed by the receiving teacher. The gifted education professional needs to monitor the personal adjustment of the accelerated student to the new setting. Richert (1985) suggests three themes of inquiry and interview:

Are you learning more or better in this placement?
Are you happier with this group of students?
Do you prefer to stay?

The student should, of course, be informed that the placement is tentative and that adjustment to the new placement could take some time. This knowledge should help the student develop reasonable expectations and re-duce pressure for immediate superior performance.

If placement is deemed unsuccessful, it is essential that counseling be provided to both student and parents to ensure they do not view it as a failure on the part of the student. On the other hand, if the placement is successful, a plan for the student's continued progress through school should be gener-ated and shared with parents and students.

Evaluation

The gifted education professional as well as other educational personnel bears the responsibility for ongoing evaluation of the intervention after a placement is deemed successful. Updating and revising the intervention plan should be done periodically. Changes in the (1) adjustment of the student, (2) achievement level attained, and (3) type and number of options available to the student may require reassessment of the placement recommendation. In cases where achievement far exceeds the norm, further acceleration may be warranted, even essential.

SUMMARY

Decisions to accelerate are never easy. They are frequently made with some ambivalence and are never free from fallibility. For those engaged in such decisions, it is imperative that a clear, well-publicized, standardized procedure be adopted. This procedure should

1. Provide mechanisms to engage those people with the expertise and interest required
2. Provide the data essential for informed decision making
3. Include provisions for informing parents and students about the po-tential benefits and drawbacks of acceleration options
4. Perhaps most importantly, provide a process to view each candidate as an individual with unique qualities and needs

The procedure that has been described is designed to meet these crite-ria. It provides for the inclusion of a variety of professionals who can consider the widest range of information about individuals under consideration. Ex-tensive review, documentation, and the existence of opportunities for flexible placement are features that categorize the decision-making process adopted herein.

On the other hand, the most careful placement policies are of little value if staff are resistant, insensitive, or inadequately trained to meet the needs of accelerants. Students need to have people with whom they can share their hopes, fears, and anxieties. They need access to role models and mentors.

To parents of accelerants, the district owes other services. The decision to move a student from steady contact with age-mates can be worrisome. Parents need assurance that the situation is being monitored and that any adjustment difficulties will be addressed. It will be necessary to provide parents with information from ongoing evaluation and to inform them when additional intervention measures should be considered. Some parents may need reassurance; others may need a contact who can provide counseling.

Skeptics, too, must be answered. The district, through the gifted education professional, must be able to provide accurate, specific data about the achievement level and adjustment of accelerants. If the process of acceleration is to remain an option for gifted education, its efficacy must be documented.

REFERENCES

Connoly, A., Nachtman, W., & Pritchett, E. (1971). *Key math diagnostic arithmetic test*. Circle Pines, MN: American Guidance Service.

Davis, G. A., & Rimm, S. B. (1988). *Education of the gifted and talented* (2nd ed.). Englewood Cliffs, NJ: Prentice-Hall.

Doll, E. A. (1965). *Vineland social maturity scale*. Circle Pines, MN: American Guidance Service.

Elkind, D. (1988). Mental acceleration. *Journal for the Education of the Gifted, 11*(4), 19–31.

Feldhusen, J. E., & Kolloff, P. B. (1986). ME: A self concept scale for gifted students. *Perceptual Motor Skills, 53*, 319–323.

Feldhusen, J. E., Proctor, T. B., & Black, K. N. (1986). Guidelines for grade advancement of precocious children. *Roeper Review, 9*(1), 25–27.

Hultgen, H. M. (1989). A case for acceleration. *Talent Development, 6*, 10–12.

Kaufman, A. S., & Kaufman, N. L. (1983). *K-ABC: Kaufman assessment battery for children*. Circle Pines, MN: American Guidance Service.

Kaufman, A. S., & Kaufman, N. L. (1985). *K-TEA: Kaufman test of educational achievement*. Circle Pines, MN: American Guidance Service.

Renzulli, J. S. (1977). *The enrichment triad model: A guide for developing defensible programs for the gifted*. Mansfield, CT: Creative Learning Press.

Richert, S. E. (1982). Ask the experts. *Gifted Children Newsletter, 3*(5), 17–18.

Ross, J. D., & Ross, C. M. (1966). *Ross test of higher cognitive process*. San Rafael, CA: Academic Therapy Publications.

Sisk, D. A. (1988). Response to Elkind. *Journal of the Gifted, 11*(4), 32–38.

Southern, W. T., Jones, E. D., & Fiscus, E. D. (1989a). *Academic acceleration: Con-

cerns of gifted students and their parents. Paper presented at the annual meeting of the National Association for Gifted Children, Cincinnati, OH.

Southern, W. T., Jones, E. D., & Fiscus, E. D. (1989b). Practitioner objections to the academic acceleration of young gifted children. *Gifted Child Quarterly, 33,* 29–35.

Torrance, E. P. (1966). *Torrance test of creative thinking.* Princeton, NJ: Personnel Press.

Wechsler, D. (1989). *Wechsler preschool and primary scale of intelligence, revised.* San Antonio, TX: The Psychological Corporation.

Woodcock, R. W., & Johnson, M. B. (1989). *Woodcock-Johnson psycho-educational battery, revised.* Allen, TX: DLM Teaching Resources.

CHAPTER 9

Evaluation of Acceleration Programs

Carolyn M. Callahan and Scott L. Hunsaker
University of Virginia

The evaluation of student outcomes, including achievement and adjustment, has often been the focus of efforts to assess the effectiveness of acceleration programs. The impacts of programs on students are certainly crucial in making judgments about the overall success of acceleration programs; however, the success (and potential longevity of a program of acceleration) must be judged by other criteria as well. Further, program evaluation so narrowly conceived as to focus on just outcome variables fails to serve its full potential as a tool for program improvement. Among the other consequences and program variables that should be considered in an evaluation are the following:

1. Impact on other school components
2. Effect on students not in the program
3. Functional adequacy of the program
4. Cost-effectiveness (Callahan & Caldwell, 1986)

Decision makers must recognize that the conclusions we can draw from evaluative data are highly dependent on where we place the focus of evaluation. Further, we must recognize that data collected on students for program evaluation purposes may be quite different from data we would collect for making individual decisions about particular students. This chapter will address *program* evaluation and provide a guide to issues to be considered in establishing systems to carry out evaluation of acceleration programs—including collection of student data for that purpose. The following chapter will focus on student evaluation and associated research.

PROGRAM EVALUATION

We will begin our discussion with a brief overview of evaluation considerations that are particularly important with regard to acceleration programs.

An overview of strategies and types of data that have been used to evaluate the major categories of acceleration programs will be followed by a critique of these methodologies and further issues that must be considered in planning an evaluation of such programs. Further discussion of general evaluation issues can be found in Renzulli (1975), Callahan (1983), and Callahan and Caldwell (1986).

What Program Evaluation Is for

The primary goal of evaluation has traditionally been to provide information that permits assessment of the overall worth or merit of the object of the evaluation. The object may be a judgment about a process, a program, or people (administrators, staff, students, etc.). However, evaluation information can be used in many ways other than in making summative judgments (Scriven, 1967; Worthen & Sanders, 1987). Understanding the potential contributions of evaluative information is vital to successful program evaluation. Four different categories of evaluation data hold potential for providing useful information to decision makers:

1. Descriptive
2. Prescriptive
3. Formative
4. Summative

Descriptive evaluation. Because it is not possible to evaluate what you cannot describe and it is impossible to replicate what you do not thoroughly know and understand, descriptive evaluation is a primary focus of thorough evaluation. The driving question of descriptive evaluation is, What exactly is the program? If we are able to address this question adequately, then we will be able at a later time to decide which components of the program function well and which do not, what to continue and what to abandon in our programs, and what to adopt or adapt from other programs. Table 9.1 illustrates the major components to include in a program description.

Prescriptive evaluation. Is this acceleration program needed and what is the best plan for implementing the program? This general question forms the basis for prescriptive evaluation. As Callahan and Caldwell (1986) point out, we need to weigh various programming options or variations on delivery in order to serve the needs of gifted students most effectively. The data collected from this aspect of evaluation include:

> Documentation on the specific needs for a program
> Documentation that the particular approach selected is most appropriate
> Documentation that the program is feasible

Formative evaluation. When we ask, Is the program functioning as intended? or Are the various components of the program contributing to achievement of our goals? we are asking formative questions. The identification of program weaknesses (e.g., lack of follow-up on diagnostic effectiveness) and strengths (e.g., counseling that results in smooth transitions) and provision of recommendations for in-progress revisions of the program are part of the formative process (Callahan & Caldwell, 1986). Formative evaluation should begin at the onset of program development and continue through the program implementation phases.

Summative evaluation. When Benbow and Stanley (1983a) ask, Was SMPY's identification procedure effective? and Do SMPY's educational facilitation procedures have long-term benefits? they are asking summative evaluation questions. These questions are summative because they assess the results or impacts of the program. Questions that address the issue of what acceleration programs are trying to accomplish, for whom, with whom, why, and (most importantly) how will we know when it has been accomplished are summative evaluation questions (Hanson, 1980).

Whereas formative evaluations provide information about program strengths, deficiencies, and potential improvements, summative evaluation questions are frequently answered with a yes or no (albeit qualified in most cases).

Table 9.1 Program Components Essential for Adequate Program Description

1. Program definition	2. Philosophy
3. Procedures and criteria	4. Program goals and objectives for identification
5. Student goals and objectives	
7. Personnel	6. Curriculum
9. Program evaluation	8. Budget
11. Instructional strategies	10. Management
13. Descriptions of relationships and interdependence of program components	12. Programming options
	14. Resources which support each program component

Adapted from Carter and Hamilton, 1985; Callahan, 1986

What Past Research and Practice Tell Us

There are at least five areas of concern that consistently emerge when evaluating programs of acceleration:

1. Thoroughness and rigor. The evaluator should be cognizant of the many questions that will arise concerning how well the students have mastered the content of the discipline in which they are accelerated. If grade skipping is an option, then concerns will arise about "missed concepts." For example, one evaluator found that a group of accelerated students had not mastered cursive handwriting, a skill considered very important by subsequent instructors (Klausmeier & Ripple, 1962). If telescoping or rapid acceleration is used, there will be questions about whether the student could have "really" learned the material in so short a period of time. Questions also arise about whether the student is mature enough to be able to benefit maximally from discussions of particular topics.

2. Social-emotional adjustment. The evaluator should be aware that constituents will be very concerned about the social and emotional adjustment of the accelerants. Repeated studies have documented that concerns over these issues are the most prevalent reasons for the dismissal of acceleration as a viable option for gifted students (Southern, Jones, & Fiscus, 1989).

3. Identification and assessment of potential accelerants. The guidelines for grade advancement that Feldhusen, Proctor, and Black (1986) have provided suggest implicitly areas of evaluation concern. Given the guidelines, it follows that an evaluation of an acceleration program should be asking:

- Are comprehensive psychological evaluations of the children's intellectual functioning, academic skill levels and socio-emotional adjustment completed by a psychologist and considered in the decision?
- Are the IQ scores of children who are accelerated at least 125, or do they score above the mean on measures of mental development for the grades they will enter?
- Do the children who are accelerated score above the mean on skill levels of the grade to which they are accelerated?
- If a child scores above the mean on only some skills, is that child placed above grade level for only that instruction?
- Are children who are accelerated free of any serious adjustment problems; do they demonstrate a high degree of persistence and motivation for learning?

- Are accelerated children in good health?
- Are children who are accelerated not unduly pressured by parents?
- Do receiving teachers have positive attitudes toward the acceleration?
- Is the transition as smooth as possible?
- Are accelerative options viewed clearly as trials with clear options presented to the child for returning to the earlier placement?

4. Teacher capability. One aspect of the evaluation of acceleration options that is often overlooked is the capability of the teachers. It is often assumed that teachers who normally teach older students will be capable of teaching these accelerated students. Experience with Advanced Placement Program courses and college courses taught in the high school have demonstrated that this is clearly a false assumption (see Stanley & Stanley, 1986). If advanced content knowledge is not sufficient, what skills and traits are necessary for teaching accelerated pupils? Are provisions made for potential instructors to develop these skills and traits?

5. Special populations. Concern about the underserved gifted (e.g., minorities, economically disadvantaged, handicapped, and women) and the lack of data on the effects of various programming options on these subpopulations will warrant specific attention in the evaluation process. Are acceleration options resented in ways that are equally attractive and supportive to these individuals? Are there provisions made for appropriate counseling and support networks? Which of these provisions are most likely to maximize the success of underserved students in these programs?

Evaluation Concerns of Interested Audiences

In deciding on the relevant issues for an evaluation of acceleration programs, it is important to examine those variables likely to be of greatest importance to the "prime interest groups" affected by the program (Renzulli, 1975). Such groups include government and funding agencies, colleges and universities, central office and school administrators, teachers and counselors, parents, students, and the general public. All prime interest groups should be consulted in the process of developing an evaluation design to ensure that the concerns of each of these groups are addressed in the evaluation process and that they can use the information gained.

Administrators. Wilbur (1982) has identified a set of questions drawn from the concerns raised by high school principals involved in cooperative programs with colleges in offering college-level courses to high school students (see Table 9.2). These concerns represent the kinds of general issues

Table 9.2 Evaluation Concerns Identified by High School Principals

- Are the specified college standards being properly maintained?
- Can other institutions be assured that grading and learning experiences on and off campus are equivalent?
- Is the credit students earn easily transferable to other colleges and universities?
- How effective are the course materials, general structure, and content sequence?
- What effect is the program having on the high school organization?
- How effective is the teaching, on and off campus?
- What teacher behaviors and course characteristics seem best to facilitate learning?
- What kinds of students are being served by the program and which are most likely to be successful?
- How do participants do in college? What are the long-term effects on student academic performance?

Adapted from Wilbur, 1982

administrators might identify because of their responsibilities with the overall implementation of programs.

Teachers. Teachers may raise concerns about the impact on their school of removing potential leaders, academic role models, and social role models. They may be concerned that programs outside of school compete with or duplicate school programs or curriculum. Information on the adequacy of the teacher-training program and any anticipated problems or expectations would certainly be important for teachers to know. Teachers will also be concerned with documenting that students master skills and concepts before they progress to the next level of instruction; that adequate attention is paid to scope and sequence; and that students are exposed to and learn the fundamental concepts of their disciplines.

Parents and students. Parents may be concerned with the savings that accelerative options may yield in both tuition payments and student time. However, their greatest concerns are likely to focus on

1. The level of achievement in the program
2. The overall adjustment of their children to new contexts
3. The quality of curriculum and instruction
4. The students' relationship with classroom peers
5. The effect of separation from age-level peers

Parents' concerns reflect a student concern for a comfortable yet interesting and challenging classroom and instructor, sufficient support, and a curriculum that is neither too easy nor too difficult.

Other audiences. Central office administrators, school boards, and the general public will be concerned about the influence of the program on overall school image, achievement, finances, and so on. (Mezynski & Stanley, 1980; Benbow & Stanley, 1983; Gudaitis, 1986).

Prioritizing Evaluation Concerns

In any evaluation, there will be multiple questions from each of the audiences interested, varying in importance from key questions to those of little import. Because evaluators and clients have limited resources, it is necessary to prioritize the questions and to limit the evaluation effort to only the most important. For example, if acceleration occurs by moving a whole class forward at a rapid pace or offering an entire class a college-level course, then there is less concern about negative social effects from being removed from age peers. Consequently, the most important issues might arise from questions of whether increased challenge and expectation of parents, teachers, and administrators might cause undesirable academic stress. In this case it would be important to consider the stress issue but not as important to collect data about social relationships (unless other indications of such problems existed). Table 9.3 provides criteria for prioritizing evaluation questions.

Prioritization does not preclude allowing other questions, issues, or concerns from being addressed that may emerge during the course of the evaluation, and evaluators should remain flexible and responsive to meet new issues.

Evaluation for Decision Making

The relationship between educational evaluators and practitioners has not always been a cordial one. Educators have generally had little use for experimental research designs and the massive technical reports produced by

Table 9.3 Criteria for Prioritizing Evaluation Questions

1. Would the findings be of interest to key audiences?
2. Would the answer to this question reduce present uncertainty?
3. Would the findings yield important information?
4. Would the results be of continuing interest?
5. Is the question critical to the study's scope and comprehensiveness?
6. Is the question answerable given financial and human resources, time, and available methods and technology?
7. Will we or can we act on the information if it does not confirm our expectations?

Adapted from Worthen and Sanders, 1987

outside evaluators. Unfortunately, alternative approaches have often rested on ill-conceived and cursory survey data. Evaluations can, however, be useful to those who make the decisions about the development, adoption, implementation, improvement, or continuation of an educational program if adequate and clear information is given to them on a timely basis.

Adequate information. An evaluation design often used, but often unsuitable for evaluation, is the controlled experimental design. Stanley and Benbow (1986) chose not to employ this design in their evaluation of SMPY because of the (1) potentially restricted populations for experimental and control groups, (2) violations of the assumptions of statistical tests, (3) the availability of alternative methods, and (4) ethical concerns, including the question of withholding potentially beneficial services from students and the desire to avoid deceiving students in a control group. (For descriptions of alternative designs, see Callahan, 1983; Callahan & Caldwell, 1986; and Carter, 1986.)

Also, the goals and objectives of many gifted programs are frequently difficult to measure in an objective, controlled manner (Renzulli & Smith, 1979; Callahan, 1983, 1986). How might one, for example, evaluate objectively whether or not the Advanced Placement Program has advanced American education by the strengthening of the secondary schools, a stated "proposition to test" of the Advanced Placement Program (Cornog, 1980)?

Evaluation information must also be comprehensive to be considered adequate. All the major evaluation issues identified by the "prime interest groups" should be considered in the evaluation design, not just student change. Heikkila (1983) suggested four general areas that would need to be covered in a comprehensive evaluation of acceleration programs:

1. The appropriateness of the selection process in matching students to programs
2. The reasonableness of goals and objectives given available human and material resources
3. The relatedness of the program to the total educational experience (i.e., the regular program and the larger body of knowledge)
4. The interrelatedness of the various components of the program

Adequacy is also judged by the degree to which evaluation information is credible. The credibility of information rests on the competence of the evaluator, the quality of instruments used, and the influence of internal and external political forces on the evaluation. If we fail to provide evidence of credibility, then we will not convince interested audiences that our conclusions or recommendations are warranted. For example, in investigating the social and emotional impact of acceleration programs on students, many programs have relied on respondents' answers to a single item on a locally produced questionnaire. Data of this nature lack credibility with many audiences.

The Joint Committee on Standards for Educational Evaluation (1981) suggested that evaluators "exhibit the training, technical competence, substantive knowledge, experience, integrity, public relation skills, and other characteristics considered necessary by . . . the users of the evaluation" (p. 24). Evaluation findings and limitations should be reported openly, directly, and honestly. Balanced reporting of program strengths and weaknesses is essential.

Informational appropriateness. Perhaps the most important consideration in determining the appropriateness of evaluation information is timeliness. Reports are timely when they are delivered to the intended audience at a time when they can best be used by that audience, not necessarily at the conclusion of a project (Joint Committee, 1981). If information is received after a decision has already been made, the information is no longer useful.

It is also important to provide information that is succinct and understandable. In the evaluation of the Advance College Project, information was shared from the beginning of the project in the form of brief reports, tables, graphs, compilations of teacher and student quotes, executive summaries, as well as through more extensive technical reports (Lave, 1984; Gudaitis, 1986). These strategies allowed for continual efforts to adapt the program to meet student needs.

According to the Joint Committee (1981), regardless of the form taken to report information, it is essential that it be concise and logical, use well-defined technical terms, include tabular or graphic representation, and include relevant examples.

ACTUAL PROGRAM EVALUATIONS

Calls for the evaluation of acceleration programs are found throughout the literature (e.g., Wilbur, 1982). The literature on evaluations of acceleration programs most often reports readily available data such as standardized test scores, grades, continued matriculation at the college level, and questionnaire, survey, or interview data. The most closely examined variables have been those related to academic achievement. Notable exceptions occur in those evaluations where efforts have been made to collect additional achievement data from specially constructed assessment instruments, sociometric data, personality data, and other adjustment data (e.g., Swiatek & Benbow, 1989; Thomas, 1989).

Reports on Early Entrance to Kindergarten or Grade Skipping

As early as 1948, Hobson reported longitudinal comparative data on an early admissions program using grades, retentions, standardized achievement test scores, and numbers of college admissions as measures of the academic success of the program. The equal physical stature of the younger children was also used as an indication of the suitability of the acceleration strategy, and the social and emotional development of the children was assessed comparing referrals for emotional problems as the criterion. In this evaluation, Hobson (1948) also examined extracurricular activities and honors and awards earned as measures of success. The criteria represent a commonly accepted set of measures of success (with the exception of physical stature). Although the academic criteria seem suitable, one must question whether referral for emotional problems represents an extreme measure of social and emotional adjustment. Birch (1954) examined academic, social and emotional, and physical adjustment through principal and teacher rating of students, and Worcester (1956) reported using reading and arithmetic grouping as assessments of success in one program and using grades, standardized test results, sociometric ratings, retentions, physical development (height) and teacher ratings of social and emotional adjustment, health, leadership, attitudes toward school, and achievement in others. He even reported on comparing the number of accelerants wearing glasses to the number of nonaccelerants wearing glasses, suggesting the wide variety of outcome measures that have been considered important by various audiences.

Klausmeier and Ripple (1962), Klausmeier (1963), and Klausmeier, Goodwin, and Ronda (1968), in a series of studies of the effects of grade skipping at the elementary level, also looked at achievement measures, attitudes toward school, teacher ratings of emotional, social, and physical development, and sociometric rankings, but added creativity measures, an ethical values inventory, measures of problem-solving ability, psychomotor skills (strength, coordination, speed, and maneuverability), participation in school activities and special programs, and a rating of handwriting. In attempts to avoid the potential biases of self-report in locally developed rating scales, Pennau (1981) used the Scales for Rating Behavioral Characteristics of Superior Students and the Devereaux Elementary School Behavior Rating Scale to assess cognitive and affective outcomes. Similarly, Mateo (1980) used a standardized measure of behavioral problems (the Hahnemann High School Behavior Rating Scale) as a measure of behavioral adjustment of early entrance students once they had achieved seventh-grade status.

More recently, the Montgomery County Public Schools (Maryland) compared grades (at later points in the junior high school and high school program) and scores on standardized achievement and aptitude tests of accelerated students (early entrance or grade skipping) with grades and scores of the general school population at the same grade level. Interviews with the students and their parents (on issues of concern including negative aspects of acceleration, satisfaction with the arrangement, and effects on social life) and a review of the number of activities in which these students participated (both within and outside of school) were also part of the program evaluation (Splaine, 1982).

Similar efforts for evaluating the effects of early entrance to kindergarten through the examination of standardized achievement test scores, grade-point averages, questionnaires to students and counselors relative to social and academic implications of acceleration, counselor comments, and participation in extracurricular activities were carried out by the Delaware City Schools (Alexander & Skinner, 1980); and standardized achievement test scores (Wide Range Achievement Test), school success as measured by promotion and retentions, and a locally constructed rating scale of social/emotional adjustment (Parent-Teacher Academic Sentiment Questionnaire), as well as student permanent records, were used to evaluate an early admissions program in Colorado (Obrzut, Nelson, & Obrzut, 1984).

Montgomery County also evaluated a plan that allowed for either early placement in first grade or a telescoping of kindergarten/first-grade curriculum (Hebbeler, 1983). Criteria used for success were the percentages of students recommended for placement in grade 2, percentages accepting that placement, achievement test scores, teacher perceptions of social adjustment and achievement, parent satisfaction with placement, and teacher and administrator attitudes. This evaluation also sought to determine the effectiveness of identification procedures (use of group standardized tests, in particular) for predicting end-of-year achievement and to collect data on the impact that the program had on the instructional climate in the classroom through interviewing teachers.

In a fairly extensive evaluation of an elementary acceleration program in the Catholic Diocese of Cleveland, Pevec (1964) first examined the reliability and validity of negative attitudes held by secondary school personnel toward the program by asking teachers to identify the accelerants (in which they were very inaccurate). Two comparison groups were established (a group who had been offered acceleration but did not accept, and a group who had not been offered acceleration). A rating scale was constructed to assess counselor perception of intelligence, academic achievement motivation, physical maturity, emotional stability, leadership, participation in school activities, and freedom from nervousness. Questionnaires were distributed to students to assess social or personal problems, truancy, conformity to school regulations, curriculum choice, participation in school activities, reading habits, nonassigned study time, and perceptions of intelligence, number of jobs, time spent watching television, time spent with hobbies, as well as perceptions of the program. A unique and positive aspect of this evaluation was the use of sociograms to assess the degree to which the number and pattern of friendships and dating habits were similar for accelerants and nonaccelerants. These measures provide a potentially less biased report of social acceptance than self-report. Scores on standardized achievement tests, grades, and "more objective" personality tests (to assess personal, social, and total adjustment) were also compared.

Acceleration Through Telescoping

Klausmeier (1963) reported on a 3-year evaluation of a program for gifted students that included provisions to complete primary school in fewer than six semesters, to condense 3 years of junior high school mathematics into 2 years wherein geometry and biology were completed in grade 9, and to complete a 3-year senior high program in less than 3 years. This evaluation was more comprehensive than most in its inclusion of the evaluation of the identification procedures and documentation of actual classroom practice as well as assessment of student outcome variables. Assessment instruments and strategies used in evaluating this program included the following:

> Individual and group intelligence tests; standardized educational achievement tests; questionnaires completed by students, parents, teachers and principals; rating scales and check lists completed by teachers; ratings of children completed by parents; logs describing instructional practices completed by teachers; personality assessments of children, including clinical interviews by school psychologists; observation of classrooms performed by U[niversity] of W[isconsin] personnel and central supervisory staff; sociometric tests of children; special tests of creativity, ethical values and character, attitudes toward school and learning, problem-solving, work-study skills, and current events administered to children. . . . Not all information gathering instruments were used with all children at all school levels each year. (p. 4)

The Hewlett-Woodmere Public Schools (Hewlett, New York) accomplished acceleration through combining the grade 5 and grade 6 curriculum into one year. Evaluation of the program was accomplished by comparing these students to a matched comparison group on the variables of major subject average for 12th-grade students, participation in honor classes, scores on the Cooperative English Test, Scholastic Aptitude Tests (Verbal and Nonverbal), the National Merit Scholarship Examination, and the New York State Regents Scholarship Examination, a Student Information Blank, and the Mooney Problem Check List (Morrison, 1970).

Another approach to telescoping curriculum is to offer courses in the summer that cover essentially the same material that would be offered during the regular year. Many of the Talent Search Programs that have grown out of the initial efforts at Johns Hopkins University offer this acceleration approach to identified students. These programs document student achievement through a variety of approaches with on-site testing used to assess immediate achievement and follow-up questionnaires being a primary source of data on later achievement and social-emotional adjustment (Thomas, 1989; Swiatek & Benbow, 1989; Benbow & Arjmand, 1989; Benbow, Perkins, & Stanley, 1983; Richardson & Benbow, 1988).

In the assessment of achievement at the conclusion of one such program at California State University, Sacramento, Thomas reported using the Cooperative Mathematics Achievement Tests to assess the mathematics courses. He used the Sequential Tests of Educational Progress, English Expression, and the Test of Standard Written English and an evaluation of students' writing samples to assess the writing classes. The National Latin Examination was used to assess the Latin classes. A 115-item questionnaire was mailed to students 4 years later soliciting data on educational attainments, school matriculation, amount of further acceleration, perceived effect of acceleration on grades, interest in school and learning, ability to get along with others, social life in general, general emotional stability, acceptance of self and acceptance of differences in others, participation in extracurricular activities, honors and awards, self-concept, locus of control, and goals and aspirations for the future.

Questionnaires mailed to participants in the original cohort groups (1972, 1973, and 1974) of the SMPY program by researchers at Johns Hopkins and later at Iowa State University sampled similar outcome variables (Benbow et al., 1983; Swiatek & Benbow, 1989; Benbow & Arjmand, 1989). These follow-up studies have also examined the degree to which participants who completed the fast-paced courses continued their participation in mathematics and science courses, pursued majors and graduate study in those fields, and remained interested compared with students who never enrolled or dropped out of the program.

Stanley and Stanley (1986) used the College Entrance Board Examination Achievement Tests in biology, chemistry, and physics (as well as AP examination results when available) to assess the programs offered in those discipline areas.

Advanced Placement Program Courses

The most obvious outcome variable in assessing the academic perform-ance of students in Advanced Placement Programs are scores on the Ad-vanced Placement examinations. However, data on the numbers of colleges accepting the credit of students (and at what level students must score to earn credit at various institutions), performance of students in more ad-vanced college courses, persistence in college, academic honors, the impact of the program on other aspects of the school program, attrition from courses, and standardized achievement tests (e.g., the ETS Cooperative Mathematic Test in calculus) have also been used to assess AP Programs (Hanson, 1980; Stanley & Stanley, 1986; Mezynski & Stanley, 1980).

With a particular question in mind relative to the success of young women in Advanced Placement Programs, Casserly and Rock (1980) used questionnaires to study the perceived articulation between high school and college work and the appropriateness to college careers of AP calculus courses and used extensive interviews and on-site observation to identify fac-tors that resulted in "successful participation" of women in AP mathematics courses (e.g., competence and attitudes of teachers, level of expectations of teachers for males and females, amount of encouragement of adults—parents and other school personnel). The addition of interviews and observations to questionnaire data in these assessments not only enriches the data but also adds credibility and additional support to the conclusions drawn.

College Courses Offered in High School

In evaluations of college courses offered in high school reported by Mer-curio (1980) and Mercurio, Schwartz, and Oesterle (1982), the only sum-mative outcome variables examined were grades earned in college (in general and in the subject areas where students had taken Project Advance courses) and continued attendance at and graduation from college as reported on follow-up surveys. However, extensive evaluations of the Project Advance Program offered documentation of the degree of correspondence between the college courses and those offered in the high school (through on-site visits and checking of papers and tests completed by students against university standards) and data on the degree to which colleges and universities will accept the Syracuse course work and/or exempt students from similar courses.

Two evaluation reports on the Advance College Project (ACP) at Indiana University, Bloomington, included data similar to those reported above. In addition, however, these reports offered information on students' satisfaction with individual courses, the degree to which they perceived that their study habits and time-management skills had improved, the degree to which they felt they would have to work harder in college than in high school, the degree to which they had gained new skills, the degree to which they would recommend ACP courses to others, and the degree to which they had gained skills that they thought would be useful in college. Further, the reports provided comparisons of the high school students' final-exam scores with those of college students for the same exam, perceptions of the high school teachers about the appropriateness of the courses and the final exams, and the degree of teachers' satisfaction with the administrative arrangements with the university (Lave, 1984; Gudaitis, 1986). Student questionnaires, teacher questionnaires, and course evaluation forms are available in the appendices to these reports.

Early College Entrance

The Early Entrance Program (EEP) at the University of Washington has approached the evaluation of program and students from several perspectives. The major evaluation of this program involved the comparison of EEP students with three other groups:

1. A group of students who qualified for the program but chose not to attend
2. National Merit finalists who had entered UW at ages 17½ to 18½
3. Students who had entered UW at ages 17½ to 18½ with preentry scores matched to those of the EEP students

The criteria used to judge success were academic achievement (GPAs) and the groups' responses to a variety of adjustment measures (N. M. Robinson, personal communication, January 24, 1989). According to Robinson, the program has also surveyed parents for their opinions of the project as well as professors, right after grades were turned in, to solicit data on academic performance, behavior, number of questions asked, and use of office hours. It has also studied underachievers and friendship patterns. Current evaluative efforts focus on comparing homework and the tradeoff with social activities and degree of student satisfaction with the program. Additionally, student performance in various lower division college-level courses has been used as the basis for modification of the courses in the transitional program both in terms of instructional strategies (math) and the institution of new courses. This program is currently doing a follow-up survey of the EEP students, the group who qualified but chose high school, and the National Merit finalists by soliciting data on available standardized scores (such as GRE or MCAT), enrollment in graduate or professional schools, majors, degrees earned, honors achieved, jobs, marital status, and children.

Stanley used age at completion of degree, grade-point averages, dean's list achievements and other academic honors and awards as criteria for judging the success of early entrants to college at Johns Hopkins University (Stanley, 1985; Stanley & Benbow, 1983; Stanley & McGill, 1986). Brody, Lupkowski, and Stanley (1988) interviewed students who had entered college early, collected data on freshman year academic achievement and social adjustment, and analyzed the data in terms of type of college selected, whether the student lived at home or not, number of years the student had been accelerated, when acceleration had occurred, and type of bridging mechanisms available between high school and college.

Evaluations of Extracurricular Accelerative Options

The Study of Mathematically Precocious Youth (SMPY) research program has conducted follow-up studies on the effects of acceleration on seventh- and eighth-grade students who were accelerated after identification as mathematically precocious. Follow-up questionnaires have been the primary assessment tool for the longitudinal study of groups identified by the talent searches and of select students within those groups who either elected to take courses offered through the Center for the Advancement of Academically Talented Youth (CTY) or were accelerated by their schools. These questionnaires (administered after the students had completed high school and then again after the students had completed college) collected data on later achievements ranging from courses completed and grades to awards and colleges attended. The questionnaires also asked students their perceptions of the effects of the SMPY program on their academic careers and the effects of acceleration on their social and emotional development. Copies of the various questionnaires can be found in Benbow (1983), Benbow et al. (1983), and Fox, Benbow, and Perkins (1983). As reported above, SMPY and its affiliated programs that have conducted talent searches and programs for the identified students have also used standardized achievement measures during and at the conclusion of these to gauge the success of courses and options used to serve the needs of gifted students.

Table 9.4 summarizes the types of instruments used by previous evaluation studies to address particular evaluation questions and concerns.

ISSUES RAISED BY THE EVALUATIONS
REPORTED IN THIS REVIEW

Given this review of evaluations of acceleration programs and current attitudes, it is important to consider a number of specific issues in developing

Table 9.4 Summary Chart: Types of Instruments Used in Prior Evaluation Studies

In the list below, the type of question asked is followed by the kinds of instruments or data used.

What is the impact of acceleration and the student's achievement—immediate?

Standardized achievement tests—general, specific
Grades in courses or classes—current
Teacher and principal ratings of student success in school
Self-report of success through questionnaire
Interviews with students, parents, and teachers
SAT scores
Creativity tests
Surveys/ratings by professors
Aptitude tests
Measures of problem-solving ability
Measures of handwriting skills

What is the impact of acceleration on the student's achievement—long term?

Grades in later courses; high school GPA; college GPA; college matriculation and completion; retentions
Honors and awards
Number and place of college admissions
Self-report (see text for details)
SAT and GRE scores
Number of AP exams
Participation in honors courses or other advanced classes
Participation in extracurricular activities

What is the impact of acceleration programs on social adjustment—immediate?

Parent ratings
Teacher ratings
Self-report on questionnaires
Sociometric data
Personality tests (objective and projective)
Referrals for emotional problems
Participation in extracurricular activities
Standardized behavior ratings
Conformance to school rules and regulations
Truancy
An ethical values inventory
Interviews with parents, students, and counselors

What are the impacts of acceleration programs on other student and program variables?

• *Physical development*

Physical stature (height and weight)
Number of students wearing glasses
Teacher ratings

Table 9.4 *(continued)*

- *Attitude toward school*
  Rating Scales
- *Attitudes toward acceleration in*
  Interviews with parents, students, teachers, and administrators
  Questionnaires
- *Influence on classroom climate*
  Interviews and observations
- *Identification procedures*
  Later ratings by teachers and parents of student success
- *Classroom differentiation*
  Logs kept by teachers
  Observations
- *Acceptance of acceleration (AP or college course credit) by colleges and universities*
  Student surveys
- *Correspondence/articulation of high school*
  On-site visits
- *AP and college courses with college programs*
  Mutual scoring of exams by high school and colleges
  Common exams

---

evaluation designs. Dealing with these issues can improve the quality and effectiveness of acceleration program evaluations.

Use of Surveys and Questionnaires

Problems with using questionnaires to assess the effects of a program on a particular student or group of students are many and need to be considered in the design of evaluations and in the interpretation of the resulting data. Although questionnaires yield considerable valuable information of certain types, especially opinions and perceptions, they fall short when used to assess certain variables that have been identified as important in acceleration, such as social and emotional adjustment. One global self-report item asking for an assessment of social and emotional adjustment is quite unlikely to be sensitive to adjustment difficulties (see Benbow, 1983).

Questionnaire use in follow-up studies is also plagued with particular difficulties—especially when one is trying to assess the outcomes of a program. First, the data are most usually derived from "successes"—those who stayed with a program or who were at least favorable enough to respond. In addition, the data are retrospective, and memory has a tendency to distort actual events and responses. Further, these students being evaluated are very intelligent and aware of the expectations others had for their success and their adjustment. Finally, are those students who have very negative reactions to a program also those who do not choose to respond to the questionnaire? Some evaluative efforts have sought to answer this question by pursuing nonrespondents by phone (e.g., Thomas, 1989). However, even if 100% response rate is achieved, we cannot be sure that responses are not biased by students' desire to appear successful and well-adjusted.

We might consider collecting questionnaire data at the time that the student is in the program. These efforts are, of course, desirable. But again, we must consider the student who is not well adjusted to a program but is under considerable pressure from parents and from a desire to appear successful to others. Will that student admit to adjustment problems or extreme difficulty in achievement?

Rating Bias

One major problem in evaluating an acceleration program is in soliciting unbiased ratings and assessments and making the distinction between the actual performance of students and the bias that individuals may have for or against acceleration in general. For example, Hebbeler (1983) points out that teachers often seemed to reflect their bias about the acceleration option rather than their opinion of the students' adjustment. Given the generally negative bias toward acceleration (Southern et al., 1989), assessments of the attitudes of teachers and administrators are likely to be biased negatively.

Comparison Groups

One of the unresolved issues in many of the evaluations reviewed above is selection of appropriate comparison groups to be used in judging the particular effects of a program of acceleration. To whom or to what standard do we compare the success of the accelerated students? Do we set absolute standards of success (certain grade equivalent scores on standardized tests, grades, involvement in minimal numbers of extracurricular activities, etc.)? Do we compare these students with age peers in general? Do we compare them with age peers of equal ability and achievement levels who were not accelerated? Do we compare them with grade-placement peers? In areas of academic achievement, it seems that we would like to demonstrate that the performance is equal to or better than that of those in the same grade. However, it might be argued that the same level of achievement might have been accomplished without acceleration, thus necessitating comparison with those who did not accelerate.

Although older comparison groups are used frequently and appropriately to assess the degree to which the cognitive achievement level of the accelerant keeps pace with grade-level achievement, the use of older groups may not be the best choice for comparison on other variables. Is it reasonable to expect best choice for comparison on other variables? Is it reasonable to expect that because a student's academic needs are advanced that he or she should be expected to behave in an advanced way in order to be considered successful in an accelerated placement? Consider, for example, the findings of Obrzut et al. (1984) in their study of an early entrance program. They found that the early accelerants who had been retained were held back for social reasons, such as "the student has a short attention span, needs constant one-to-one attention, doesn't listen to directions" (pp. 75–76). In cases such as this some value decisions will be made by virtue of the evaluation questions asked and the way in which these data are interpreted. Do we evaluate teachers' ability to adjust to these differences and try to alter their expectations? Or do we hold children to the criterion of social and emotional adjustment of the grade level to which they are accelerated?

On the one hand, it seems unreasonable to expect that students with advanced cognitive abilities and substantially advanced achievement will necessarily have correspondingly advanced emotional maturity, social skills, and physical development [although studies such as those of Klausmeier (1963) and Klausmeier & Ripple (1962) indicate that they often do]. It seems that it may be appropriate simply to affirm that the accelerant is developing at a normal pace. On the other hand, it is quite likely that teacher and administrator objections to programs for the gifted that provide accelerative options stem more from differences that occur in these areas of classroom adjustment and grade-appropriate behaviors than from concerns about the academic achievement of the students. Disruptions in classes or observations of "immature behavior" or even worry over the degree to which the accelerant "fits in" with the class may be disruptive to teachers and result in negative judgments about the program.

If educators believe that children should be allowed age-appropriate behavior, then a program should take steps to ensure that teachers are familiar with such behavior. It should provide teachers of accelerants with skills in working with children who are younger than those with whom they normally work. It should closely monitor the classroom situation and teacher and administrator attitudes as part of the evaluation to ensure that unrealistic expectations are not coloring the perceptions of the student and the program. On the other hand, if one accepts the premise that the accelerant's behavior should be on a par with that of the older students, then the program must be evaluated in light of the procedures for selecting students who meet that criterion.

Required Versus Voluntary Assessment

Interpretation of missing data is an issue that arises repeatedly in the review of evaluations of acceleration programs. For example, in seeking to assess the effects of the programs in biology, chemistry, and physics offered through CTY, Stanley and Stanley (1986) examined AP examination scores on exams taken 1 or 2 years later. Many students did not elect to take the examination; therefore, the data were incomplete. We might consider requiring all students to take the exam, or we might regard the decision not to take the exam as evidence of a nonsuccess because the student has not demonstrated enough confidence or interest to take the exam. Either approach fails to address the evaluation issue. To require all students to take the exam may result in disastrous results if students are not motivated to succeed. To assume that the student who does not elect to take a particular exam has been unsuccessful is not warranted. A student may choose not to take an AP exam for many reasons (e.g., AP credit not given at college of choice, dislike for examinations, schedules, priority to invest time in preparation for other subject-matter examinations or assessments). To encourage students to participate, incentives can be offered for completion (e.g., payment for the exam by the school) or examinations can be required for course credit. An investigation through interview or questionnaire as to the reasons exams are not taken would also be an aid to addressing the evaluation problem.

Criteria for Success

A major consideration in evaluating an accelerated program is, of course, the degree to which acceleration accomplishes the stated and implied goals and objectives. One such goal is the opportunity to complete at least one phase of one's education at an earlier age, an achievement that is readily and repeatedly documented in the literature.

Another stated goal of such programs as the Advanced Placement Programs and college courses offered in the high school is that students have the opportunity to earn credits and thereby save time and money in achieving their baccalaureate degree. Often this goal is not reached because students elect to earn far more than the number of hours required for graduation. For example, Stanley (1985) reports that only 2 of 11 accelerated general-honors students at Johns Hopkins elected to earn fewer than 131 credits (minimum of 120 required), and Mercurio et al. (1982) report that most of the students in the Project Advance Program of Syracuse University did not seek time-shortened degrees.

Another claim of acceleration programs is that they may "prevent social and emotional difficulties" that may arise from students' being so different as to be outcasts or so bored as to develop unacceptable outlets for that boredom. The findings of "no detrimental social or emotional effects" of acceleration do *not* support such claims of such programs. To show that acceleration really accomplishes that goal would require documentation that those who are not accelerated do experience such difficulties. That evidence does not exist in the extant literature and would be extremely difficult to obtain. It is more realistic to evaluate the ways in which interventions, both academic and counseling, are monitoring students' individual social or emotional adjustment and to assess the degree to which appropriate modifications are made if and when difficulties arise.

DIFFERENTIATING SUCCESSFUL AND UNSUCCESSFUL STUDENTS AND PROGRAMS: LACK OF ATTENTION TO SIGNIFICANT VARIABLES

Little effort has been made to identify which factors (other than initial ability level) might have accounted for the differences in levels of achievement, adjustment, or satisfaction with programs. For example, in studying Academic Talent Search students, Thomas (1989) found that 14% of the participants reported a decrease in general emotional stability, but no attempt was made to identify reasons for these changes in certain students.

One of the most serious concerns raised by the review of evaluations presented in this chapter is the lack of attention to those children who were not successful in the programs evaluated. The evidence that acceleration was not suited to all students is ample, but little attempt has been made to identify those factors that contribute to the success of some children but not others. The recent report by Brody, Lupkowski, and Stanley (1988) on the variability of success among early college entrants is a beginning of such important evaluation efforts.

A related problem in many of the evaluations reported in this chapter is the inability to attribute outcomes to the program or other variables within the student or the students' experiences. For example, in the reports on the Academic Talent Search students, those completing the fast-paced classes showed very high achievement and greater involvement and interest in math and science careers. The tendency is to credit the fast-paced mathematics courses with this outcome, and the credit may well be due to those courses. However, it may also be that greater initial interest and desire to succeed in mathematics and science motivated these students to enroll in the first place and to work harder to complete the courses. Or other intervening variables (increased expectations of others because of a student's successful completion of such courses) may account for these differences. The significant numbers of students who simultaneously participate in other forms of educational programming designed for gifted students (e.g., Thomas, 1989) also make it difficult to examine the effects of one particular intervention.

CONCLUSION

Raising these issues is not an exercise in identifying concerns in order to devalue acceleration or evaluation. Rather, we raise them in hopes that those planning to evaluate acceleration programs will give the issues serious attention in the planning process. All too often, inadequate evaluation data are presented because of inadequate consideration of these issues. We should also point out that the administrator or parent considering implementation or revision of programs of acceleration is likely to gather more useful information from carefully executed program evaluations than from the published research literature. In local decision making we must carefully consider the context we are dealing with and base decisions about program modification or individual student placement on specific, locally applicable information.

REFERENCES

Alexander, P. J., & Skinner, M. E. (1980). The effects of early entrance on subsequent social and academic development. *Journal for the Education of the Gifted, 3,* 147–150.

Benbow, C. P. (1983). Adolescence of the mathematically precocious: A five-year longitudinal study. In C. P. Benbow & J. C. Stanley (Eds.), *Academic precocity: Aspects of its development* (pp. 9–37). Baltimore: Johns Hopkins University Press.

Benbow, C. P., & Arjmand, O. (1989). *Predictors of high academic achievement in mathematics and science by mathematically talented students: A longitudinal study.* Unpublished manuscript.

Benbow, C. P., Perkins, S., & Stanley, J. C. (1983). Mathematics taught at a fast pace: A longitudinal evaluation of SMPY's first class. In C. P. Benbow & J. C. Stanley (Eds.), *Academic precocity: Aspects of its development* (pp. 51–78). Baltimore: Johns Hopkins University Press.

Benbow, C. P., & Stanley, J. C. (1983). An eight year evaluation of SMPY: What was learned? In C. P. Benbow & J. C. Stanley (Eds.), *Academic precocity: Aspects of its development* (pp. 205–214). Baltimore: Johns Hopkins University Press.

Birch, J. W. (1954). Early school admission for mentally advanced children. *Journal of Exceptional Children, 21,* 84–87.

Brody, L. E., Lupkowski, A. E., & Stanley, J. C. (1988). Early entrance to college:

A study of academic and social adjustment during freshman year. *College and University, 63,* 347–359.

Callahan, C. M. (1983). Issues in evaluating programs for the gifted. *Gifted Child Quarterly, 27,* 3–7.

Callahan, C. M. (1986). Asking the right questions: The central issue in evaluating programs for the gifted and talented. *Gifted Child Quarterly, 30,* 38–42.

Callahan, C. M., & Caldwell, M. S. (1986). Defensible evaluations of programs for the gifted and talented. In C. J. Maker (Ed.), *Critical issues in gifted education: Defensible programs for the gifted* (pp. 277–296). Rockville, MD: Aspen.

Carter, K. R. (1986). Evaluation design: Issues confronting evaluators of gifted programs. *Gifted Child Quarterly, 30,* 88–95.

Carter, K. R., & Hamilton, W. (1985). Formative evaluation of gifted programs: A process and model. *Gifted Child Quarterly, 29,* 5–11.

Casserly, P. L., & Rock, D. (1980). *Factors related to young women's persistence and achievement in advanced placement mathematics.* Princeton, NJ: Educational Testing Service. (ERIC Document Reproduction Service No. ED 214 798)

Cornog, W. H. (1980, Spring). The Advanced Placement Program: Reflections on its origins. *The College Board Review,* pp. 14–17.

Feldhusen, J. F., Proctor, T. B., & Black, K. N. (1986). Guidelines for grade advancement of precocious children. *Roeper Review, 9*(1), 25–27.

Fox, L. H., Benbow, C. P., & Perkins, S. (1983). An accelerated mathematics program for girls: A longitudinal evaluation. In C. P. Benbow & J. C. Stanley (Eds.), *Academic precocity: Aspects of its development* (pp. 113–138). Baltimore: Johns Hopkins University Press.

Gudaitis, J. L. (1986). *Advance College Project final evaluation report, 1984–1985 school year.* Bloomington: Indiana University. (ERIC Document Reproduction Service No. ED 267 097)

Hanson, H. P. (1980, Spring). Twenty-five years of the Advanced Placement Program: Encouraging able students. *The College Board Review,* pp. 8–13, 35.

Hebbeler, K. M. (1983). *Follow-up study of students in early admission program.* Rockville, MD: Montgomery County Public Schools, Department of Educational Accountability. (ERIC Document Reproduction Service No. ED 228 360)

Heikkila, F. L. (1983). An evaluation model for middle school programs for high ability mathematics students. *Dissertation Abstracts International, 44,* 2700a. (University Microfilms No. DA8329797)

Hobson, J. R. (1948). Mental age as a workable criterion for school admission. *Elementary School Journal, 48,* 312–321.

Joint Committee on Standards for Educational Evaluations (1981). *Standards for evaluations of educational programs, projects, and materials.* New York: McGraw-Hill.

Klausmeier, H. J. (1963). Effects of accelerating bright, older elementary pupils: A follow-up. *Journal of Educational Psychology, 54,* 165–171.

Klausmeier, H. J., Goodwin, W. L., & Ronda, T. (1968). Effects of accelerating bright, older elementary pupils: A second follow-up. *Journal of Educational Psychology, 59,* 53–58.

Klausmeier, H. J., & Ripple, R. E. (1962). Effects of accelerating bright, older pupils from second to fourth grade. *Journal of Educational Psychology, 53,* 93–100.

Lave, J. (1984). *Advance College Project final evaluation report.* Bloomington: Indiana University. (ERIC Document Reproduction Service No. ED 258 977)

Mateo, J. (1980). A study of overt classroom behavior of public and nonpublic seventh graders with early school entrance experiences in comparison with their older classmates. *Dissertation Abstracts International, 41,* 1499A. (University Microfilms Order No. 8021712)

Mercurio, J. (1980). College courses in the high school: A follow-up study. *College and University, 56,* 83–91.

Mercurio, J., Schwartz, S., & Oesterle, R. (1982). College courses in the high school: A four-year follow-up of the Syracuse University Project Advance Class of 1977. *College and University, 58,* 5–18.

Mezynski, K., & Stanley, J. C. (1980). Advanced Placement oriented calculus for high school students. *Journal for Research in Mathematics Education, 11,* 347–355.

Morrison, W. A. (1970). A comparative study of secondary school academic achievement and social adjustment of selected accelerated and non-accelerated elementary pupils. *Dissertation Abstracts International, 31,* 2015A–2016A. (University Microfilms Order No. 70–21, 166)

Obrzut, A., Nelson, R. B., & Obrzut, J. E. (1984). Early school entrance for intellectually superior children: An analysis. *Psychology in the Schools, 21,* 71–77.

Pennau, J. E. E. (1981). The relationship between early entrance and subsequent educational progress in the elementary school. *Dissertation Abstracts International, 42,* 1478A. (University Microfilms Order No. 8115026)

Pevec, A. E. (1964). Some problems of academically accelerated senior boys in selected high schools of Catholic diocese of Cleveland. *Dissertation Abstracts International, 25,* 6350A–6351A. (University Microfilms Order No. 65-2331)

Renzulli, J. S. (1975). *A guidebook for evaluating programs for the gifted and talented.* Ventura, CA: Ventura County Superintendent of Scols.

Renzulli, J. S., & Smith, L. H. (1979). Issues and procedures in evaluating programs. In A. H. Passow (Ed.), *The gifted and talented: Their education and development, 78th yearbook of the National Society for the Study of Education* (pp. 289–307). Chicago: University of Chicago Press.

Richardson, T. M., & Benbow, C. P. (1988). *Long-term effects of acceleration on the social-emotional adjustment of mathematically precocious youths.* Unpublished manuscript, Iowa State University, Study of Mathematically Precocious Youth, Ames.

Scriven, M. (1967). The methodology of evaluation. In R. Tyler, R. Gagne, & M. Scriven (Eds.), *Perspectives of curriculum evaluation* (pp. 39–83). Chicago: Rand McNally.

Southern, W. T., Jones, E. D., & Fiscus, E. D. (1989). Practitioner objections to the academic acceleration of gifted children. *Gifted Child Quarterly, 33,* 29–35.

Splaine, P. (1982). *A study of the effects on adolescents of skipping a grade or starting school early.* Paper presented at the annual meeting of the American Educational Research Association, New York.

Stanley, J. C. (1985). Young entrants to college: How did they fare? *College and University, 60,* 219–228.

Stanley, J. C., & Benbow, C. P. (1983). SMPY's first decade: Ten years of posing problems and solving them. *Journal of Special Education, 17,* 11–25.

Stanley, J. C., & Benbow, C. P. (1986). Youths who reason exceptionally well mathematically. In R. J. Sternberg & J. E. Davidson (Eds.), *Conceptions of giftedness* (pp. 361–387). Cambridge: Cambridge University Press.

Stanley, J. C., & McGill, A. M. (1986). More about young entrants to college: How did they fare? *Gifted Child Quarterly, 30,* 70–73.

Stanley, J. C., & Stanley, B. S. K. (1986). High-school biology, chemistry, or physics learned well in three weeks. *Journal of Research in Science Teaching, 23,* 237–250.

Swiatek, M. A., & Benbow, C. P. (1989). *Effects of fast-paced mathematics courses on the development of mathematically precocious students.* Unpublished manuscript, Iowa State University, Study of Mathematically Precocious Youth, Ames.

Thomas, T. A. (1989). *Acceleration for the academically talented: A follow-up of the academic talent search class of 1984.* Unpublished manuscript, California State University, Academic Talent Search Project, Sacramento.

Wilbur, F. P. (1982, September). College courses in the high school: New opportunities for the twelfth year. *The Practitioner,* pp. 1–12.

Worcester, D. A. (1956). *The education of children of above-average mentality.* Lincoln: University of Nebraska Press.

Worthen, B. R., & Sanders, J. R. (1987). *Educational evaluation: Alternative approaches and practical guidelines.* New York: Longman.

CHAPTER 10

Student Assessment and Evaluation

Scott L. Hunsaker and Carolyn M. Callahan
University of Virginia

In spite of all the evaluation studies on accelerants in general, it is important to remember that each gifted student is unique. The most recent studies of these students emphasize the wide variations in factors that influence the success of any given gifted student within an acceleration program. As Stanley and Benbow (1983) have stated,

> The strongest moral we can draw is that each exceptionally able youth must be treated on an individual basis. Full consideration must be given to his/ her pattern of abilities, family circumstances, local opportunities, and— most of all—the youngster's own considered assessment of the situation and of his/her eagerness to move one way or another. Getting the young student into the educational decision-making process early, while in elementary school, seems crucial. Many sensitive parents and teachers know this intuitively. Others must train themselves to consult the youth about his/her wishes on all important decisions after providing the necessary information. (p. 16)

IDENTIFYING THE APPROPRIATE STUDENT FOR ACCELERATION

According to Robinson (1983), one of education's most trite, but often ignored, truisms is the need to match the educational program of a child with the child's skill level. "Effective teaching must involve a sensitive assessment of the individual's status in the learning process and the presentation of problems that slightly exceed the level already mastered. Too-easy tasks produce boredom; too-difficult tasks cannot be understood" (p. 140). Feldhusen, Proctor, and Black (1986) assert that when new learning tasks are presented to the student at the right level, the task is learned well, is more effectively remembered, and is generalized to other relevant problems. The question becomes, then, How can we identify the appropriate level at which a child should be learning? Which students can most benefit from acceleration?

Assessing Intellectual Characteristics and Appropriate Academic Achievement Levels

Different approaches have been employed to assess student intellectual characteristics and academic achievement levels in order to determine if acceleration options are appropriate. These approaches vary according to the acceleration option being considered.

Early entrance to kindergarten. In a review of studies on early admission policies in the schools, Proctor, Black, and Feldhusen (1986) noted that the principal criteria for early admission to kindergarten or first grade were chronological age, advanced mental age as measured on an intelligence test, superior attention span, and advanced language facility. They then raised the question, "Would different criteria or screening methods maximize the success rate of those admitted" (p. 72)?

An evaluation of a Maryland program to allow 5-year-olds admission to first grade yielded the following recommendations for identifying qualified students:

1. Use multiple criteria—such as test scores, teacher observations, and the like—to determine eligibility
2. Place student in kindergarten initially and for a while so the teacher can observe and rate the child
3. Avoid overreliance on testing
4. Do not use chronological age in September or preschool experience as an identifier (Hebbeler, 1983)

Grade skipping. Feldhusen et al. (1986) recommend the following policies relative to intellectual and academic factors guiding decisions about the academic readiness of a pupil to be advanced to a grade at a younger than normal age:

1. A comprehensive psychological evaluation of the child's intellectual, academic, and social-emotional functioning
2. A mental development level above the mean for the target grade (e.g., a minimum IQ of 125)
3. Academic skill levels above the mean for the target grade

As an alternative to skipping an entire grade, they suggest the possibility of placement in the advanced grade only for those academic areas in which the student excels. Placement in other areas would be in the age-appropriate grade. [Recommendations made by Feldhusen et al. (1986) relative to non-intellectual factors will be discussed later.]

Telescoping the curriculum. Perhaps the most well known of programs that telescope the curriculum are those using the talent search model of Study of Mathematically Precocious Youth (SMPY). Each year interested seventh graders—and a few qualifying older sixth graders or younger eighth graders—take the Scholastic Aptitude Test (SAT) to establish their eligibility for a number of services offered by the talent search, including fast-paced math classes that permit students to complete the precalculus sequence in a few summers.

> The talent searches rely on the SAT because as a reasoning test, [it] would predict success in later mathematics, at least through differential equations, far better than would items measuring learned concepts, learned algorithms, and computational speed and accuracy. (Stanley & Benbow, 1986, p. 364)

Further, according to Stanley and Benbow, the test would have a high enough "ceiling" to permit students' full abilities to be tested. Even though the SMPY program at Johns Hopkins is primarily a math program, both SAT-Quantitative (SAT-Q) and SAT-Verbal (SAT-V) scores have been used to identify potential students in order to "avoid identifying mere calculating freaks" (p. 365).

However, the use of SAT scores for identification purposes should be consistent with the intended content of the fast-paced course. Bartkovich and Mezynski (1981) reported that, for a fast-paced math course for junior high students, correlations between the SAT-V score and the number of math courses subsequently completed were very low. They recommended that only the SAT-Q score be used when selecting for accelerated mathematics courses.

VanTassel-Baska (1984) has made specific recommendations relative to the types of options that should be made available to students based on their scores on the SAT subtests. Those in the 200 to 390 range should be considered for honors-level work in the content area of qualification, for enrichment seminars, and for academic counseling. Those in the 400 to 520 range should be provided fast-paced course work during the school year in their area of strength as well as academic counseling and enrollment in university summer programs. Those in the 530 to 650 range should have options for individualized diagnostic-prescriptive teaching in the area of strength, university programs of fast-paced instruction, academic counseling, early access to Advanced Placement courses, and grade acceleration. Finally, those in the 650 to 800 range would benefit from the same options as those in the previous range, plus they should be considered for early admission to college with advanced standing, mentorships, and career counseling. Although the breakdown into the various score ranges may be arbitrary, it illustrates the point that, even among the gifted, there are differences in ability levels and that these differences should be considered in accelerative programming.

Stanley and Benbow (1986) cautioned that it is illogical and inefficient to believe that a measure of overall ability such as an intelligence test can be used to place students in an accelerated option because students are likely to differ in the amount of acceleration they need across academic disciplines. Nonetheless, a telescoping project in the public schools of Milwaukee used a cutoff score of 125 on an individually administered intelligence test as well as achievement test scores above the 75th percentile in at least two areas and a high score on a teacher rating scale. Qualifying students were placed in an accelerated track in a nongraded elementary school with the intent of eliminating at least two semesters from their educational career (Klausmeier, 1962b). Although Klausmeier (1963) reported that students successfully completed this acceleration program without the predicted gaps in knowledge in the content areas, it seems more sound to use content-specific aptitude scores and specific academic achievement assessments for students— especially in secondary schools where content areas are more highly departmentalized.

Advanced Placement Programs. Many high schools permit enrollment in Advanced Placement courses either on an open basis, on minimum general grade-point average requirements, and/or on grades in the content area of the courses. The evidence available on the success of various assessments in predicting the achievement of accelerated students points out the need for program decision makers to collect and evaluate data on students before jumping to conclusions about appropriate screening instruments. For example, Mezynski, Stanley, and McCoart (1983) found that for science and mathematics courses, SAT-Q scores were a good predictor of continued course enrollment and of scores on the AP exam. Achievement tests in the content area also predicted continued enrollment. A mechanical reasoning test administered to the students prior to the beginning of an AP physics course, however, bore little relationship to the scores students eventually earned on the actual AP exam. This seems reasonable in light of the highly verbal nature of the AP examination in contrast to the more nonverbal mechanical reasoning test.

For students in chemistry and physics, previous enrollment in the corresponding lower level high school courses did not predict successful performance in the AP course, but previous enrollment in fast-paced math classes was predictive of success in the AP calculus course (Mezynski et al., 1983). Further, concurrent enrollment in the high school calculus course during the first semester was found to be important (Mezynski & Stanley, 1980).

College courses in high school. Wilbur (1982) reported on a number of programs that permit high school students to enroll in college courses. Eligibility requirements included having completed the 11th grade, earning and maintaining a minimum grade-point average, and, in cases involving dual enrollment, meeting the admission requirements of the university or college granting credit. These included submitting high school transcripts, aptitude test scores, and letters of recommendation from high school administrators or faculty. Other programs had similar requirements, including the Syracuse University Project Advance (Mercurio, 1980; Mercurio, Schwartz, & Oesterle, 1982) and the Indiana University Advance College Project (Lave, 1984; Gudaitis, 1986). Further, some of the Advance College Project high schools added their own academic requirements (not specified in the reports) to those required by Indiana University Bloomington.

Early entrance to college. Karnes and Chauvin (1982) conducted a survey of 190 colleges and universities to determine their policies for admitting younger than average students. Of the responding schools, 78% stated they had specific policies guiding the admission of younger than average students. These policies included the employment of a specific person to oversee early admissions, provision of scholarship funds for younger than average students, and availability of all majors. Admission requirements included a minimum age in only 25% of the schools, minimum ACT or SAT scores in 45%, minimum grade point averages in 70%, a minimum number of completed high school Carnegie units in only 26%, recommendations from the high school in 72%, an admissions interview in 40%, and parental permission in 39%. Because of the wide variability in policies, Karnes and Chauvin recommended that students interested in early college admission begin gathering information and preparing for taking aptitude and placement tests early in their high school career—even in the freshman year.

Cautionary note. It is important to note that standardized tests are frequently biased against students from underserved populations such as ethnic minorities, women, or socioeconomically disadvantaged students. However, alternative means of using testing and alternative tests are available (see also Silverman, 1986; Maker & Schiever, 1989).

Assessing Appropriate Nonintellectual Characteristics

In addition to assessing intellectual and academic characteristics of candidates for acceleration, many programs evaluate various nonintellectual characteristics to ascertain if acceleration is appropriate for a specific student. Feldhusen et al. (1986) recommend that the following nonintellectual areas be assessed:

1. The child's social and emotional maturity (including the student's persistence and motivation)
2. The child's physical health (including size only if competitive sports are considered important in later years)
3. The receiving teachers' attitudes about acceleration and accelerated students
4. The timeliness of the transition between grades and schools
5. The possibility of a trial period with counseling but without excessive expectations

Social and emotional maturity (including persistence and motivation). The majority of early entrance to kindergarten or first-grade programs reviewed by Proctor et al. (1986) required social and emotional maturity or skills equal to those of age-appropriate students. How these attributes were assessed was unclear.

Mezynski and Stanley (1980) suggested that students permitted to enroll in an AP calculus class demonstrate high motivation. However, they gave no indication of how they assessed high motivation. A concurrent enrollment program in Oklahoma universities seeks to serve three kinds of students, (a) students who wish to take a course the high school doesn't offer, (b) students who are older and seeking a more mature environment, (c) students who wish to pursue special interests (Wilbur, 1982). Again, however, the methods for determining who these students are were not described.

Feldhusen et al. (1986) suggest that students be free of social or emotional problems. However, they also point out that the accelerative option may be the solution to such problems.

Because of the great weight put on social and emotional development and adjustment and the negative view of acceleration held by many educators (Southern, Jones, & Fiscus, 1989), it is imperative that a careful analysis be made to ensure that the student is likely to adjust socially and emotionally. As a minimum, data should be collected on (1) the child's willingness to accelerate, (2) the likelihood that the child will be able to adjust to older students and the stress of higher expectations, and (3) the child's current emotional adjustment and stability. Because no systematic research base exists to support the choice of particular instruments or assessment tools, it seems imperative that a school psychologist or counselor develop a case study that will allow for a reasonable judgment relative to these points.

Health (including physical size). In most of the programs reviewed by Proctor et al. (1986), superior health and coordination were required for early entrance to kindergarten or first grade. Some programs required that physical development be on a par with age-appropriate students. However, Klausmeier (1962a, 1962b) pointed out that physical characteristics such as height and weight are not highly correlated with academic ability and cautioned against using them in the identification process.

Teacher attitudes. Feldhusen et al. (1986) suggest that receiving teachers' attitudes toward acceleration and the accelerated student be positive and characterized by a willingness to help the student adjust. This is especially important in light of evidence about pessimism many educators still hold for acceleration as an appropriate option for highly gifted students. Cramond and Martin (1987) surveyed teachers about their attitude toward imaginary students described on three dichotomies; athletic-nonathletic, studious-nonstudious, and brilliant-average. Combined, these dichotomies yielded descriptions of eight students. In all cases, teachers preferred the athletic student regardless of other descriptors. The least preferred student was the brilliant, studious, nonathletic one. This finding is particularly important because the accelerated student, with the possibility of physical development a year or two behind that of classmates, will frequently fit that description.

Southern et al. (1989) reported the greatest concern of educators was social and emotional adjustment and concluded that this concern was based on selective memory of students who had difficulty in an accelerated setting. This feeling was reinforced for the educators by familiarity with the literature opposed to acceleration (e.g., Elkind's writings); yet few educators could cite references from the pro-acceleration literature. Personal or family experience with acceleration, however, modified educators' feelings about acceleration in a favorable direction. Thus, student readiness is certainly not the only factor to be considered in discussions or decisions relative to acceleration.

Timeliness and ease of the transition. Feldhusen et al. (1986) suggest that transitions occur at natural points (e.g., at the beginning of the school year, between semesters, etc.), when potential disruption for the student, his or her peers, and teachers is minimal. Such a transition permits communication between sending and receiving teachers and programs and decreases the likelihood of skipping important content, a major concern teachers have about acceleration (Klausmeier, 1963).

In an interesting reversal of the age issue discussed concerning early admission to kindergarten, some talent search and early college entrance programs have *maximum* age requirements. Gregory (1985) indicates that students must be tested for the Early Entrance Program at California State University Los Angeles prior to the completion of seventh grade.

SMPY requires that talent search participants be tested prior to the completion of seventh grade. Although there is this maximum age cutoff, minimum age requirements are not relevant for the fast-paced math courses. Learning mathematics is more dependent upon instructional experiences than on either personal experiences outside of the classroom or maturation that is closely associated with chronological age.

Whatever the reasons for selecting a particular time for a transition, communication between the sending and receiving teachers and/or programs is essential. It is important to communicate information about the child's skill level in the various disciplines, permitting the receiving teacher to plan a program based on student strengths and weaknesses. It is also valuable to provide the receiving teacher with data relative to student interests, motivation, and potential adjustment. Clear and complete information about program components, expectations, schedules, and so on, must also be communicated to the students and their parents.

Possibility of trial period with counseling. A major finding of an evaluation of a telescoped kindergarten/first-grade program in Rockville, Maryland, was that early placement in first grade should be portrayed as tentative. Indeed, it was recommended that the program be called Kindergarten-First Grade instead of Early Admission.

For early college entrance, Kearney (1989) suggested that families weigh the loss of parental influence in adolescent years against the gains in academic and social life. She suggested part-time commuter enrollment as a possible trial before full-time residential enrollment. This is an important possibility to consider in light of Karnes and Chauvin's (1982) finding that only 36% of the colleges and universities surveyed provided special counseling services for younger than average students.

Feldhusen et al. (1986) suggested a 6-week trial period for accelerated students. During this period, and after its successful completion, counseling should be provided for the child, and excessive expectations of teachers, parents, and the child should be held in abeyance. The child should be made aware of the trial nature of the placement and be informed that he or she may choose to return to the previous setting without fear of being labeled a failure.

The content of a counseling program for accelerated students should include information about and help with heightened achievement expectations, increased academic workload, the new social milieu, different physical development, increased independence and responsibility, potential school and career opportunities, and possible resentment from those jealous of or opposed to acceleration. Parents should be included in the counseling program as well. They need information on supporting students without pressuring them, providing times for relaxation, using available community resources to supplement students' education, and preparing financially for future schooling opportunities.

MONITORING THE ACCELERATION EXPERIENCE

To increase the possibility that the acceleration experience will be a successful one for the student, it is necessary to monitor the student's academic progress and social and emotional adjustment on a continuing basis. In this way, problems can be identified and corrected early.

Monitoring Academics

For the most part, academics for accelerants are monitored through some system of testing. Ideally, test results are then used to design programs for students and to determine their success. Much of the work in this area has been done through the SMPY program at Johns Hopkins University. However, when students are simply accelerated by skipping grades or entering school early, they will often not be part of a carefully developed diagnostic/prescriptive program. Teachers and parents must exercise caution that early and frequent assessment be the basis for educational decisions.

Providing and using diagnostic information. Stanley and Benbow (1986) maintain that many educators, after having assessed a student's need for acceleration, provide at least four kinds of inappropriate options for the student. These include busy work, irrelevant academic enrichment, relevant but inconsistent academic enrichment, and programmed self-pacing.

As an alternative, SMPY has suggested diagnostic testing followed by prescribed instruction ($DT \rightarrow PI$). According to Stanley and Benbow (1982),

> The basic principle is to determine what the knowledgeable student does *not* know about a given subject and then help him or her to learn just that, without having to take an entire course or wade through a textbook containing material already known. (p. 5)

Stanley and Stanley (1986) reported that the model has also been applied to Advanced Placement courses where pretests provided the instructor with information about group knowledge as well as individual student strengths and weaknesses.

Bartkovich and Mezynski (1981) described the $DT \rightarrow PI$ approach as follows:

> In brief, the DT $\rightarrow$ PI classroom approach begins with diagnostic testing. Each student is administered a standardized test in the subject that follows the last precalculus mathematics course for which credit was obtained in school. Testing in succeeding courses is continued to the point where a student does not score well (better than the 75th percentile on national norms) on the test. This is the initial course in that individual's program of instruction.
>
> After the level of instruction has been determined for each student, an individualized program of "prescriptive" instruction can be devised. By using an item content classification chart (based on course concepts), the instructor can scrutinize missed test items to determine which mathematical concepts are not already known. The resulting instruction should include only those topics not yet learned. Little or no class time is spent on concepts already acquired. Review of such topics can be done through homework reinforcement. (p. 73)

Obviously a great deal of unnecessary repetition is avoided by using this approach. Minimal review is necessary to maintain skills already learned, but the focus is on topics not yet mastered by the student.

Caution should be exercised, however, in using a norm-referenced test in place of a domain-referenced test as described above. Although an item analysis based on course concepts provides some idea of concepts not mastered, skipping through several levels of instruction based on norm-referenced tests could result in gaps in knowledge given that such tests sample from the total domain of concepts.

Assessing and improving student effort. Where motivation is used as an identifying characteristic to place students in an acceleration program, problems with student effort do not frequently arise. However, in programs such as SMPY that identify based on scores on an ability test only, such problems sometimes occur. Stanley and Stanley (1986) cautioned teachers in fast-paced AP courses to watch carefully for students who were not achieving as would be expected. They reported that some students spent excessive periods of time studying. This resulted from poor reading skills, poor study habits, simple anxiety, or inappropriate assignments. They suggested teaching students how to skim less important material and to focus on critical areas and advised teachers to be willing to modify assignments for individual students where necessary.

When students began falling behind in another AP class as a result of insufficient study, a general letter was sent to all students encouraging them to attend class and complete assignments or be asked to withdraw. Students complied with this request by increasing their efforts (Mezynski et al., 1983). Because of limited resources and personnel, SMPY frequently provides such academic counseling by mail. Individual counseling is provided as requested (Stanley & Benbow, 1986).

Greater parental attention to student study habits would also be appropriate. Stanley and Benbow (1982) found that

> Parents allow their children to put off their homework until the last minute and then to do it poorly. Often there are no systematic study plans and routines in the home. We need to study carefully the setting in which each student works so that plans can be devised to prevent failing from lack of focused effort. (p. 8)

Thorough interviews with parents and students can often signal a problem in this area. Parents can then receive counseling in how to provide appropriate times and places for students to work. Students could be guided in how to organize time and materials to accomplish academic tasks.

Assessing and reporting student progress. Homework is frequently reported as a principal means for assessing student progress. In fast-paced math courses for junior high students, the minimum 4 hours of homework per week were used to reinforce newly acquired concepts and skills, as a learning device, and to inform teacher judgment about completion of the course (Bartkovich & Mezynski, 1981). Mezynski et al. (1983) reported that, even though homework's correlation with performance on the AP test was surprisingly low, they still felt it was necessary to emphasize the importance of homework (see also Mezynski & Stanley, 1980).

To certify completion of a course and to provide school personnel with enough information to inform placement and credit decisions, SMPY has provided school officials with packets containing evaluations of the students. These packets have included a brief course description and syllabus, an individual evaluation based on teacher judgment (which is in turn based on homework, in-class tests, and quizzes), and a report of scores on a standardized test (such as a CEEB achievement test) as post-test data.

Monitoring Social and Emotional Adjustment

In reviewing the literature on acceleration programs, one is struck by the lack of systematic efforts to monitor the social and emotional adjustment of accelerated students. The most frequently used method for monitoring students in the public schools seems to be teacher observation. Sometimes teachers are provided with rating scales that facilitate and direct their observation. (See, e.g., Hebbeler, 1983.) The most frequently used method in the concurrent or early college programs is student self-report. Although much of the literature on acceleration indicates the lack of social and emotional adjustment problems, teachers and administrators continue to be concerned, based on their selective memory, often of famous cases (see Southern et al., 1989). Instead of trying to convince educators that there are no social or emotional drawbacks to acceleration, it may be more useful to develop systems by which educators can watch for difficulties and assist accelerated students with any problems that may arise.

For students entering college early, the change from public school can be quite dramatic. Consider the report by Karnes and Chauvin (1982) that 64% of the colleges surveyed would permit younger than average students to live in the regular college dormitories. Only 9% would place any restrictions on the students with regard to social activities. Kearney (1989) reminds us that "gone are the days of nosy housemothers and midnight curfews; today's college dormitories are often the scene of heavy drinking, drug use, and casual sex" (p. 13). Accelerated students and their parents are faced with making important decisions about housing, dating, recreational activities, peer-group relations, and careers at a much earlier age.

SMPY has provided career counseling through informal sessions with faculty members from various fields and through individual counseling with students and their parents (Bartkovich & Mezynski, 1981), and high school counselors work with concurrent enrollment students in the Advance College Project (Lave, 1984; Gudaitis, 1986). Nonetheless, only 36% of the colleges and universities surveyed by Karnes and Chauvin (1982) reported providing special counseling for younger than average students. Even without special counseling services, young students in college should be encouraged to use the regular counseling services that are available. Kearney (1989) emphasizes the importance of a support system for young college students. She suggests a number of options, including "a college advisor with a talent for cutting bureaucratic red tape" (p. 13), tutors, enthusiastic parents, and other young college students.

The effort to monitor social and emotional adjustment in other accelerative options, such as grade skipping or fast-paced classes, needs to be expanded. Teachers and parents need to be trained to detect signs of maladjustment in order to make proper referrals to counselors. Students should be made aware of resources available when they feel in need of help.

The Need for Systematic Approaches

The problem of developing systematic approaches for identifying accelerated students and monitoring their social and emotional adjustment and academic progress is exacerbated by the lack of well-reported methodologies and instrumentation in the literature. Most reported acceleration programs failed to describe their specific method for identifying and monitoring students. Usually only a list of criteria was provided. Locally produced instruments were sometimes mentioned but were not described or included in appendices. Reliability and validity information was almost never provided. (Except in the area of monitoring social and emotional adjustment, SMPY is a notable exception.) Robinson (1983) has criticized enrichment programs as "piecemeal, inconsistent from one year to the next, and sometimes conflicting" (p. 141). Without greater dissemination of descriptions of systematic approaches, acceleration will not find itself immune from similar criticisms.

An Exemplary Program

Efforts have been made at the Early Entrance Program (EEP) run by the Center for the Study of Capable Youth at the University of Washington to develop and report a system for monitoring student academic, social, and emotional adjustment. Students who are 14 years or younger and/or have not yet entered the 10th grade, who have had exceptional achievement in their schooling, and who obtain qualifying scores on the Washington Pre-College Test are admitted to the university as part of a Transition Program. This permits the students to take college courses on a part-time basis while they become acclimated to the demands of college life and learn basic study skills such as note taking, cursive writing, and time management (Robinson, 1983; Janos et al., 1988).

Subsequently, students enroll full-time at the University of Washington. During their first year, they meet with both departmental and college advisors as well as an EEP counselor to check their program and make any necessary changes. Group meetings are held twice weekly (mandatory during the first year, encouraged during the second) that orient students to the university and help them develop social and study skills.

Students are required to live at home (or in a family setting if they are from out of town) during the first year. This facilitates parental influence in developing appropriate skills for succeeding in a university. Parent conferences are held as needed. At the time of full-time enrollment, many students choose to live in the dormitories; however, quarterly group sessions for parents are held to help them deal with their child's emerging independence—

particularly for the parents of girls. The girls generally want independence; the boys generally aren't ready for it.

A mid-quarter interview is conducted with the student to monitor progress and resolve problems. At the end of the quarter, contact is made with faculty who have worked with the students to discuss any problems, and students write a course evaluation.

KNOWING THE FACTS

Feldhusen et al. (1986) recommended that decisions about acceleration be made on the facts about acceleration. It is the purpose of evaluation to provide decision makers with those "facts," be they about a program or about a child. Is the child ready and willing to be accelerated? What challenges and needs is the child likely to face? What benefits will accrue to the child from being accelerated? Of the two, the "facts" about the child are probably the more important.

Important questions to ask about the program will generally have to be asked in consideration of information acquired about the child. For example, Is this program right for this child? How will the program help the child meet the needs and challenges and maximize the benefits? Given the claims of benefits made by proponents of acceleration, this last question is of particular importance. Stanley and Benbow (1986) have listed a number of benefits, including increased desire to learn, reduction of boredom, better attitude toward education, enhanced feelings of self-worth, reduction of egotism and arrogance, better educational preparation, earlier entrance into a career, increased opportunity to explore interests and hobbies, reduced costs, and greater success in life. This is an impressive list. Exactly how these benefits are actually secured to the child is not really clear. We have few facts available for us to use as a basis for decision making. We have a set of interpretations of self-report responses to inadequately described questionnaires.

A broad-based evaluation program could provide such data. Academic progress can be assessed daily by the teacher through homework and a comprehensive testing program that includes teacher-made tests, mid-unit and final exams, and standardized tests. Teachers and parents should make daily behavioral observations and consult with one another on a regular basis to discuss academic and social-emotional problems that may arise. Counselors, administrators, and teachers should develop a systematic counseling program that includes school group, individual, and family components, thus permitting prevention of or timely intervention in problems. Program administrators and staff should use data on a regularly scheduled basis to determine program effects on students with an eye to modifying the program to maximize benefits to the students.

Obviously, no one should or does take the decision to accelerate a student lightly. Nor should we accept vague evidence about acceleration programs in general as the definitive statement as to the appropriate placement for a specific child. What has come to light about acceleration is that some programs are beneficial to some children and not to others. Only when psychologists, counselors, administrators, parents, and the potential accelerants consider information about the program alongside information about the child can enlightened decisions be made. Such decisions are what evaluation is all about.

REFERENCES

Bartkovich, K. G., & Mezynski, K. (1981). Fast-paced precalculus mathematics for talented junior high students: Two recent SMPY programs. *Gifted Child Quarterly, 25*, 73–80.

Cramond, B., & Martin, C. E. (1987). Inservice and preservice teachers' attitudes toward the academically brilliant. *Gifted Child Quarterly, 31*, 15–19.

Feldhusen, J. F., Proctor, T. B., & Black, K. N. (1986). Guidelines for grade advancement of precocious children. *Roeper Review, 9*(1), 25–27.

Gregory, E. (1985). Early Entrance Program at California State University, Los Angeles. *Gifted Child Quarterly, 29*, 83–86.

Gudaitis, J. L. (1986). *Advance College Project final evaluation report, 1984–1985 school year.* Bloomington: Indiana University. (ERIC Document Reproduction Service No. Ed 267 097)

Hebbeler, K. M. (1983). *Follow-up study of students in the early admission program.* Rockville, MD: Montgomery County Public Schools, Department of Education Accountability. (ERIC Document Reproduction Service No. ED 228 360)

Janos, P. M., Robinson, N. M., Carter, C., Chapel, A., Cufley, R., Curland, M., Daily, M., Guilland, M., Heinzig, M., Kehl, H., Lu, S., Sherry, D., Stoloff, J., & Wise, A. (1988). A cross-sectional developmental study of the social relations of students who enter college early. *Gifted Child Quarterly, 32*, 210–215.

Karnes, F. A., & Chauvin, J. C. (1982). A survey of early admission policies for younger than average students: Implications for gifted youth. *Gifted Child Quarterly, 26*, 68–73.

Kearney, K. (1989, July). The highly gifted: The early college option (Part III). *Understanding Our Gifted*, p. 13.

Klausmeier, H. J. (1962a). *Report of research on educational provisions for children and youth of superior abilities, 1958–61.* Unpublished manuscript.

Klausmeier, H. J. (1962b). *Proposed program for children and youth of superior ability.* Unpublished manuscript.

Klausmeier, H. J. (1963). Effects of accelerating bright older elementary pupils: A follow-up. *Journal of Educational Psychology, 54*, 165–171.

Lave, J. (1984). *Advance College Project final evaluation report*. Bloomington: Indiana University. (ERIC Document Reproduction Service No. Ed 258 977)

Maker, C. J., & Schiever, S. W. (Eds.). (1989). *Critical issues in gifted education: Defensible programs for cultural and ethnic minorities*. Austin, TX: Pro. Ed.

Mercurio, J. (1980). College courses in the high school: A follow-up study. *College and University, 56*, 83–91.

Mercurio, J., Schwartz, S., & Oesterle, R. (1982). College courses in the high school: A four-year follow-up of the Syracuse University Project Advance Class of 1977. *College and University, 58*, 5–18.

Mezynski, K., & Stanley, J. C. (1980). Advanced Placement oriented calculus for high school students. *Journal for Research in Mathematics Education, 11*, 347–355.

Mezynski, K., Stanley, J. C., & McCoart, R. F. (1983). Helping youth scores well on AP examinations in physics, chemistry, and calculus. In C. P. Benbow & J. C. Stanley (Eds.), *Academic precocity: Aspects of its development* (pp. 86–112). Baltimore: Johns Hopkins University Press.

Proctor, T. B., Black, K. N., & Feldhusen, J. F. (1986). Early admission of selected children to elementary school: A review of the research literature. *Journal of Educational Research, 80*, 70–76.

Robinson, H. B. (1983). A case for radical acceleration. Programs of the Johns Hopkins University and the University of Washington. In C. P. Benbow & J. C. Stanley (Eds.), *Academic precocity: Aspects of its development* (pp. 139–159). Baltimore: Johns Hopkins University Press.

Silverman, L. K. (Ed.). (1986). The IQ controversy [Special issue]. *Roeper Review, 8*(3).

Southern, W. T., Jones, E. D., & Fiscus, E. D. (1989). Practitioner objections to the academic acceleration of gifted children. *Gifted Child Quarterly, 33*, 29–35.

Stanley, J. C., & Benbow, C. P. (1982, May). Educating mathematically precocious youths: Twelve policy recommendations. *Educational Researcher*, pp. 4–9.

Stanley, J. C., & Benbow, C. P. (1983). SMPY's first decade: Ten years of posing problems and solving them. *Journal of Special Education, 17*, 11–25.

Stanley, J. C., & Benbow, C. P. (1986). Youths who reason exceptionally well mathematically. In R. J. Sternberg & J. E. Davison (Eds.). *Conceptions of giftedness* (pp. 361–387). Cambridge: Cambridge University Press.

Stanley, J. C., & Stanley, B. S. K. (1986). High-school biology, chemistry, or physics learned well in three weeks. *Journal of Research in Science Teaching, 23*, 237–250.

VanTassel-Baska, J. (1984). The talent search as an identification mode. *Gifted Child Quarterly, 28*, 172–176.

Wilbur, F. P. (1982, September). College courses in the high school: New opportunities for the twelfth year. *The Practitioner*, pp. 1–12.

CHAPTER 11

Conclusions About Acceleration: Echoes of Debate

Eric D. Jones and W. Thomas Southern
Bowling Green State University

It must be said that the views on the subject of academic acceleration held by the authors of the preceding chapters are not unanimous in support or praise of its unrestricted application. Even so noted and strong a proponent as Julian Stanley, along with his colleague Linda Brody, issues some cautionary advice (see Chapter 5). The tone of the other authors ranges from cautious endorsement to careful skepticism. The reasons for their conservatism may lie in the fact that despite decades of research, definitive answers are in short supply. One culprit seems to be the uncontrollability of some of the research questions.

Certainly the most vexing issue seems to be whether acceleration is harmful to a student's social and emotional well-being. As Cornell, Callahan, Bassin, and Ramsay (Chapter 4) reveal, the commonly stated proposition that acceleration has been proved harmless is not so firmly grounded as many experts may think. Studies that have examined these issues have lacked rigor and appropriate controls. As Feldhusen (Chapter 6) points out, there have been very few studies that assessed long-term benefits and harm. On the other hand, the case that harm results from the practice is not particularly compelling either. Jones and Southern (Chapter 3) argue that much of the existing literature in early admission is methodologically unsound and probably inapplicable to populations of gifted students admitted early.

At least three factors affect the tenuousness of results in this area:

1. Designing the experiment
2. Measuring social and emotional adjustment
3. Determining the effects of acceleration on individuals

A major problem of experimental design in real educational settings is that no modern district will allow students who are shown to have a demonstrated need for an educational intervention to be assigned randomly to receive it. That is, establishing a comparison group that would *not* receive necessary treatment would be insupportable, even if a researcher would propose such an experiment. Without such a procedure, however, the problem of comparability of groups noted by Callahan and Hunsaker (Chapter 9) becomes quite thorny. Students who are accelerated are quite different in many potentially important ways from students who are not accelerated. Comparisons with same-age peers with equal IQs ignore the experimental, social, and familial background that led one group of youngsters and their parents to choose acceleration.

Another problem arises in applying the concepts of social and emotional adjustment. In a number of the chapters in this volume, the authors have pointed out that issues of social and emotional adjustment are complex and the concepts vary with development and across school and extracurricular settings. To complicate matters further, the terms have different connotations when used by different people. When parents or teachers define social or emotional maturity, for example, they are likely to name widely divergent behaviors. Students characterized as immature can be too quiet, too active, too inattentive, too boisterous, or too withdrawn. One teacher described a child as immature because she talked only with adults at school. Although this behavior may indicate poor integration with peers, it is difficult to characterize engaging adults in conversation as a sign of immaturity.

Finally, as nearly every author has pointed out, the effects of acceleration probably vary widely for different students. Concentrating on whether groups were or were not harmed disguises effects on individuals. Unfortunately, it is not any easier to determine the extent of social and emotional harm done to individuals than it is to do so for groups. As stated in Chapter 1, the students who are accelerated in modern schools are students who are already quite different from their peers in achievement and performance. To what can we attribute abnormalities in their social or emotional development? It seems impossible to disentangle the treatment from the condition that suggested the treatment when assigning causes. This problem is compounded when we note that some students are accelerated because they appear maladjusted in their current placement. Boredom, school phobia, and lack of peer relations are characteristics attributed to students who are considered for acceleration (Sisk, 1986). Some claim that these may be symptoms of the lack of appropriate placement and instruction for these students and that acceleration is the treatment. Yet, to be redundant, no child can function as his or her own control. We can never be certain that the presenting problem or the treatment is at fault for subsequent maladjustment. Hence, examining the way individuals respond to acceleration leaves us with a classic chicken-and-egg dilemma.

Despite the apparent pessimism of these observations, there are some definite conclusions that can be drawn from the literature of acceleration and the presentations in this book. For example, it is probably justifiable to discard concerns about the academic progress of accelerated students in advanced placements. The research literature seems very clear on this issue, and most writers in the field tend to agree. Students are going to succeed and probably excel in accelerated placements. That this is true is not surprising, given the nature of the students who are normally considered for the process. A student who is identified as a potential candidate for acceleration generally exceeds the current grade placement demands by a considerable amount. If school personnel concur in acceleration, these students have probably demonstrated competence at a level far above any grade for which they are likely to be considered. It is unlikely that they will feel undue pressure or stress, or that there will be serious problems with "basic skill gaps."

It should also be possible to lay to rest concerns about the effect of "mental acceleration." Most programs in schools are administrative in nature providing mechanisms to place a student at a level commensurate with current levels of achievement. Very few actively increase the pace or demand of instruction through an agency external to the student. Once again, the nature of the student considered for these programs is such that acceleration will result in no great leap in cognitive demand. Where it is employed, acceleration is approached conservatively. Despite some eye-catching publicity, radical acceleration is still relatively rare. When students do skip grades, it is likely that they will skip only one and that the process will not be repeated. For students achieving two, three, or four grade levels in advance of current placement, most accelerative options will represent only a marginal increase in school demands.

If this is the case, why consider acceleration at all? Since the issue of social and emotional adjustment is difficult, even impossible to resolve, should schools not simply seek alternate methods of dealing with the needs of the gifted and talented? There seem to us to be at least three compelling reasons why districts must employ accelerative options:

1. Economy
2. Inevitability
3. Honesty

With regard to economy, the district will be unable to furnish teachers with appropriate time and expertise to meet the needs of students who are highly, positively deviant. Every district will encounter a few students who tax the ability of the teacher to meet their learning needs in classrooms with age-level peers. Because the rate at which these students learn is considerably greater than that of their peers, the teacher would be forced to spend an increasing percentage of time planning for an individual. Teacher time is a limited resource. When a student is viewed as too substantial a drain on that resource, teachers will reduce their concern and involvement with the student (Gerber & Semmel, 1984). Many teachers also lack the expertise and training to deal with the needs of highly gifted and talented students under the best of circumstances. As students advance in their ability within content areas, it becomes increasingly unlikely that the teacher will have the knowledge required to carry out instruction. Schools generally have subject-matter specialists at the secondary level. Students at the elementary level lack access to them. Even secondary teachers have limitations in the sophistication and currency of their knowledge, and for many students, the university may be the most likely source of access to appropriate knowledge. Nor is it likely that teachers at any level have the training or expertise to guide students in mentorships or independent study indefinitely. Eventually, for some students, some form of acceleration may be the only economical answer to the problem.

As for inevitability, it is nearly impossible to design an intervention that simultaneously challenges all students and avoids any accelerative implications. At some point, good enrichment always engages the student with advanced content and skills. Students who read extensively will eventually need to be exposed to the tools of literary analysis. Students who show interest and facility in a foreign language will eventually require some systematic instruction. Some students who pursue intuitive geometry, or who do informal proofs in studying tesselations, will eventually need the terms and procedures of more formal proof. Districts whose goal is the enrichment of all students, and the retention of all exclusively with grade-level peers, have set themselves an impossible task.

Which brings us to honesty. If a district indeed sets as its goal the exclusion of accelerative options, then it will invariably waste the time and talent of some of its students. The materials used with highly capable students must be either divorced from content or repetitive. In either case, the materials will not serve the intellectual needs of the students, and the district will not be educating some of its most talented students.

Acceleration, therefore, is a tool that must be employed. There are some guidelines, however, that need to be followed. Robinson and Weimer (Chapter 2), Piper and Creps (Chapter 8) and Van Tassel-Baska (Chapter 7) address some of the procedural issues in their chapters; Brody and Stanley (Chapter 5) offer some guidance for radical acceleration; and Callahan and Hunsaker (Chapters 9 and 10) provide some valuable guidance for monitoring the effectiveness and suitability of programs and student placement. It remains for us to say only that there are a series of issues concerning the administrative impact of acceleration that should be rationally addressed any time these options are used.

When a district attempts to provide some administrative recognition of a student's current performance, the district should be aware of the consequences of program options and decisions. Problems often arise from one of three sources:

1. The placements may have unanticipated effects at subsequent levels of school
2. The programs place the student at risk in potentially keener competition with other capable students for scholarships or admission to selective schools
3. The programs may reduce rather than increase student opportunities

Unanticipated effects for students can arise because the schools tend to compartmentalize student curriculum and record keeping. High school personnel may be unlikely to systematically review elementary and junior high records for evidence of advanced skills or course taking. Demands for days and hours of instruction, Carnegie units, and numbers of courses for meeting minimal graduation standards are generally confined to each level, and a broader view of student progress is unlikely. Schools need, minimally, to examine how acceleration may affect records, graduation demands, and availability of advanced course options before implementing it. It would be better to develop an integrated plan for addressing these sorts of issues at the time a student is counseled into accelerative options.

Schools should also take pains to see that the student is not penalized for the acceleration in terms of scholarships or college admission. This entails providing support and oversight in initial placements so that if the placement is too difficult, the student may leave without penalty. It also means being certain that the student's records and recommendations clearly indicate the unusual age for taking such courses and the demanding nature of the options selected. Although one cannot guarantee that a college admissions officer will pay adequate attention to these details, the school should make them difficult to overlook.

Schools should ensure that the accelerative options open doors for the student. College credit courses that eliminate a student from honors tracks, or advanced courses that bring a student to a dead end in terms of more advanced work at the high school level, close rather than open opportunities. For example, if a school district telescopes math instruction in the junior high, it is incumbent on the district to offer sufficient math courses at the high school level to allow a student to continue in his or her study of higher mathematics. Schools must make sure that students who are beginning to amass advanced credit receive timely advice and counseling in terms of college application, admission, and career choice. Ignoring these issues may allow students to miss important deadlines for applications and entry testing or to make naive decisions in course taking that may screen them from potential careers. Finally, schools should prepare students for the eventuality that some experiences may be truncated or missed altogether. Eligibility for and full-scale participation in varsity athletics may be affected by decisions to accelerate a student. In the case of some sports, the opportunity to participate at all may be ruled out. Where rules can be changed to eliminate penalties, they should be. But some impediments are natural (less time for growth and development), and some rules are beyond the district's power to intervene (those set up by state athletic associations, for example).

Perhaps the one thing we may be surest of is that the student who is considered for acceleration must want to be accelerated. If the student feels that remaining with peers or participating in a full 4 years of high school athletics or activities is the most important point, then the student's wishes should be respected. Forcing a student to accelerate will probably not be successful, and it may bring about those negative outcomes so feared from acceleration. Parents, too, must support the adoption of accelerative interventions. Beyond the legal requirements for their permission, parents must provide support for the student and information about the student's adjustment to the district. They are key to the success of any intervention, and acceleration is no exception.

For all practical purposes, the debate over acceleration will probably never be totally resolved. School personnel, parents, and students must be aware, however, that for many gifted and talented students, it is an option that must be considered. Care and forethought can reduce harmful consequences from its use. But, if a district is to fulfill its responsibility of educating all students to their potential, it is too valuable a tool to discard.

REFERENCES

Gerber, M. M., & Semmel, M. I. (1984). The teacher as imperfect test: Reconceptualizing the referral process. *Educational Psychologist, 19*(3), 137–148.
Sisk, D. A. (1988). Response to Elkind. *Journal of the Gifted, 11*(4), 32–38.

About the Contributors

Laurie Bassin is a doctoral candidate at the University of Virginia studying education of the gifted and talented. She received an MEd in the education of gifted and talented students from the University of Virginia and a BS in astronomy from Penn State University. She is currently teaching gifted and talented third and fourth graders in the Quest Program in Charlottesville, Virginia.

Linda Brody is associate director of the Study of Mathematically Precocious Youth (SMPY) at Johns Hopkins University. Her research focuses on understanding how talent develops in highly gifted students and evaluating program alternatives for them. Mathematically and/or verbally talented females are also a special interest of hers. Previously, she worked with the Intellectually Gifted Child Study Group at Johns Hopkins on a variety of research studies that culminated in two books with Lynn Fox and Dianne Tobin, *Women and the Mathematical Mystique* and *Learning Disabled/Gifted Students: Identification and Programming*.

Carolyn Callahan is a Professor of Education in the Department of Educational Studies in the Curry School of Education at the University of Virginia. She teaches courses in the education of the gifted and is executive director of the Summer Enrichment Program. She has authored more than 40 articles, 10 book chapters, and several monographs on topics that include creativity, program evaluation, and issues faced by gifted female students. She is a past president of The Association for the Gifted and serves on the executive board of the National Association for the Gifted. In 1988 she was selected Outstanding Faculty Member in the Commonwealth of Virginia and in the following year received the Distinguished Scholar Award from the National Association for Gifted Children.

Dewey G. Cornell is a clinical psychologist and assistant professor in the Curry School of Education at the University of Virginia. His research interests include the psychological adjustment and family relationships of highly able children. In 1989 he received the Early Scholar Award from the National Association for Gifted Children. He has given numerous presentations and published many articles in the area of gifted education.

Karen Creps is a coordinator of gifted education at the Wood County Office of Education in Bowling Green, Ohio. She received her BS and MA in elementary education from Bowling Green State University. She has presented at state, local, and national conferences for gifted education and initiated summer day programs for the gifted. She is currently working on a grant-funded training project for teachers who serve gifted and talented students in the regular classroom and is very active in the Odyssey of the Mind competition at regional and state levels.

John F. Feldhusen is Distinguished Professor of Education at Purdue University where he is responsible for the graduate program and the development and administration of the Purdue Gifted Education Resource Institute. His research interests include the education of gifted and talented children, and the nature of creativity and problem solving. He has authored two books on gifted education as well as numerous articles and book chapters. He is currently the editor of *Gifted Child Quarterly.*

Scott L. Hunsaker is a doctoral student specializing in the evaluation of programs for gifted and talented children and a research assistant at the Bureau of Educational Research at the University of Virginia. He is chair of the Creativity Division of the National Association for Gifted Children and is co-author of the Virginia State Department of Education's *Suggestions for Program Development in Gifted Education.* He has presented at numerous conferences in gifted education, served as a district coordinator of gifted education, and worked as a classroom teacher in his home state of Utah.

Eric D. Jones is associate professor of special education at Bowling Green State University in Ohio. He earned his doctorate in special education at the University of Virginia. His training included extensive work in program evaluation and an extended internship at the Northwest Educational Research Laboratory in Portland, Oregon. Prior to graduate school, he taught Navajo and Hopi Indian children with mild learning handicaps in northern Arizona. He teaches courses in curriculum development, applied behavior analysis, research methods, and mental retardation. He has written several chapters and articles and has presented many papers on direct instruction, mathematical problem solving, behavioral assessment, program evaluation, and the academic acceleration of gifted children.

Sylvia Piper has been coordinator of gifted education in the Wood County Office of Education since 1980, working with resource room and regular classroom teachers in multiple school districts. She is active in gifted education at the state level, serving as a member of The Executive Committee of the Consortium of Ohio Coordinators of the Gifted. She has presented at national and state conferences on the gifted and is also an educational consultant for a national learning styles network. She is currently involved in a grant-funded project designed to train teachers in how to accommodate the gifted learner in the regular classroom.

Shula Ramsay is a doctoral student at the University of Virginia, studying educational psychology. She has presented at numerous state and national conferences and has worked as a teacher of the gifted, a program development consultant, and an inservice instructor. Current research interests include the research of gifted scholars and appropriate programming and instruction for gifted students.

Nancy Robinson is professor of psychiatry and behavioral sciences and director of the Center for the Study of Capable Youth at the University of Washington. Since her graduate student days at Stanford University, where her mentor was Maud Merrill, the co-author of the Stanford-Binet, Professor Robinson has maintained an interest in the intellectual and social development of gifted children and youth. In 1981 she assumed the directorship of the Center for the Study of Capable Youth that had been founded by her late husband, Halbert Robinson. Her research interests include the precocious development of preschool children, family issues such as sibling relationships when one or more children is intellectually advanced, and the development of adaptive versus maladaptive "perfectionism."

W. Thomas Southern is assistant professor of special education, and coordinator of gifted education at Bowling Green State University in Bowling Green, Ohio. He currently directs programs for the gifted and talented at Bowling Green and serves as a consultant for the Office of Gifted Programs at Indiana University. He has been a junior high school teacher, a program coordinator, and a program evaluator. His current research interests include the effectiveness of simulation for the gifted, the effects of accelerative options, and the identification and programming needs of special populations of gifted children.

Julian C. Stanley is professor of psychology and director of the Study of Mathematically Precocious Youth (SMPY) at Johns Hopkins University. Dr. Stanley had a distinguished career in the fields of psychological testing, research methodology, and statistics before devoting himself to working on behalf of mathematically gifted youth. Since 1979, he has devoted himself almost exclusively to work with boys and girls who before their 13th birthday had scored at least 700 on the mathematical portion of the Scholastic Aptitude Test. Dr. Stanley and his staff have been seeking sorely needed accelerative opportunities for these children.

Joyce VanTassel-Baska is the Jody and Layton Smith Professor of Education at the College of William and Mary in Virginia where she has developed a graduate program and research and development center for gifted education. Formerly, she initiated and directed the Center for Talent Development at Northwestern University and served as state director of gifted programs for Illinois and as a regional director of a gifted service center in the Chicago area. She has worked as a consultant in over 40 states and is past president of The Association for the Gifted. She co-authored *Comprehensive*

Curriculum for Gifted Learners with John Feldhusen, and *Excellence in Educating the Gifted* with John Feldhusen and Ken Seeley. She also edited *Patterns of Influence: The Home, The Self, and The School.*

Linda Weimer is a clinical psychologist and assistant professor of clinical psychiatry and behavioral sciences at the University of Washington. Since 1978 she has been associated with the Center for the Study of Capable Youth where she has served as research assistant, psychologist, and clinical consultant. Her primary responsibilities include assessment and parent counseling in the Diagnostic and Counseling Center with families of gifted children with whom there were behavioral, emotional, or educational concerns. She is currently special consultant to two Seattle schools in the area of gifted education.

Index